D0583519

WARREN BUFFETT

WARREN BUFFETT

INVESTOR AND ENTREPRENEUR

TODD A. FINKLE

Columbia Business School
Publishing

Columbia University Press
Publishers Since 1893
New York   Chichester, West Sussex
cup.columbia.edu

Copyright © 2023 Todd A. Finkle
All rights reserved

Library of Congress Cataloging-in-Publication Data
Names: Finkle, Todd A., author.
Title: Warren Buffett : investor and entrepreneur / Todd A. Finkle, Ph.D.
Description: New York : Columbia University Press, [2022] | Includes bibliographical references and index.
Identifiers: LCCN 2022021406 | ISBN 9780231207126 (hardback) | ISBN 9780231556828 (ebook)
Subjects: LCSH: Buffett, Warren. | Capitalists and financiers—United States—Biography. | Businesspeople—United States—Biography. | Entrepreneurship—United States. | Investments—United States.
Classification: LCC HG172.A3 F56 2022 | DDC 338.092 [B]—dc23/eng/20220914
LC record available at https://lccn.loc.gov/2022021406

♾

Columbia University Press books are printed on permanent and durable acid-free paper.
Printed in the United States of America

Cover design: Noah Arlow
Cover image: Getty Images

I would like to thank my wife, Patti Livingstone, for her love and encouragement during the writing of this book. I would also like to dedicate this book to all the teachers that have had an impact on me in my life, especially Warren Buffett.

CONTENTS

PART IV: WARREN BUFFETT: THE PERSON

PREFACE

When I met Warren Buffett for the first time, someone asked him what he would do if he were not chairman and chief executive officer (CEO) of Berkshire Hathaway. Buffett quickly responded—a teacher. When asked why, he said:

> There have been so many teachers that have had a significant impact on my life.

Having been a professor at the university level for over thirty years, I want to share with everyone in the world the knowledge I have learned about one of the most successful entrepreneurs and investors of all time. I grew up in Omaha, Nebraska, and went to Omaha Central High School, the same high school as Buffett's children, his first wife, Susie, and his father, Howard. I went to high school at the same time as Buffett's son, Peter. He was two years older than me. I, however, had many friends who were also friends with Peter, and we would often eat lunch together. I have been fortunate enough to build a personal relationship with Warren Buffett, which I will talk about in the book. In 2008, during the worst financial crisis since the Great Depression, I decided to learn as much as possible about arguably the smartest businessperson since J. P. Morgan.

This book examines the behaviors that have made Warren Buffett so successful. I relate, in chronological order, how he has accomplished this. To develop these themes, I have combined my knowledge of Buffett, Charlie Munger (and other influencers), Omaha, finance, investments, entrepreneurship, and other factors. I introduce you to a variety of topics that will assist you in your personal and financial life, emphasizing how entrepreneurship has transformed Buffett's life.

The book is a compilation of information (from both primary and secondary sources) about Buffett's life and his investing philosophy. It includes interviews with a variety of people, personal statements, shareholder letters, books, and my own interpretations.

I have made six visits to see Buffett with my university students. Upon our return to campus, I asked them what they considered to be the most important lesson that they had learned from Buffett. To my surprise, they always highlighted not his accomplishments or investments, but his values.

Buffett grew up in the Great Depression and subsequently became one of the richest men in the world. Many call him the most prolific investor of all time. This book explores how he earned this label and how you can integrate his keys to success to enhance your own life.

Beginning with Buffett's childhood, the book tells how he was affected by his family and two major mentors, Benjamin Graham and Phil Fisher. The book takes you through his entrepreneurial ventures from grade school through high school. It then examines Buffett's college years and entrepreneurial experiences, including the creation of his own investment partnerships.

Chapter 3 is devoted to Charlie Munger, Buffett's business partner, a man whose brilliance and wit matches that of the "Oracle of Omaha." Munger's fresh perspective on investing and his voracious intellect challenged Buffett to change Berkshire's business philosophy. The next three chapters are devoted to Buffett's investment methodology (margin of safety, key factors, valuation, and recommendations to investors).

This is followed by chapter 7, on behavioral biases, which Buffett considers critical to the success of any investor. This chapter defines several biases, gives a few examples, and then tells you how to overcome them.

The following two chapters of the book, chapters 8 and 9, examine the history of Berkshire Hathaway. This is followed by chapter 10, on Buffett's investing mistakes. Next, chapter 11 focuses on Buffett's keys to success, values, views on happiness, and philanthropy, and then chapter 12 explores Buffett as a person. What is it like being in the same room with him? It is based on my own experiences of bringing my classes to Omaha. The chapter takes you through the question-and-answer time with Buffett.

Finally, chapter 13 updates you with what is happening today in investing, with a focus on financial services technology (fintech), cryptocurrencies, Bitcoin, and other digital currencies. This will be part of the future for Berkshire Hathaway.

As I look back on the many years it took for me to write this book, I realized that few (if any) authors writing about Buffett have discussed a real-world example of how Buffett values investments and the strategies he follows through a step-by-step process. My goal is to give the layperson the ability to value companies as Buffett does. This way, they can use this process when making their own investment decisions.

Furthermore, few books written on Buffett have explored behavioral biases. In this book, I examine what behavioral biases are and how they affected certain investment decisions that Buffett made. Specifically, I examine Buffett's investment mistakes and discuss how behavioral biases may have affected his decisions. In doing so, we can all learn from these mistakes.

My ultimate goal is to educate the reader about Buffett's life and the various things that he has done to become successful. I hope the book is both enjoyable and useful.

Disclaimer: I own shares of Berkshire Hathaway outright and also have some via one or more of my index funds. In no way does the content of this book represent my investment views, nor does it represent any direct investment advice to readers.

ACKNOWLEDGMENTS

I often urge my friends not to write a book. It takes an enormous amount of work, more than you realize. However, I loved the subject, Warren Buffett. Writing this book has transformed my life. The book would not have been possible without the support and guidance I received from several people. First and most important, I want to thank Warren Buffett for allowing me the opportunity to meet him and study him. You are truly an inspiration. I also want to thank his daughter, Susie Buffett, for allowing me the opportunity to interview her and gain an insight into the Buffett family dynamics. Thank you also to Jim Weber, the chief executive officer (CEO) of Brooks Sports, and Professor Donald F. Kuratko (Indiana University) for allowing me to interview you for the book.

I would never have had the opportunity to meet Warren if not for my cousin Steve Nogg from Omaha. In 2007, he told me that Warren was inviting university classes to spend a day in Omaha with him. I promptly applied—and was rejected immediately—but I was persistent and formed a relationship with Warren. Writing this book has given me an opportunity to create a closer relationship with Steve, which I am extremely grateful for.

I want to thank Mark Pigott and his family for endowing an entrepreneurship professorship at Gonzaga University. Without Mark's support, this book would never have happened. I also want to thank my dean, Dr. Kenneth Anderson, for giving me the opportunity to study Warren Buffett.

Thank you to Brian Smith and Myles Thompson at Columbia University Press for guiding me through the publication process. Because of them, I was fortunate to find two excellent editors, Claudia Rowe and Greg Shaw of Clyde Hill Publishing, who were both essential to creating a quality book. They are both dynamic writers and helped me enormously.

Several people assisted me in the creation and revision of the book. Matt Kaufler, chartered financial analyst (CFA), and Charles Fishkin are both at the top of the list. Matt and Charles volunteered to help me work through the long, arduous process of getting the book published. Matt also recommended that I add a section on behavioral biases, which eventually led to a chapter on Buffett's mistakes. They both constantly pushed me to look deeper. Charles, a friend of mine since the third grade at Harrison Elementary School and my classmate at Omaha Central High School, was an ongoing source of support. He reviewed the entire draft twice and guided me through the editorial process.

There were several professors who helped me at various stages of writing and reviewing the book. Thank you to Kathleen Allen, Reinhold (Rinnie) Lamb, Rick Zuber, Tom O'Brien, Kent Hickman, Mark Shrader, Paul Buller, and Bud Barnes. I also want to thank Professor Andrew Thomas, who has published numerous books and gave me constant positive feedback and guidance.

I also want to thank a few friends of mine in the financial industry. Pat Terrion (Founders Capital Management) has guided me for several years on writing articles and this book on Buffett. Adam Mead (Mead Capital Management) reviewed the book and gave me valuable insights. Jon Shane (Merrill Lynch) sends me material on current events that are happening with Buffett. Finally, I want to especially thank John Hemmingson (Lakeside Companies), who volunteered to take three groups of students to the annual Berkshire Hathaway meeting on his own dime. Thanks to all of you for taking the time to help me in the development of my book.

Other people who helped me in the journey of getting the book published included Evan Conrad, Ken Walters, Brad Petersen, and Marc Blumenthal. Thank you to my former graduate assistants who helped me in the development of the book over the years: Hieu Tran, Jose Lopez, Joseph Syren, Greg Sinclair, and Hunter Pribyl-Huguelet were all valuable in putting together parts of the book and doing research. Hunter, who is now in a PhD program, worked especially hard to revise the book. Thank you for everything you did.

I also want to thank my brother Dr. David Finkle and Richard Kucirek, a high school friend, who went with me to numerous shareholder meetings. Richard also gave me some insights into Buffett through his family interactions with him. David, Richard, and I would stay up all night, wait in line talking to people from all over the world, and then race to get to the front of the arena, next to the stage.

I want to thank all of the people who believed in me and had a positive impact on my life. There were numerous professors, teachers, coaches, teammates, bosses, colleagues, former students, and friends who have made me what I am today.

Most important, I want to thank my family for putting up with me during the writing of this book. Especially my wife, Patti; my ninety-year-old mother, Barbara; my late father, Maynard, who taught me the value of hard work; my three brothers and their wives and kids, Scott and Karen, David and Judi, and Terry and Sue; my stepson, Joe Ritzo, and his wife, Emily, and my stepgrandchildren, Benjamin and Elijah; and finally, my brother-in-law and sister-in-law, Keith and Nancy Livingstone.

My wife would see me disappear into my office for days on end and then ask me, "When are you going to be done?" That was on and off for the past fourteen years! Well, I'm finally done.

WARREN BUFFETT

PART I

EARLY LIFE

CHAPTER 1

WARREN E. BUFFETT'S BACKGROUND

It takes twenty years to build a reputation and five minutes to ruin it. If you think about that, you'll do things differently.[1]

WARREN BUFFETT

On the first day I teach an entrepreneurship course, I always draw a picture of a refrigerator with an open door on the whiteboard. Then I ask my students, "What is that?" Usually, none of them answer the question correctly, which I attribute to my less-than-stellar artistic ability. I tell them and then ask what they notice about the refrigerator. Usually, no one answers this correctly either.

"It's empty," I point out.

Entrepreneurs are hungry. Their refrigerator is empty. I cannot teach students how to be hungry; they either possess that quality or they don't. But after the first lecture, there are always a handful of students who seek me out afterward. They are full of energy and usually have a bunch of ideas that they want to share. Some are already entrepreneurs. I don't need to do anything to motivate them. But being hungry is not the same thing as being successful.

By the end of the semester, another handful of students have decided that they too want to be entrepreneurs. But the ones who surprise and hearten me most of all are the students I never would have pegged as entrepreneurs. I learn of their progress only when they check back with me five or ten years after graduating. Often, they tell me that something I said motivated them, underscoring the impact of a teacher. It's no coincidence that Warren Buffett himself loves to teach. He has often said that if he had not gone into finance and investing, he might have become a teacher.

Maybe that's hard to believe, coming from a multibillionaire. But Warren E. Buffett often confounds expectations and stereotypes. His stratospheric success, paired with his humble personal style, have mesmerized people all over the world for decades. Buffett, the chief executive officer (CEO) and chair of Berkshire Hathaway, is the J. P. Morgan of the late twentieth- and early twenty-first centuries. By the time he dies, Buffett will have given more than $100 billion to charity. Part of his mystique is how someone so wealthy and intelligent can be so humble, gentle, and generous.

During times of worldwide crisis, Buffett time and again has demonstrated courage, wisdom, and restraint. When the world was in shock during the Great Recession, Buffett spoke with calmness, rationality, and integrity. Prior to that, he had been the voice of reason during other major calamities, such as the 1987 stock market crash, the Gulf wars, the tech bubble of 2000, and the 9/11 terrorist attacks.

I came to know Buffett after learning that the financier with the heart of an educator was inviting university students and their professors to Omaha for a day to teach students how to live their lives both personally and financially. I applied immediately—and was promptly rejected. But I was persistent, and eventually Warren and I built a relationship. Part of my interest in him was rooted in my own personal history. I grew up in Omaha, Nebraska, and went to Omaha Central High School, the same school that Buffett's children, his first wife, Susie, and his father attended. Buffett's son Peter and I often ate lunch together in the school cafeteria. I had no indication then that Peter's father was wealthy.

That might have remained an interesting footnote from my past were it not for the global financial crisis that struck in 2008. During the worst financial crisis since the Great Depression of the 1930s, I decided to learn as much as possible about the person I viewed as the smartest businessman since J. P. Morgan. That is when I realized that there was a connection between my passion as a professor of entrepreneurship and my fascination with the Buffett family. Buffett, however else he may be remembered, is at heart a brilliant entrepreneur.

The standard definition of an entrepreneur is someone who creates their own business for the sake of profit. But there are many nuances and other ways of understanding this particular personality type and that approach to business. Typical of entrepreneurs, Buffett started an investment partnership and grew it through his entrepreneurial skills into one of the most respected companies in the world. His investment career and leadership of Berkshire Hathaway display the hallmarks of entrepreneurship, and these were the products of a mind that was engaged in entrepreneurial ventures from an early age.

One of the most interesting aspects of Buffett's life was his early desire to be self-employed. From the age of six, Buffett was making money on his own in various enterprises. By the time he was twenty-six, Buffett was a millionaire (in today's dollars). He was already quite successful, though unknown outside the business world, when he purchased Berkshire Hathaway in 1964. But many founders flame out. Buffett, by contrast, saw the market value of his company grow by 3,641,613 percent per share, compared with a 30,209 percent gain for the S&P 500 stock index (with dividends).[2] Berkshire Hathaway had beaten the S&P 500 by an average of 10.4 percent annually from 1964 through 2021.

While Buffett's financial accomplishments are well documented and his philosophy and style have been mimicked by many, this book views Buffett through the lens of his entrepreneurship and how his background and mentors helped to shape his astounding trajectory.

An early story illustrates his unusual humility and tenacity. While earning his master's at Columbia in 1951, Buffett learned that his mentor, Benjamin Graham, had purchased a 50 percent stake in GEICO and was chairman of the board. To learn more about GEICO, Buffett traveled from New York City to Washington, D.C., on a Saturday in January. He knocked on the door of its headquarters until a janitor let him in. On the sixth floor, Buffett found an executive named Lorimer "Davy" Davidson, then the assistant to the president. Today, it may be difficult to imagine that an executive would not immediately call security and have Buffett escorted from the premises. But I imagine that Buffett introduced himself as Graham's student and, as Graham's stake in the company effectively made him Davidson's boss, it's a bit less surprising that Davidson would entertain questions from the ambitious young man standing before him. Either way, the story is a classic example of Buffett's initiative and drive. He managed to talk with Davidson for five hours.

Davidson explained that there were two ways to make money in the insurance industry. The first was through premiums on policies. The second was investment returns on the premiums (a concept known as "float," which I explain in more detail in chapter 6). Davidson also shared that GEICO's method of selling, through direct marketing, gave it a cost advantage of 10 to 25 percent over competitors that sold through agents, a form of distribution so ingrained in the business of these insurers that it was impossible for them to give it up. This session with Davidson made Buffett more excited about GEICO than he had ever been about a stock.[3] He later said that he'd learned more in five hours with Davidson (who eventually ascended to become CEO of GEICO) than he had throughout his entire college career.

I recount this story to demonstrate Buffett's entrepreneurial hunger. It has become a cliché to trace a businessperson's success all the way back to their first lemonade stand. But in Buffett's case, it is warranted. Even as a six-year-old, he displayed the hustle, motivation, and drive to be independent that entrepreneurs have. Of course, social currents play a role as well. Buffett was growing up during the Great Depression, where it was common to see kids going door to door selling whatever they could. In his case, it was chewing gum:

> I had this little green tray, which had five different areas in it. I'm pretty sure my aunt Edie gave me that. It had containers for five different brands of gum, Juicy Fruit, Spearmint, Doublemint, and so on. I would buy packs of gum from my grandfather and go around door to door in the neighborhood selling this stuff. I used to do that in the evening, largely. I remember a woman saying, I'll take one stick of Juicy Fruit. I said, we do not break up packs of gum, I mean, I've got my principles.[4]

Buffett recalls that he made two cents of profit per pack. Selling one stick was tempting, but not tempting enough because, the child reasoned, if he sold one stick to the woman, he would have four individual sticks left to sell—not worth the risk of no takers.[5]

Not many six-year-olds would make that kind of calculation. But Buffett had the bug. After his venture into chewing gum, he started his next entrepreneurial venture with Coca-Cola. Buffett got the idea for selling Coca-Cola based on all of the bottle caps he was collecting at gas stations. Out of 8,000 caps he collected, a great majority were Coca-Cola. Hence began his venture of purchasing six-packs of Coca-Cola from his grandfather's store for 25 cents and selling individual bottles door-to-door for 5 cents each—earning a 20 percent profit.[6] He also juggled three paper routes for two rival newspapers. He once said, "I liked to work by myself, where I could spend my time thinking about things I wanted to think about . . . I could be sitting in a room thinking, or I could be riding around flinging things and thinking."[7]

EARLY YEARS

Warren Buffett's family background and experiences in childhood provided the foundation for his values, demeanor, and attitude. Entrepreneurialism was part of his heritage. His family's history in America dates back seven generations, to the 1600s, when his earliest relatives moved from France and settled on Long Island, New York, as farmers. Two hundred years later, his great-grandfather, Sidney Homan Buffett, aspiring to something more than the hard life and meager wages of farming, moved west to Nebraska, where he eventually opened his own grocery store in downtown Omaha. Even then, in the 1860s, the Buffetts were dispensing business advice. Sidney's father wrote him letters with the following counsel: "Try to be punctual in all your dealings. You will find it difficult to get along with some men, deal as little as possible with such. . . . Save your credit, for it is better than money. . . . If you go on in business, be content with moderate gains. Don't be too hasty to get rich. . . . I want you to live so as to be fit to live and fit to die."[8]

Sidney married Evelyn Ketchum in 1870, and they had six children. Their sons Ernest and Frank helped to run the grocery store. Born in 1877, Ernest married Henrietta Duval in 1898. The couple had four sons and a daughter: Clarence, George, Fred, Howard, and Alice. Ernest, grandfather to the future richest man on the planet, was known as a hard worker who demanded much of his employees. And he was given to spouting the kinds of financial aphorisms so often attributed to the future Oracle of Omaha: "Spend less than you make" and "do not go into debt,"[9] he often advised his grandson Warren.

The Buffetts were frugal people who insisted on the value of education. This was particularly true for Ernest, who left school in the eighth grade to work in the grocery business due to the Panic of 1893, an economic depression in the United States that lasted from 1893 to 1897.[10]

Ernest insisted that all his children, including his daughter Alice, earn college degrees. So they did, a rare achievement at the time—especially for a girl.

Manual Labor

Ernest Buffett was as hard on his kin as on any other employee. Warren worked for him, unloading trucks, stocking shelves, managing wartime rations, and keeping the sidewalks in front of Buffett & Sons clear of snow during the punishing

Nebraska winters. Ernest paid him $2 a day for twelve hours of work (about 17 cents per hour, or $2.65 per hour in today's dollars). It was during these years that the young Buffett became certain that he wanted a life that did not involve manual labor, and that, whatever work he eventually did, he would be his own boss.[11]

As Charlie Munger said, "There was no minimum wage in those days on Saturday,"[12] nor were there child labor laws. Social Security was a new concept, and it disgusted Ernest, who believed that it discouraged self-reliance. After working Warren, his friend John Pescal, and Warren's eventual right-hand man Charlie Munger to the bone, Ernest demanded that they each fork over two pennies from their $2 pay, as their contribution to Social Security.

Today, Buffett recalls those years, and a key lesson that his grandfather imparted:

> The worst job was when he hired me and my friend John Pescal to shovel snow. We had this huge snowstorm, a foot of super wet snow. We had to shovel out the whole bank of snow, in front where the customers parked and in the alleyway behind the store, in the loading dock, and by the garage where we had the six trucks. We worked at this for about five hours—shoveling, shoveling, shoveling, shoveling. Eventually, we couldn't even straighten our hands. And then we went to my grandfather. He said, "Well, how much should I pay you boys? A dime's too little and a dollar's too much!" I'll never forget—John and I looked at each other. . . .[13]

Their stomachs dropped. Ernest was talking about pay that they would have to split between them. Buffett remembers this as the moment he learned a key adage: "Always know what the deal is in advance."[14]

In the early years of the twentieth century, Omaha was run by a few prominent families, and the Buffetts were decidedly not among them. Ernest's son Howard, attending public schools and wearing hand-me-downs, felt his outsider status acutely. As soon as he was able, Howard escaped to attend college at the University of Nebraska in Lincoln, where he majored in journalism. As editor of the school newspaper, the *Daily Nebraskan*, Howard hired a bright young woman named Leila Stahl, and the two eventually married in 1925. Within two years, the couple had moved back to Omaha, where they had three children: Doris (born in 1928), Warren (born in 1930), and Roberta (known as "Bertie," born in 1934). Initially, Howard sold insurance. Then, two years before the stock market crash of 1929, he decided to become a stockbroker for Union State Bank. Howard died young, at age sixty, but not before turning to politics and serving four terms as a Republican congressman. The Buffetts were moving up in the world.

Buffett and the Great Depression

One of the biggest early influences on Warren Buffett's life was the Great Depression. On September 3, 1929, the Dow Jones Industrial Average peaked at 381.17. By November, the market had crashed to 220.39, a drop of 42 percent. But the ride was not yet over. Although stocks had regained much of their value through the early months of 1930, creeping back up to 294.07 by April 17, the market finally bottomed out at 41.22 on July 8, 1932. In the end, 89 percent of its value was lost, plunging millions of people into poverty and touching off an economic depression that rocked the world and haunts history to this day. Into this financial maelstrom, Warren Buffett was born on August 30, 1930.

The following year, two days after Warren's first birthday, his father was laid off. Howard, now ousted from his stockbroker's job, had also lost all of his family's savings. (The period following the market crash saw more than 4,000 bank failures.) Could he work at the grocery store? Howard asked his father. Ernest had no money to hire him with. Instead, he supplied his son and grandchildren with food—on credit.

Undefeated, Howard opened his own stock brokerage, selling municipal bonds, utility stocks, and other securities that he deemed safe. The business thrived, and slowly the firm began to make money. But that did not mean all was smooth. The Buffetts' financial stress began to show up in the behavior of Warren's mother, Leila, who verbally abused her three children. (Warren's older sister, Doris Buffett, later came to believe that Leila suffered from undiagnosed bipolar disorder.)[15] Around the same time, Howard was diagnosed with a heart condition that also took a toll. Warren and his siblings later said they could tell what type of day it was going to be by the tone of Leila's voice in the morning.[16] Both Leila's grandmother and mother had a history of mental illness.[17] Her mother, Stella, had a nervous breakdown and was mired in depression, which had caused the children to look after the household. Her sister died by suicide,[18] and Leila's grandmother died in a mental institution.

The result of these hard early years on Buffett will surprise few: He was determined to never again endure poverty. He would remain independent of others and be his own boss. By age thirty, Buffett vowed, he would be a millionaire. In fact, he beat the deadline by four years.

Later in life, Buffett spoke fondly of his parents. They were intelligent people who talked about interesting things and sent him to solid schools. But he also recognized the role of luck. "I was born at the right time and place. I won the 'Ovarian Lottery,' "[19] he has said. "I've had it so good in this world, you know. The odds were fifty-to-one against me being born in the United States in 1930. I won the lottery the day I emerged from the womb by being in the United States instead of some other country where my chances would have been way different."[20]

Early Adventures in Entrepreneurship

For Warren's tenth birthday, his father took him to New York City. The nation's financial capital interested Warren for three specific reasons. He wanted to see the Scott Stamp and Coin Company, the Lionel Train Company, and the New York Stock Exchange. The scene from the stock exchange dining room—and the power of the wealth he was looking at—were embedded in his mind. Even decades later, Buffett recalled:

> We had lunch at the Exchange with a fellow named At Mol, a Dutchman, a member of the stock exchange, and a very impressive-looking man. After lunch, a guy came along with a tray that had all these different kinds of tobacco leaves on it. He made up a cigar for Mr. Mol, who picked out the leaves that he wanted. And I thought, this is it. It doesn't get any better than this. . . . [Money] could make me independent. Then I could do what I wanted to do with my life. And the biggest thing I wanted to do was work for myself.[21]

An avid reader, Buffett was riveted by any book that had the words "investment" or "finance" in the title, or implied the same. One of his favorites was *A Thousand Ways to Make $1,000*.[22] At ten, he was already doing whatever he could to make a buck. Selling peanuts and popcorn during football games at what is now the University of Nebraska–Omaha, he would call out, "Peanuts, popcorn, five cents, a nickel, half dime, fifth of a quarter, get your peanuts and popcorn here!" gleefully demonstrating his facility with figures.[23]

More profitable than concessions was Buffett's golf venture. He walked the nearby courses, gathering up golf balls that had been lost in the underbrush, and then he cleaned them up and resold them for $6 a dozen. Eventually, the police got wise and kicked him out. But when the authorities spoke to Buffett's parents, Howard and Leila were unconcerned. This was merely another sign of their son's precocity and ambition, they felt. Warren's sisters saw it somewhat differently. Their brother seemed to walk beneath a halo of approval and for that reason got away with pushing boundaries.[24]

The dustup over his golf scheme hardly deterred the young Warren. Although he was still too young to gamble, the future Oracle of Omaha frequently visited the local Ak-Sar-Ben (Nebraska spelled backwards) Racetrack and Coliseum, looking for discarded tickets that might be worth money. Buffett later described the practice with glee:

> They called that "stooping." At the start of the racing season, you get all these people who had never seen a race except in the movies. And they would think that if your horse came in second or third, you did not get paid, because the emphasis was on the winner, so they would throw away place and show tickets. The other time you would hit it big was when there was a disputed race. . . . By that time, people had thrown away their tickets. Meanwhile, we were just gobbling them up.[25]

Even then he was using knowledge—or another person's lack of it—to gain a financial advantage. Buffett also sold a racer's tip sheet, combining his skill at math and his love of gathering information to handicap the horses. He hawked Stable-Boy Selections for twenty-five cents, undercutting the official Blue Sheet, which went for a bit more.[26]

Every one of these ventures required an ability to make rapid calculations on the spot, in his head. To this day, Buffett claims that he does not use a computer or calculator when figuring profits and losses.

First Investments in Stocks and Real Estate

In 1942, at age eleven, Buffett purchased his first stock: three shares of Cities Service for $38.25 per share (a total investment of $114.75, presumably earned through his racetrack schemes). The price bottomed at $27 and then rose to $40. So he sold it—only to watch the stock price soar to $200 a share.[27] This was a key early lesson about the importance of patience in investing. The performance of the stock market over the next seventy-seven years illustrates everything you need to know about Buffett's positive outlook on American investing. Today, that young boy's investment would be worth more than $600,000.[28]

Howard Buffett, always interested in politics and public affairs, got elected to Congress when Warren was twelve, and the family moved to Washington, D.C. Although the future financier missed his friends in Omaha, he thrived in D.C., continuing his entrepreneurial endeavors. He earned $175 a month delivering the *Washington Post* and filed his first tax form with the Internal Revenue Service (IRS) in 1944,[29] deducting his bicycle as a $35 business expense. At age fifteen,[30] he purchased forty acres of Nebraska farmland for $1,200[31] and leased it out. By the time he entered ninth grade, Buffett had amassed $14,275 in today's dollars.

BUFFETT THE ENTREPRENEUR IN HIGH SCHOOL

The comfort that Warren Buffett derived from making money was surpassed only by the energy he felt through even these early forays into entrepreneurialism. Each success made him more ambitious for the next. While a student at D.C.'s Woodrow Wilson High School, Buffett and his friend Don Daly went into business by purchasing a used pinball machine for $25 (the original price was $300) and installing it in a barbershop.[32] They charged 5 cents to play and split the proceeds 50-50 with the owner. Calling it the Wilson-Coin-Operated Machine Company, the teens' little venture quickly grew to seven machines in different stores and earned them $50 a week. In 1947, they sold the business for $1,200 to a war veteran.[33] Daly and Buffett also rented out a 1928 Rolls Royce, which Daly had bought for $350 from a scrapyard and repaired himself, for $35 per day.[34]

By age sixteen, Buffett had graduated. He was sixteenth in his class of 350[35] and had already made $6,000 (or $76,366 in 2022 dollars) through his various entrepreneurial ventures. His high school yearbook photo was captioned "likes math: a future stock broker."[36] The yearbook editors were certainly pointed in the right direction. But they could hardly have guessed how soundly their predictions would be knocked out of the park. As of March 2022, Buffett has a personal net worth of $126 billion. (See appendices 1–3 for financial statements for Berkshire Hathaway from 2016–2021, and table 1.1 for the companies that it owns as of March 2022.)

TABLE 1.1 List of companies that Berkshire Hathaway owns as of March 2022

No.	Company	No.	Company
1	Acme Brick Company	32	HomeServices of America
2	Ben Bridge Jeweler	33	IMC International Metalworking Companies
3	Benjamin Moore & Co.	34	International Dairy Queen, Inc.
4	Berkshire Hathaway Automotive	35	Johns Manville
5	Berkshire Hathaway Direct Insurance Company (THREE)	36	Jordan's Furniture
		37	Justin Brands
6	Berkshire Hathaway Energy Company	38	Kraft Heinz
7	Berkshire Hathaway GUARD Insurance Co.	39	Larson-Juhl
8	Berkshire Hathaway Homestate Companies	40	LiquidPower Specialty Products Inc. (LSPI)
9	Berkshire Hathaway Specialty Insurance	41	Louis–Motorcycle & Leisure
10	biBERK Business Insurance	42	Lubrizol Corporation
11	BNSF Railway	43	Marmon Holdings, Inc.
12	BoatUS	44	McLane Company
13	Borsheims Fine Jewelry	45	MedPro Group
14	Brooks	46	MiTek Inc.
15	Business Wire	47	MLMIC Insurance Company
16	Central States Indemnity Company	48	National Indemnity Company
17	Charter Brokerage	49	Nebraska Furniture Mart
18	Clayton Homes	50	NetJets
19	CORT Business Services	51	Oriental Trading Company
20	CTB Inc.	52	Pampered Chef
21	Duracell	53	Precision Castparts Corp.
22	Fechheimer Brothers Company	54	RC Willey Home Furnishings
23	FlightSafety	55	Richline Group
24	Forest River	56	Scott Fetzer Companies
25	Fruit of the Loom Companies	57	See's Candies
26	Garan Incorporated	58	Shaw Industries
27	Gateway Underwriters Agency	59	Star Furniture
28	GEICO Auto Insurance	60	TTI, Inc.
29	General Re	61	United States Liability Insurance Group (USLI)
30	Helzberg Diamonds	62	XTRA Corporation
31	H. H. Brown Shoe Group		

Source: Berkshire Hathaway, Inc. Subsidiaries: Retrieved from https://www.berkshirehathaway.com/subs/sublinks.html.

THE ROLE OF ROOTS

I recount these high points from Warren Buffett's early life to underscore his belief in the importance of place, and family, in shaping a person's trajectory. I also do so to share my personal perspective on his story. As I have mentioned, I too grew up in Omaha and attended Omaha Central High School, the alma mater of Warren's father, Howard; his first wife, Susan Thompson Buffett; and his three children, Susie, Howard, and Peter. Buffett's legendary right-hand man and business partner, Charlie Munger, also graduated from Omaha Central, in 1941. (We'll learn more about him and his influence on Warren Buffett in chapter 3.)

The largest city in Nebraska, Omaha is midwestern in its culture and values. Its 1.3 million residents value hard work and humility. Omaha Central High School today educates some 2,500 students. When I attended, in the late 1970s, the school was open to anyone in the city. As such, it was culturally and ethnically diverse, with students who were Black, Hispanic, Jewish, Asian American, and Native American. Today, Omaha Central is 60 percent minority students.

When I attended Central, it was housed in an old building with creaky floors. The doors from the courtyard no longer shut, and in winter the cold prairie air would whistle inside. There were four floors, with separate staircases for girls and boys. The bathrooms were tiny, lacking in privacy, and often full of cigarette smoke.

Peter Buffett

When I attended Central, Buffett's youngest son, Peter (Pete) Buffett, was a senior. We often ate lunch together, members of a loose group of friends who would grow up to become some of the most prominent intellectuals in our city. Several were on Omaha Central's math team, which consistently placed among the top three nationally. Some of these students went on to Harvard, the Massachusetts Institute of Technology (MIT), or the University of Chicago. One grew up to run two public companies in Silicon Valley. Excellence in mathematics was an important part of the culture at Central. But I had no idea about Pete's background or the wealth of his father. Neither did anyone around us. Warren Buffett maintained a low profile in the community, as well as in the financial markets.

Even his children were unaware of Buffett's remarkable investment success. He came home from work every evening and ate dinner with them. To the kids, he was just Dad.

Today, Pete is a musician, author, philanthropist, composer, and Emmy winner. The author of the *New York Times* bestseller *Life Is What You Make It: Find Your Own Path to Fulfillment*, Pete is often asked about his upbringing. How did growing up in Omaha, as the son of the world's wealthiest man, shape him? In a 2011 interview, Peter had this to say about his community:

> I know what worked for me was that it wasn't noisy—there wasn't a lot of distraction. There weren't a lot of people thinking you had to be this way to be cool or that way to be whatever. I talk about this in my show, that the simplicity and integrity of my upbringing—it wasn't about my father having money or any of that stuff—because when we were kids, we didn't know he did. It was about my grandparents living a few blocks away. It was about going to the same school, where I had the same English teacher my mother had. It was all these things that created a safe environment. I mean, I know they say that musicians and artists have to struggle and be miserable. First of all, I don't think that's true, although it does give you things to work with in terms of writing songs and things. I think it's the environment's lack of distraction that allows you to [produce art], and that's why my dad stayed in Omaha, because he could focus on his version of art. I really think the environment—what some people might think, "Geez, this isn't very exciting"—actually can be a great incubator for great ideas.[37]

Omaha was home to the world's largest stockyard from 1955 to 1971. It opened in 1884, with 7,000 head of cattle, and had expanded to have 7.7 million by the late 1940s. Although the stockyards shut down in 1999, the old Livestock Exchange building still exists. Today, the city is the home of Boys Town and the College World Series. Aside from Berkshire Hathaway, several other Fortune 500 and Fortune 1000 companies are located there, including Aflac (insurance and financial), Union Pacific (the largest railroad in the United States), Peter Kiewit Sons (construction), Mutual of Omaha (insurance and financial), TD Ameritrade (financial), Green Plains Renewable Energy, Werner Enterprises (transportation and logistics), and Valmont Industries (manufacturing).

Omaha Health Care and Berkshire Philanthropy

From my perspective, what feels particularly notable about our hometown is the role of health care in Omaha and its relationship to philanthropy. In 2009, 2011, and 2017, I took three groups of students and four professors to Omaha to meet with Buffett. I showed them Central High School, Buffett's home, and Berkshire Hathaway's corporate headquarters. But they were most dazzled by the city's health-care complex in Midtown. Creighton University and the University of Nebraska Medical Center (usually referred to as the "Med Center") both have a medical school and a pharmacy school. In 2018, Creighton opened a new dental school as well. In addition, Omaha boasts six nursing schools. Together, these institutions position Omaha as one of the top health-care communities in the country.

Amid all of it, we could not miss a huge new building—the Fred and Pamela Buffett Cancer Center. Warren's cousin Fred Buffett, one of the earliest investors in Berkshire Hathaway, died of kidney cancer twenty-five years ago. After his passing, Fred's widow led a drive to raise $370 million for the new center.

Dick Holland, a prominent local businessperson, was an early investor with Buffett who made millions. He has stated that at least $1 billion in Berkshire-related money has been donated or pledged to the betterment of Omaha. Holland himself became a major donor to the city's $90 million Holland Performing Arts Center. Other early Berkshire investors who have funneled their earnings back into Nebraska institutions include Carl and Joyce Mammel, Bill and Ruth Scott, Lee and Willa Seemann, Dan Monen, John and Janice Cleary, Leland and Dorothy Olson, Stanley and Dorothy Truhlsen, and Donald and Mildred Topp Othmer. Their projects include a business college, a classroom building in Lincoln, medical research and teaching facilities in Omaha, and the football stadium at Omaha Central High School.[38]

BUFFETT THE ENTREPRENEUR

So far, I have sketched some of the building blocks of personal background and social history that have contributed to Warren Buffett becoming one of the most successful entrepreneurs of all time. His personality and values were undoubtedly shaped by the entrepreneurial tradition within his own family: the print shop owned by his maternal grandparents and the grocery store founded by Ernest Buffett. To the general public, the humility and frugality so often associated with Buffett may obscure his dynamism. But make no mistake: Warren Buffett had a vision for his life that he pursued relentlessly. He also possesses many of the traits shared by all entrepreneurs.

As a personality type, entrepreneurs have a strong drive to achieve, and they are willing to own their mistakes rather than blaming others. They are risk-takers, tolerant of ambiguity but with a keen sense of pragmatism about the probability of success in a given venture. In other words, they are not reckless. Most also have a high need for independence, rock-solid self-confidence, and stubborn optimism. They persevere, even in the face of early failures, and they are oriented toward creative problem-solving. Always, they are highly energetic people who pride themselves on their resourcefulness. Almost always, they are team builders.

Above all, entrepreneurs are not followers. They are unafraid of moving in a direction opposite to that of the crowd, the masses. That's where they find innovation. This orientation is one that Buffett and his partner Charlie Munger emphasize constantly: To be successful, entrepreneurs must think for themselves rather than passively following a direction or cues set by others.

CAN YOU BECOME AN ENTREPRENEUR?

I have spent a large part of my academic career observing Warren Buffett, whether through my work teaching entrepreneurship or from growing up in Omaha alongside his children. Aside from the entrepreneurial personality traits I've listed here, the one characteristic I see in all entrepreneurs is appetite: Put simply, entrepreneurs are hungry! Hungry for money, hungry for success, hungry for independence—however you couch it, all of them have an overweening hunger to chase down their goals.

Many also come from families with a tradition of entrepreneurship. In Buffett's case, the combination of his rough experience working for Grandpa Ernest in the grocery store—convincing young Warren that he wanted a life free from manual labor—and the role model of Ernest as self-reliant and independent provided the requisite spark of inspiration.

Buffett's longtime partner, Charlie Munger, also started several entrepreneurial ventures at a very young age. There is a term for these intense, highly driven individuals. No matter how much they have achieved, they remain ever-interested in new ideas, ever-hungry for new ventures. We call them "serial entrepreneurs."

Any type of organization can be entrepreneurial (e.g., corporations, small businesses, family businesses, franchises, social ventures, and fast-growth enterprises), and all organizations need the creativity of an entrepreneurial mindset at the helm. However, as I've demonstrated through Buffett's early-life history, most entrepreneurs prefer to work on their own rather than for other organizations.

The motivations powering men and women toward entrepreneurship are similar, but not the same. For men, the primary driver tends to be independence and money. For women, who have been historically restricted from rising into the upper echelons of management, the motivation is often a need for greater job satisfaction, while money is fourth. For both genders, their bottomless hunger and seemingly endless energy may imply that entrepreneurs are necessarily young. But that isn't always the case.

When Is the Right Age to Become an Entrepreneur?

There is no age restriction or ideal moment for launching your own business, although younger people tend to be more tolerant of risk and at ease with ambiguity. The following entrepreneurs created their companies at a wide variety of ages:

- Facebook: Mark Zuckerburg (cofounder: twenty)
- Apple: Steve Jobs (cofounder: twenty-one)
- Tesla, PayPal, Neuralink, Open AI, and Zip2: Elon Musk (founder or cofounder from the age of twenty-four)
- Nike: Phil Knight (cofounder: twenty-six)
- Google: Sergey Brin and Larry Page (cofounders: twenty-seven)
- Spanx: Sara Blakely (founder: twenty-seven)
- Robinhood: Vladimir Tenev and Baiju Bhatt (cofounders: twenty-seven and twenty-eight)
- Merrill Lynch: Charles Merrill (cofounder: twenty-eight)
- Alibaba: Jack Ma (cofounder: thirty-one)
- Amazon: Jeff Bezos (founder: thirty-one)
- Twitter: Jack Dorsey (founder: thirty-two)
- Urban One: Cathy Hughes (founder: thirty-three)

- Charles Schwab Corporation (founder, Charles Schwab: thirty-four)
- Appaloosa Management: David Tepper (founder: thirty-five)
- IBM: Thomas Watson and Charles Flint (cofounders: thirty-six and sixty)
- Ford Motor Company: Henry Ford (founder: forty)
- Walmart: Sam Walton (founder: forty)
- Home Depot: Bernie Marcus (cofounder: fifty)
- eTrade: Bill Porter (cofounder: fifty-four)
- Kentucky Fried Chicken (KFC): Harlan Sanders (founder: sixty-two)

As far as perseverance and tolerance for failure, there may be no better example than Jack Ma, who had to overcome numerous hurdles before he became the world-famous billionaire we know today. For starters, to learn English, he spent nine years giving foreigners tours of his hometown, Hangzhou, China. He started the job at age twelve or thirteen, riding his bike seventeen miles in the rain, sleet, or snow to get to work. He failed an important primary school test twice and failed a comparable middle school test three times. As a young man, he was one of twenty-four people to apply for a job at Hangzhou's first KFC—and the only one rejected. That was just one of dozens of job rejections. Ma also failed his entrance exams to college, although he eventually got in. Still, he labored. Ma applied to Harvard Business School ten times and never made it. Today, he is worth billions.[39]

What the Most Successful Entrepreneurs Did

- Participated in new ventures
- Gained start-up experience
- Knew where to seek advice (social networks)
- Acquired skills in a line of business
- Focused on making their businesses profitable
- Continuously read and learned
- Surrounded themselves with creative, resourceful, and intelligent people and then got out of their way
- Were good to their employees (e.g., shared the profits)
- Knew they had weaknesses (Buffett, for example, famously invests only in industries he understands, thereby admitting that he does not understand everything)

What Can You Do to Become a Successful Entrepreneur?

- Build a network of people with a wide variety of skill sets
- Get a few mentors
- Seek education; many failures occur if you have experience and no education—you do not need a master of business administration (MBA) degree, but do take some courses to help you with marketing negotiations, accounting, and finance
- Get work experience in marketing, finance, and/or operational work
- Participate in new ventures and learn from your mistakes

Motivations for Becoming an Entrepreneur

Your desire to become an entrepreneur can stem internally, from your own ambition, or it can be touched off by an unexpected external event, such as a divorce, a layoff, or even a pandemic. Or you may simply come upon an opportunity and become inspired to take a calculated risk.

I offer this advice to my students: If you really want to be an entrepreneur, go work for someone in the industry you're focused on. Learn everything you can. Ask questions and look for niches. Save your money so you will have enough when the time is right to leave.

Even if you feel that you are not an entrepreneur at heart, there might be points in your life when you have no choice but to become one. For example, the COVID-19 pandemic resulted in the sharpest spike in unemployment since the Great Depression. Millions of people have reevaluated their options and their values, plunging into independent, gig-economy work that edges toward the entrepreneurial: driving for Uber, blog writing, independent consulting, online tutoring, sales via the Internet, building online businesses, recording audiobooks, pet-sitting, house-sitting, and many more. But it takes a self-starter with confidence to move from independent side gigs into full-fledged entrepreneurialism. Even if you are not an entrepreneur, all signs suggest that in the America of the twenty-first century, you'll need to think and act like one.

CHAPTER 2

EARLY INFLUENCES, COLLEGE, AND PARTNERSHIP YEARS

There is one all-important law of human conduct. If we obey that law, we shall almost never get into trouble. In fact, that law, if obeyed, will bring us countless friends and constant happiness. But the very instant we break the law, we shall get into endless trouble. The law is this: Always make the other person feel important. John Dewey . . . said that the desire to be important is the deepest urge in human nature; and William James said: "The deepest principle in human nature is the craving to be appreciated."[1]

DALE CARNEGIE

HOW TO WIN FRIENDS AND INFLUENCE PEOPLE

As a youngster, Warren Buffett had been socially awkward. To address this problem, he sought to learn as much as possible from successful people. One of his most significant influences was Dale Carnegie, the author of the now-legendary *How to Win Friends and Influence People* (1936).

Carnegie, an expert on salesmanship and public speaking, built his own career as an entrepreneur on training others in those skills. Buffett practiced Carnegie's principles throughout high school. Buffett confidante Alice Schroeder reports, "By high school, he had accumulated a few more friends, joined the Woodrow Wilson golf team, and managed to make himself inoffensive if not popular. Dale Carnegie's system had honed his natural wit; above all, it enhanced his persuasiveness, his flair for salesmanship."[2] These qualities would serve Buffett well throughout his career.

He has often quipped that one of the best decisions he ever made was spending $100 on a Dale Carnegie class in public speaking. At the time, he was twenty-one years old, fresh out of graduate school and working as a stockbroker for his father's investment firm. He was also teaching a course on investing at the University of Nebraska–Omaha. Buffett's students were, on average, twice as old as their youthful professor.

To this day, you will not find his diplomas from college or business school on Buffett's office wall, but you will find his certificate from the Carnegie course. I have excerpted here the Carnegie principles that Buffett found so meaningful. All come verbatim from Carnegie's book.[3]

Become a Friendlier Person

1. Do not criticize, condemn, or complain.
2. Give honest and sincere appreciation.
3. Arouse in the other person an eager want.
4. Become genuinely interested in other people.
5. Smile.
6. Remember that a person's name is to that person the sweetest and most important sound in any language.
7. Be a good listener. Encourage others to talk about themselves.
8. Talk in terms of the other person's interests.
9. Make the other person feel important—and do it sincerely.

Win People to Your Way of Thinking

1. The only way to get the best of an argument is to avoid it.
2. Show respect for the other person's opinions. Never say, "You are wrong."
3. If you are wrong, admit it quickly and emphatically.
4. Begin in a friendly way.
5. Get the other person saying "yes, yes" immediately.
6. Let the other person do a great deal of the talking.
7. Let the other person feel that the idea is his or hers.
8. Try honestly to see things from the other person's point of view.
9. Be sympathetic with the other person's ideas and desires.
10. Appeal to the nobler motives.

11. Dramatize your ideas.
12. Throw down a challenge.

Be a Leader

1. Begin with praise and honest appreciation.
2. Call attention to people's mistakes indirectly.
3. Talk about your own mistakes before criticizing the other person.
4. Ask questions instead of giving direct orders.
5. Let the other person save face.
6. Praise the slightest improvement and praise every improvement. Be "hearty in your approbation and lavish in your praise."
7. Give the other person a fine reputation to live up to.
8. Use encouragement. Make the fault seem easy to correct.
9. Make the other person happy about doing the thing you suggest.

Here is some additional guidance from Carnegie's book that Buffett incorporated into his life and work:

> Benjamin Franklin, tactless in his youth, became so diplomatic, so adroit at handling people, that he was made American Ambassador to France. The secret of his success? "I will speak ill of no man," he said, ". . . and speak all the good I know of everybody."[4]
>
> Any fool can criticize, condemn and complain—and most fools do. But it takes character and self-control to be understanding and forgiving.[5]
>
> A great man shows his greatness by the way he treats little men. [Carnegie attributed this statement to Thomas Carlyle.][6]
>
> I consider my ability to arouse enthusiasm among my people . . . the greatest asset I possess, and the way to develop the best that is in a person is by appreciation and encouragement. There is nothing else that so kills the ambitions of a person as criticisms from superiors. I never criticize anyone. I believe in giving a person incentive to work. So, I am anxious to praise but loath to find fault. If I like anything, I am hearty in my approbation and lavish in my praise. [Carnegie attributed this to Charles Schwab.][7]
>
> The only way on earth to influence other people is to talk about what they want and show them how to get it.[8]

Alfred Adler, the famous Viennese psychologist, wrote a book entitled *What Life Should Mean to You*. In that book he says: "It is the individual who is not interested in his fellow men who has the greatest difficulties in life and provides the greatest injury to others. It is from among such individuals that all human failures spring."[9]

Charles Schwab told me that his smile had been worth a million dollars. And he was probably understating the truth. For Schwab's personality, his charm, his ability to make people like him, were almost wholly responsible for his extraordinary success; and one of the most delightful factors in his personality was his captivating smile. Actions speak louder than words, and a smile says, "I like you; you make me happy. I am glad to see you."[10]

BUFFETT AND HIGHER EDUCATION

Buffett did not want to go to college.[11] He thought that he could get just as good an education by reading on his own, and he was certain that hands-on experience in business would always be more valuable than sitting in a lecture hall. Buffett applied this belief to others as well. For example, when Berkshire Hathaway purchased Borsheims jewelry store in Omaha, Buffett allowed the company to retain a chief executive officer (CEO) who had no college degree. When I brought twenty-six of my students to visit with Buffett, he repeated the edict. "I do not remember the name of the study, but there was a paper written on the correlation between IQ, GPA, and school attended, with business success," Buffett told my students during a visit in November 2009. "The findings indicated that the best correlation with success was when the person got started in business. Experience was the most important determinant in success."

From the Ivy League to the University of Nebraska

Under pressure from his father, Buffett enrolled in the Wharton School of Business at the University of Pennsylvania. He was only seventeen when he enrolled, and complained almost immediately that he knew more than his professors did. This was not adolescent hyperbole—one of Buffett's roommates marveled at his ability to ace exams with only fifteen minutes of studying.

Young Warren's greatest complaint, however, was the theoretical nature of academia. Fellow students later recalled that he had no fear of using his own early experiences with entrepreneurialism to correct his professors in front of the whole class. More interested in putting his practical knowledge to use, after a year at Wharton, Buffett told his father that he planned to quit school and start his own business. But again his father prevailed, convincing Buffett to give Wharton one more year. He did, then transferred to the University of Nebraska–Lincoln, and earned enough credits to graduate with a bachelor of science in business administration at the end of his junior year. He was nineteen. Buffett's famously unflashy tastes were evident even when it came to something as formative as education.

After returning to Nebraska, Buffett immediately put his belief in the value of life experience into practice. While taking a full course load, he worked as a circulation manager for the *Lincoln Journal*, where he organized more than fifty workers and their newspaper routes.

BUFFETT AND BENJAMIN GRAHAM

Despite his antipathy toward academia, Buffett applied to Harvard University for graduate studies after earning his undergraduate degree. The result? Rejection. Harvard's interviewer suggested that Buffett get more significant business experience.

Despondent, Buffett dove into self-study. Always an avid reader, he buried himself in books on investing methodology. One book, *The Intelligent Investor* (1949) by Benjamin Graham, impressed him so much that Buffett decided he needed to study under Graham, who taught at Columbia University's Graduate School of Business in New York City. Later in his career, Buffett called *The Intelligent Investor* the most significant book ever written on investing. He mentioned that to my students every time we met with him. But the summer that Buffett was rejected by Harvard, he was particularly taken with a book called *Security Analysis*, by Graham and his colleague at Columbia University David Dodd.

Buffett, perusing the course catalog for Columbia Business School, noticed their names and immediately dashed off a letter that might read as brash by today's standards, even rude. "Dear Professor Dodd," he wrote, "I thought you guys were dead, but now that I find out you're alive and teaching at Columbia,

I would really like to come." His retelling of this moment many years later may have been somewhat tongue-in-cheek.[12] But whatever he wrote, it was enough to get Buffett admitted to the master's program.

In the fall of 1950, he moved to one of the cheapest places to live in New York City. (Unfortunately, he could not find university housing due to his late application.) He joined the YMCA for a dime a day and paid a dollar a day for a room at the Y's Sloane House on West 34th Street, by Penn Station.[13] He studied one year under Graham and graduated in 1951.

Graham's Background

Born Benjamin Grossbaum in London, Graham moved to New York City in 1895, when he was a baby. By age twenty, he had changed his identifiably Jewish name to avoid anti-Semitism. Graham's father died in 1903, when the boy was only eight, and his mother lost most of the family's money in the stock market panic of 1907.

Graham's childhood traumas had a lifelong influence on him. Feeling that he had few options, he devoted all of his energies to school. He was a driven young man, earning a scholarship to Columbia University, where he graduated second in his class at age twenty. Prior to leaving school, Graham was invited to join the faculty of three departments: math, philosophy, and English. He rejected all three offers and went to work on Wall Street.

Graham's beginnings there were humble. He worked as a messenger for Newburger, Henderson & Loeb, where he posted bond and stock prices for a mere $12 a week. But he rose quickly. At age twenty-six, Graham was tapped to write research reports and soon was awarded a partnership, at an annual salary of $600,000.[14] This was the equivalent of $9.6 million in 2022.

Graham Becomes an Entrepreneur

Seven years later, at thirty-two, Graham cofounded his own investment partnership with Jerome Newman. This early venture into entrepreneurialism, the Graham-Newman Corporation, rewarded him handsomely. The value of the firm's assets grew by an average of 17.4 percent annually, beating the stock market by 5.5 percentage points. While running his firm, Graham taught a class at Columbia (donating his salary back to the school) and was writing a book with the help of his colleague and assistant, David Dodd. The result, called *Security Analysis* (1934), is still arguably one of the most influential books on investing.

Although Graham-Newman managed to survive two world wars, the firm lost 70 percent of its value during the Great Depression, and that experience of financial precarity—the second in Graham's life—led him to take a comparatively cautious approach toward investing. He followed two principles: (1) purchase a business for less than two-thirds of its net asset value, and (2) purchase stocks with low price-to-earnings ratios.[15] Today, we would call this operating within the margin of safety. In sum, Graham emphasized a company's numbers over any qualitative considerations.

Buffett and Graham at Columbia

Buffett was one of twenty students selected to study under Graham and Dodd in 1950. He was the youngest in the class but became one of Graham's prize pupils—the only student ever to earn an A+ from the revered professor. It's hardly surprising. Both men were independent-minded and entrepreneurial. Buffett had grasped the value of having a mentor, and Graham welcomed talented students. He made such a powerful impression that Buffett later modeled his own mentorship of students on Graham's example.

Under Graham, Buffett immersed himself in *Security Analysis* and *The Intelligent Investor*. He often calls chapters 8 and 20 from the latter book the best two ever written on investing. I discuss both chapters at length later in this book.

In 1951, Buffett left Columbia with a master of science in economics.

BUFFETT ON WALL STREET

Buffett immediately applied to work at the firm founded by his new intellectual guru—even offering to work at the Graham-Newman Corporation for free. But Graham rejected his application. He wanted to hire only Jews, who were unwelcome at many Wall Street firms. As a result, Buffett moved back to Omaha and worked as a stockbroker for his father's investment firm from 1951 to 1954.

It was during this time that Buffett took the Carnegie course on public speaking and taught his investments class at the University of Nebraska–Omaha. But he kept in touch with Graham, sharing savvy investment recommendations and patiently nurturing their connection. (Throughout his career as a successful financier, Buffett would never forget his love of teaching. While he lived in New York, Buffett offered an adult education class in investing at a suburban public school, and he continued this tradition in Omaha, teaching a free course at Creighton University into the 1970s.)[16]

Graham-Newman Corporation

Graham finally hired his star pupil in 1954. He was twenty-four and earning $12,000 a year ($126,500 in today's dollars). More important, he was learning. Graham taught Buffett about arbitrage—the simultaneous purchase and sale of an asset that allows an investor to profit from the smallest discrepancies in price. As explained by investor Jason Fernando on the website Investopedia:

> Arbitrage is the simultaneous purchase and sale of the same asset in different markets in order to profit from tiny differences in the asset's listed price. It exploits short-lived variations in the price of identical or similar financial instruments in different markets or in different forms. As a simple example of arbitrage, consider the following. The stock of Company X is trading at $20 on the New York Stock Exchange (NYSE) while, at the same moment, it is trading for $20.05 on the London Stock Exchange (LSE). A trader can buy the stock on the NYSE and immediately sell the same shares on the LSE, earning a profit of 5 cents per share. The trader could continue to exploit this arbitrage until the specialists on the NYSE run out of inventory of Company X's stock, or until the specialists on the NYSE or LSE adjust their prices to wipe out the opportunity.[17]

The job at Graham-Newman would prove to be short-lived. When Buffett was twenty-five, Graham announced his retirement plans, and he offered his longtime protégé a chance to replace him as a junior partner. (Jerome Newman's son Mickey would step into his own father's shoes as the senior partner.) The firm's fund was relatively small—only about $7 million, or $75 million in today's dollars—but it was well respected. Warren Buffett, not yet thirty, suddenly faced a pivotal life choice: "This was a traumatic decision," Buffett recalled in 2012. "Here was my chance to step into the shoes of my hero—I even named my first son Howard Graham Buffett. (Howard was for my father.) But I also wanted to come back to Omaha. I probably went to work for a month thinking every morning that I would tell Mr. Graham I was going to leave. But it was hard to do."[18]

Graham closed the partnership in 1956 and retired at age sixty-one. Buffett returned to Omaha with $127,000—approximately $1.3 million in today's dollars. He had enough money to retire. The key to this plan was compound interest, something that Buffett calls "the eighth wonder of the world." Compounding is the increase in the value of an asset due to the interest, dividends, or both earned on both a principal and accumulated interest. As Buffett said years later, in *Forbes* magazine: "I thought, I'll go back to Omaha, take some college classes, and read a lot—I was going to retire! I figured we could live on $12,000 a year, and off my $127,000 asset base, I could easily make that. I told my wife: Compound interest guarantees I'm going to get rich."[19]

PHILIP A. FISHER

If Benjamin Graham was Buffett's first major influence, his second was Philip Arthur Fisher, an investor whose *Common Stocks and Uncommon Profits and Other Writings* (1958) became the first book on investing to make the *New York Times* bestseller list. Fisher's basic modus operandi was to buy high-quality companies at an undervalued price and hold them forever. He focused his research on finding firms that had the ability to grow their profits and sales at rates that beat the industry average.[20]

Over the long term, Fisher emphasized, the stock market always works in an investor's favor. This conservative approach to investing neatly dovetailed with Graham's, so it is little surprise that Buffett was influenced by it. But where Graham was quantitatively oriented, Fisher employed the inherently qualitative "scuttlebutt methodology"—that is, gathering firsthand knowledge about a company from various sources. For example, before Buffett invested in Apple in 2016, he could not help noticing that his grandchildren and their friends were on their iPhones all day long. He would take them out to Dairy Queen and watch as they sat there, sending messages to each other without talking, even though they were sitting next to each other.

Another famed proponent of using scuttlebutt methodology is Peter Lynch, the famous investor from Fidelity Investments. Lynch was a good observer of the obvious. When he saw long lines at a retail establishment, he would get excited about an investment opportunity. His investment in Dunkin Donuts (now Dunkin') is an excellent example of this. He noticed the long lines at Dunkin Donuts. He drove all over town and went into the stores and realized the customers loved their coffee. He realized the firm had a lot of room to replicate their stores and grow into a national chain. He eventually made ten to fifteen times his money on the investment.

Lynch supposedly also would take his family to the local mall and simply watch what his wife and kids would gravitate toward and generate investment ideas that way. Lynch's approach was only one tool in his toolkit, but it served him well. The moral of this story is that many great investment opportunities are hiding in plain sight.

The Education of an Entrepreneur

Unlike Buffett's family, which believed ardently in public systems, Fisher's parents had little faith in public schools—at least for young children. Philip, born in San Francisco in 1907, was privately tutored up through elementary school. He graduated from the prestigious Lowell High School in 1923 at sixteen (the same age as Buffett) and enrolled at the University of California–Berkeley.[21]

Fisher eventually transferred to Stanford and began graduate studies there. But by twenty-one, he had dropped out of school to work as a securities analyst with the Anglo-London Paris National Bank in San Francisco. In 1931, as the Great Depression was leveling brokerage houses, Fisher started his own investment counseling firm, Fisher & Company.[22] He was twenty-four years old and managed the company's affairs until his retirement in 1999, at ninety-one.

Fisher was selective about whom he worked with. His management philosophy entailed hiring the best and then don't tell them what to do.

Entrepreneurial Personality

Buffett based much of his management philosophy on Fisher's approach to hiring. Typically, Berkshire Hathaway will buy 80 percent of a company's stock and let management retain 20 percent. This 20 percent is enough incentive for managers to keep the company running profitably while also allowing them tremendous autonomy. Aside from requesting monthly financial statements, his ownership can best be described as hands-off. In chapter 4, I expand on Fisher's investment rules, which provided a foundation for the unprecedented financial success of Berkshire Hathaway.

BUFFETT THE ACCIDENTAL ENTREPRENEUR

After Graham closed his investment partnership in 1956, Buffett pondered his next career move. He did not like the questionable behavior of Wall Street, which in his view did not put the interests of its clients first.[23] But Omaha espoused a vastly different ethos. Buffett liked its sense of community, easy pace, and deep-rooted relationships. All four of Buffett's grandparents lived in Omaha, as well as several of his uncles and aunts. Omaha was free of the "noise" (i.e., questionable information) that choked such financial hot spots as New York, Boston, and San Francisco. Compared to them, Omaha felt more stable. Moreover, Buffett now had two children of his own, Howard and Susie. A small city seemed like a good place to raise them.

So Buffett returned home to Omaha and rented a house for $175 a month at 5202 Underwood Avenue, close to the former site of his family's grocery store.

Buffett recalled:

> I had no plans to start a partnership, or even have a job. I had no worries if I could operate on my own. I certainly did not want to sell securities to other people again. But by pure accident, seven people, including a few of my relatives, said to me, you used to sell stocks, and we want you to tell us what to do with our money. I replied, I am not going to do that again, but I will form a partnership like Ben and Jerry had, and if you want to join me, you can. My father-in-law, my college roommate, his mother, my aunt Alice, my sister, my brother-in-law, and my lawyer all signed on. I also had my hundred dollars. That was the beginning—totally accidental.
>
> When I formed that partnership, we had dinner, the seven of them plus me—I am 99 percent sure it was at the Omaha Club. I bought a ledger for 49 cents, and they brought their checks. Before I took their money, I gave them a half sheet of paper that I had made carbons of—something I called

the ground rules. I said, there are two or four pages of partnership legal documents. Do not worry about that. I will tell you what is in it, and you will not get any surprises.

I did no solicitation, but more checks began coming from people I did not know. Back in New York, Graham-Newman was being liquidated. There was a college president up in Vermont, Homer Dodge, who had been invested with Graham, and he asked Ben, what should I do with my money? Ben said, well, there is this kid who used to work for me. So, Dodge drove out to Omaha, to this rented house I lived in. I was 25, looked about 17, and acted like 12. He said, what are you doing? I said, here is what I am doing with my family, and I will do it with you.

Although I had no idea, age 25 was a turning point. I was changing my life, setting up something that would turn into a fairly good-size partnership called Berkshire Hathaway. I was not scared. I was doing something I liked, and I'm still doing it.[24]

Creation of the Partnerships: 1956–1969

In 1956, when Buffett was twenty-five, he founded the Buffett Partnership Limited. He would be the general partner, with seven limited partners that eventually spun off as seven individual partnerships. The first of these, which included that original core group of seven friends and family members, was Buffett Associates Ltd. Buffett contributed only $100; the others kicked in a total of $105,000. His first outside investor was Homer Dodge, a physics professor and the president of Norwich University in Northfield, Vermont. Dodge, who had heard of Buffett's talent from Graham, drove 1,500 miles to give his family's $120,000 in savings to Buffett. When Dodge died in 1983, his investment was worth tens of millions of dollars.[25]

Buffett eventually bought a home, a three-story Dutch colonial for $31,500, where he still lives today. Now valued at more than $1 million, the house is adjacent to busy Farnam Street and has a handball court in the basement. Buffett had no actual office space and ran his affairs from a tiny sitting room off his upstairs bedroom, with neither a secretary nor a calculator.[26]

The limited partners received 6 percent annually on their investments and 75 percent of any profits above that amount, while Buffett earned the other

25 percent. From 1957 to 1961, the partnership gained 251 percent, as opposed to the Dow's 75 percent.[27]

By 1958, Buffett had five partnerships. Two years after that, he had expanded to seven, worth $7 million (including $1 million of his own money). These were the years that Buffett began penning his now-famous letters to the partners. He would explain the performance of their fund, the current investment climate, and any moves he had made during the previous year. In effect, the young Buffett was employing today's hedge fund model, where the general partner (Buffett) puts his own money at risk, alongside that of his limited partners. His incentives align with theirs; he makes money only if they do.

However, in contrast to today's hedge funds, there is no evidence to suggest that Buffett focused primarily on asset gathering. He kept the funds small, which enabled him to operate efficiently and remain focused—a hallmark of successful entrepreneurs. Flipping it around, this alignment of incentives also informs what Buffett looks for when investing in companies. Do the operating managers think and act as owners of the business, or are they actually working at cross-purposes to the owners?

Purchase of American Express Stock

In 1963, Buffett made $20 million for the partnership by investing in American Express. The credit card company had just absorbed a $58 million operating loss because it had invested in the Allied Crude Vegetable Oil Company, which was embroiled in fraud. Allied Crude, led by a man named Anthony De Angelis, had falsified the contents of its salad oil containers. These were enormous drums, but they contained salad oil only in their top portion. The rest was filled with water. De Angelis was sentenced to seven years in prison. American Express, one of Allied's three major investors, saw its stock value plummet more than 50 percent.

Buffett, using Phil Fisher's scuttlebutt methodology, saw an opportunity. Were people still using their American Express cards to pay for restaurant meals? Buffett did some dining out and found that indeed they were. He saw the same thing when he browsed in department stores: shoppers were still paying with their American Express cards. What about banks—were travelers still buying American Express traveler's checks? Decidedly, yes. Based on his confidence in this street-level knowledge, Buffett invested 25 percent of the partnership assets in American Express. Over the next two years, as the shares of American Express doubled in value, he made his investors $20 million.[28]

Purchase of Berkshire Hathaway: 1962–1964

In 1962, Buffett moved his office out of the upstairs bedroom and into the Kiewit Building, which was four minutes from his house and a few more minutes from downtown Omaha. He also began buying shares in a Massachusetts-based textile manufacturer called Berkshire Hathaway.

Within two years, Buffett owned 7 percent of the company. That same year, 1964, Berkshire Hathaway's management offered to buy back Buffett's stake at $11.50 a share. Buffett agreed. But two weeks later, the paperwork arrived. On it, the share price showed up as $11.375—twelve and a half cents less than the agreed-upon number. Infuriated, Buffett turned around and bought the whole company. By the end of 1965, he controlled Berkshire Hathaway, Inc., and its stock price was $18 per share.[29] Additionally, Buffett received a note that said "include me in" scribbled by respected investor Laurence Tisch along with his contribution of $300,000 to Buffett's partnership. Tisch would go on to form the extraordinarily successful Loews Corporation. He described Buffett as one of the greatest investors of his generation.[30]

By 1966, Buffett had become chairman of Berkshire Hathaway, spending 25 percent of his partnership's capital on the acquisition. He would later concede that this emotion-fueled move was probably the biggest investment mistake he ever made; it ended up costing him billions in today's dollars when Berkshire failed as a company. His longtime business partner, Charlie Munger, wondered if Buffett's judgment hadn't been clouded by his father's death five days before the acquisition. But Buffett hung on to the name all the same.

Good deals are hidden gems. And in 1969, when it became increasingly difficult to find them, Buffett liquidated his partnership, transferring all the assets into shares of Berkshire Hathaway. He gave the partners their shares and would now use Berkshire Hathaway as a holding company through which to purchase other companies and investments.

TABLE 2.1 Performance of Buffett Partnership Limited (1957–1968)

Year	Dow Jones Industrial Average + dividends[1]	Partnership[2]	Limited partners[3]
1957	-8.4%	10.4%	9.3%
1958	38.5%	40.9%	32.2%
1959	20.0%	25.9%	20.9%
1960	-6.2%	22.8%	18.6%
1961	22.4%	45.9%	35.9%
1962	-7.6%	13.9%	11.9%
1963	20.6%	38.7%	30.5%
1964	18.7%	27.8%	22.3%
1965	14.2%	47.2%	36.9%
1966	-15.6%	20.4%	16.8%
1967	19.0%	35.9%	28.4%
1968	7.7%	58.8%	45.6%
Annual Compounded Rate	**9.1%**	**31.6%**	**25.3%**

1. Based on yearly changes in the value of the Dow plus dividends that would have been received through ownership of the Dow during that year. The table includes all complete years of partnership activity.
2. For 1957–1961, these figures consists of the combined results of all predecessor limited partnerships operating throughout the entire year after all expenses, but before distributions to partners or allocations to the general partner.
3. For 1957–1961, these figures are computed on the basis of the preceding column of partnership results, allowing allocation to the general partner based upon the present partnership agreement, but before monthly withdrawals by limited partners.

Source: Buffett Partnership Ltd. letter, January 22, 1969.

Where the Dow Jones Industrial Average generated an average compounded rate of return of 9.1 percent, Buffett's partnership reaped an average annual return of 31.6 percent (see table 2.1).[31] By 1969, the partnerships were worth $100 million, of which $25 million was Buffett's.[32]

CHAPTER 3

CHARLIE MUNGER

In my whole life, I have known no wise people (over a broad subject matter area) who didn't read all the time—none, zero. . . . You'd be amazed at how much Warren reads—and at how much I read. My children laugh at me. They think I am a book with a couple of legs sticking out.[1]

CHARLES T. MUNGER

BUFFETT AND MUNGER

A great businessperson like Warren Buffett needs a fantastic supporting cast. Generally, that includes some mix of family, friends, and colleagues. In Buffett's case, the costar who rightfully shares top billing at Berkshire Hathaway is Charlie Munger, the company's vice chair. Investors know Munger for his charisma, quick wit, and straightforward wisdom doled out in pithy, Benjamin Franklin–style aphorisms. About Munger, Buffett says this (only partly tongue-in-cheek):

> As for myself, I would like to offer some "Advice on the Choice of a Partner." Pay attention. Look first for someone both smarter and wiser than you are. After locating him (or her), ask him not to flaunt his superiority so that you may enjoy acclaim for the many accomplishments that sprang from his thoughts and advice. Seek a partner who will never second-guess you nor sulk when you make expensive mistakes. Look also for a generous soul who will put up his own money and work for peanuts. Finally, join with someone who

will constantly add to the fun as you travel a long road together. All the above is splendid advice. (I have never scored less than an A in self-graded exams.) In fact, it is so splendid that I set out in 1959 to follow it slavishly. And there was only one partner who fit my bill of particulars in every way—Charlie.[2]

Born six years apart, both men are Omaha natives. Their Nebraska roots stretch back several generations. As teens, both worked in the grocery store owned by Buffett's grandfather in downtown Omaha. But despite sharing similar childhood experiences in the same city, these two financial luminaries did not cross paths in business until 1959, when they met at a dinner party. Each had already racked up substantial business success and quickly recognized the other as a fellow reader, with broad curiosity about the world.

In the relatively small city that Omaha was at the time, it struck people as unusual that the two men did not already know one another. Omaha locals now investing with Buffett kept telling him that he reminded them of a lawyer they knew—Charlie Munger. And those who knew Munger often noted that he reminded them of Buffett. Buffett had heard of the Munger family, of course. Charlie's grandfather had been a federal judge nominated by President Theodore Roosevelt, and his father was a well-known local lawyer. And at the party, which was a setup arranged by their mutual friends, the twenty-nine-year-old Buffett and the thirty-six-year-old Munger got on famously, dominating conversation at the dinner table. Buffett recalled: "Munger was rolling on the floor laughing at his own jokes. I have been known to do that myself, so I decided there is not many guys like us in the world, and I better hook up with him."[3]

Their common sense of wit and intellect would form the foundation for a friendship lasting more than sixty years. The same qualities would eventually inform their cerebral approach to investing. And although Munger's role in their partnership came to be one of devil's advocate, interrogating Buffett's ideas, the two men say that they have never in six decades of collaboration had a real argument. On the contrary, Munger's probing questions often nudge Buffett to dig deeper into the details of an investment before plunging in. A major benefit of this approach is its help in uncovering behavioral biases that may creep in and unduly influence investment decisions (a topic I explore in depth in chapter 7).

But you wouldn't necessarily realize this from watching the two men in public. At annual shareholder meetings, Buffett and Munger sit on stage together for hours, fielding questions from the audience. While Buffett tends to give long-winded answers to questions ranging from Berkshire Hathaway's finances to larger global trends in finance, Munger's specialty is quips. He is known for dropping in poignant observations or perfectly timed moments of deadpan humor. They make an entertaining, as well as hugely successful, team.

MUNGER'S BACKGROUND

Munger's position at the zenith of the investing world comes from an upbringing of relative affluence, which aided him in becoming highly educated. But the social-historical context of crushing poverty brought about by the Great Depression nevertheless left an indelible mark on the mind of young Charlie. It fanned his hunger for education as a kind of insulation against destitution. And education is what ultimately led to his elite position in the world of finance.

"I am one of the very few people still alive who deeply remembers the Great Depression, and that has been very helpful to me," Munger said in a 2017 interview. "It was so extreme that nobody had any money. Rich people did not have any money. People would come and beg for a meal at the door."[4]

Born in Omaha on New Year's Day 1924, Charles Thomas Munger was the son of Alfred Munger, a Harvard-educated lawyer who made a comfortable living, providing for his wife, Florence "Toody" Munger (née Russell), and his children, Charlie, Mary, and Carol.

Munger's grandfather, the honorable Thomas Charles Munger, had practiced law in Nebraska for decades by then, and his example set the career path for both son and grandson. But Thomas had risen from nothing, the son of two schoolteachers who would give their young son a nickel to buy meat. Munger recalled of his grandfather:

> He would go to the butcher shop, and he would buy the parts of the animal nobody else would eat. And that is what two schoolteachers lived on in those days. And the very indignity of it bothered him so much that he was just determined to get out of poverty and never go back. And he did. He got ahead like Abe Lincoln—educated himself in lawyers' offices and so on. He had to leave college because he could not pay the tuition anymore. But he educated himself, and since he was utterly brilliant, it was not all that hard.[5]

Charlie Munger inherited much of his grandfather's drive, especially regarding education, something he describes with extraordinary pride:

> He had an attitude that was pretty damned extreme. I would say his attitude was that you have a moral duty to make yourself as unignorant and as unstupid as you possibly can, and that it was pretty much your highest moral duty—maybe taking care of your family came first. . . . He was conventionally religious, so it may have been a religious duty to him. But he really believed that rationality was a moral duty, and he worked at it, and he scorned people who did not do it.[6]

EDUCATION

Schooling in the Great Depression

Despite the Depression, Charlie's father, Alfred Munger, was able to sustain his legal practice and support his family, while "Toody" Munger encouraged her children to read. Young Charlie did so enthusiastically. He was particularly enamored of biographies chronicling the lives of illustrious people. And while still a schoolboy, Munger began breeding hamsters to trade with other kids. This early venture into entrepreneurialism and negotiating ended when the boy's stock of hamsters grew too large to manage. With thirty-five rodents running around the house, Toody finally put her foot down.

Munger graduated from Omaha Central High School in 1941, just when the Great Depression was about to be "fixed by the accidental Keynesianism of World War II," as he puts it. Although small in stature, young Charlie participated in four years of infantry ROTC in high school and rose to be a second lieutenant. He says, "I was about 5-feet-2, I got my growth late, so I was not your idea of a manly soldier in high school."[7]

College and World War II

Although Munger had his eye on attending Stanford University, his father, worried about saving money, wanted Charlie to stay in the area.[8] But both father and son were extremely ambitious men, angling for a college with more prestige than the University of Nebraska. In the Midwest, that meant one option: the

University of Michigan. Munger has put it as follows: "What was I going to say, 'screw you, send me to Stanford?' Well, I didn't say that. I went to Michigan. I have never regretted that at all."[9]

At the University of Michigan, Munger studied math and dabbled in physics. But after just two years, with the United States entering World War II, the army sent Munger to study science and engineering at the University of New Mexico in Albuquerque, and then to the California Institute of Technology in Pasadena en route to becoming a meteorologist for the U.S. Army Air Corps. During the final years of the war, Munger, stationed in Nome, Alaska, served as a meteorologist. He also met Nancy Huggins during this deployment, and they married. He was discharged in 1946.[10]

As a schoolkid, Munger had been seen by teachers as something of a wise-ass. The same attitude was apparent during his military service. He was outspoken. He did not enjoy working on menial tasks, nor did he like taking orders—especially from people he considered to be less intelligent than himself—and he made little effort to hide his feelings. As he tells it, "Well, my senior officers could tell I thought they were wrong. And I tried to hide it. And they could still . . . I never got in any serious trouble, but they—who in the hell likes a junior officer? You look over there and he is plainly indicating that he thinks you're an idiot? . . . Well, it worked out all right. I did my work well enough, so they didn't bother me. But it was not a milieu where I was going to succeed."[11]

Harvard Law

Although Munger had not officially completed his undergraduate degree, he managed to use his GI Bill benefits to attend law school at Harvard University. Officials were understandably hesitant to admit Munger without a bachelor's degree, but a Munger family friend and former dean of the law school vouched for him. The recommendation paid off; Munger graduated magna cum laude from the Harvard University School of Law in 1948. He was twenty-four.

Law was a natural career path, not just because it continued the professional heritage handed down by Munger's father and grandfather, but because the practice of law seemed to offer both a greater challenge and more independence than many other corporate pursuits: He says, "I knew I didn't want to go to the bottom of a big organization and crawl my way up. . . . I'm a natural contrarian—that wasn't going to work for me—and I found that people could tell when I thought they were idiots, and that isn't a way to rise in a big organization."[12]

Those surrounding Munger may have seen his attitude in these days as a refusal to conform. But in hindsight, it seems likely that Munger's apparent contrarianism was just his entrepreneurial spirit beginning to emerge.

EARLY WORK YEARS

Munger, his wife, and his young son, Teddy, moved to California. Rather than joining his father's law practice in Omaha after law school, he passed the California bar exam and began practicing at the firm of Wright & Garrett. He was thrifty and hardworking, always worried about making enough to support his family: "I had no alternative. I had an army of children almost immediately. I painted myself into quite a corner."[13]

As the 1950s wore on, Munger began to feel the need for more income. Part of it was alimony; Charlie and Nancy Huggins divorced in 1953, and she kept their Pasadena home. Munger earned an estimated $350,000 in his first thirteen years as a lawyer. While this was a very good salary, practicing law was beginning to bore him. Munger found himself more interested in investing in ventures created by his clients: "I hated sending other people invoices and needing money from richer people. I thought it was undignified. I wanted my own money, not because I loved ease or social prestige, I wanted the independence."[14]

MUNGER'S ENTREPRENEURIAL VENTURES

While Munger's intellect was beginning to envision new career paths, his personal life transformed as well. In 1956, he met Nancy Barry Borthwick on a blind date. Nancy was from Los Angeles and had earned a degree in economics from Stanford University in 1945. She was previously married, with two children, William and David. Nancy loved to serve others and was committed to improving many institutions. She was a modest, quiet, and unassuming person.

Munger and Nancy married later in the same year they initially met. By the end of the decade, Munger had begun to invest in the stock market and the electronics businesses of his clients. Still, he did not give up his day job.

Not until 1962 did the entrepreneurial bug bite fully. But when it did, Munger struck out on his own in grand style. He founded the real estate law firm of Munger, Tolles & Hills (later renamed Munger, Tolles & Olson LLP),

TABLE 3.1 Munger partnership performance vs. Dow Jones and the S&P 500

Year	Munger partnership	Dow Jones	S&P 500
1962	30.1%	-7.6%	-8.8%
1963	71.7%	20.6%	22.6%
1964	49.7%	18.7%	16.4%
1965	8.4%	14.2%	12.4%
1966	12.4%	-15.8%	-10%
1967	56.2%	19.0%	23.8%
1968	40.4%	7.7%	10.8%
1969	28.3%	-11.6%	-8.2%
1970	-0.1%	8.7%	3.6%
1971	25.4%	9.8%	14.2%
1972	8.3%	18.2%	18.8%
1973	-31.9%	-13.1%	-14.3%
1974	-31.5%	-23.1%	-25.9%
1975	73.2%	44.4%	37.0%
Total return	**1156.7%**	**96.2%**	**102.6%**
Average annual return	**19.8%**	**4.9%**	**5.2%**

and cofounded an investment firm, Wheeler, Munger and Company, the same year with his old poker buddy and investor, Jack Wheeler, in Los Angeles. The investment firm purchased a seat on the Pacific Coast Stock Exchange. Within four years, Munger had earned $4 million.

Their investment strategy was similar to Buffett's—they emphasized arbitrage, cigar butts, and acquired businesses. "Cigar butt investing" is when you purchase cheap stocks that still have a few puffs left for you to profit from. Graham, Buffett, and Munger all did this.

However, Munger was different in that he also preferred quality businesses with strong management and a competitive advantage (a moat). He emphasized that he did not want to invest more capital into a company, but he wanted cash to flow out. This was similar to an investment that he eventually made at Berkshire called See's Candies, which will be explained later in this chapter.

Three years later, Munger had given up the practice of law to focus full time on managing investments (although he did consult with the law firm on occasion). By concentrating on just a few securities, his fund did well for several years (table 3.1). Munger partnered with Franklin "Otis" Booth, a real estate developer, and the pair later became investors in Berkshire Hathaway.

Not every call that Munger made turned to gold. In 1973, his firm lost 32 percent on its investments in the stock market due to corrections. Then, in 1974, it lost 31 percent. But he held on, and in 1975, Munger's small investment fund produced a 73.2 percent return in compounded annual returns. Over the 1962–1975 time period, Buffett observed, Munger's partnership generated average returns some 15 points higher than the Dow (table 3.1).[15]

TWO ENTREPRENEURS COLLIDE

A Handshake Partnership

Munger had met Buffett at the beginning of this period, during a visit back to Omaha for his father's funeral in 1959. After their dinner party introduction, the two formed a fast friendship, and when Munger returned to his California law firm, he and Buffett stayed in touch. Each week, they spent hours on the phone discussing investment opportunities. In between conversations, Munger often wrote lengthy letters sharing more of his musings. With no written agreement, Buffett and Munger had become de facto business partners. The timing was a key element here. Buffett's longtime mentor, Benjamin Graham, had recently retired from investing, and he felt the absence keenly. Munger provided a new sounding board, and although he espoused a very different attitude toward investing, his personal style reminded Buffett of Graham—honest, realistic, profoundly curious, and unfettered by conventional thinking.

An example of this plainspoken approach comes through in Munger's assessment of the decision to buy the Berkshire Hathaway textile mill: "Buffett had been taught by Ben Graham to buy things for less than they were worth, no matter how lousy the business was. You cannot imagine a lousier business than New England textile mills. Buffett should have known better than to buy into a totally doomed enterprise, but it was so damn cheap, we could get a big discount from liquidating value."[16]

But where Graham had strictly followed a value-investing approach, focusing on bargain-basement opportunities, the core of Munger's belief was avoiding such cigar butt companies in favor of well-run firms that needed minimal oversight. As for any lackluster holdings that Berkshire Hathaway already owned, Munger advised Buffett to do whatever he could to convert them into moneymakers or sell them off. This was no minor shift. Graham had been a formidable influence on Buffett, and it had paid off handsomely. The pivot toward Munger's approach is testament to "the power of Charlie's mind," as Buffett put it. "He expanded my horizons."[17]

MUNGER'S INFLUENCE ON BUFFETT

No More Cigar Butts

It was Munger who pointed Buffett toward such investments as See's Candies, Blue Chip Stamps, GEICO, Coca-Cola, and Gillette—all well-established businesses. Meanwhile, as he watched the textile factory that was Berkshire Hathaway dwindle into obsolescence in 1970, Munger advised his friend and partner on the best tactic for making lemonade out of the proverbial lemon: "The only way to go forward from there was to wring enough money out of this declining textile business to have more money than [Buffett] paid to get in, and use it to buy something else. That is a very indirect way to proceed, and I would not recommend it to any of you. Just because we did some dumb thing that worked, you do not have to repeat our path."[18]

Despite their success as a team, Munger remained modest about what he brought to his collaboration with Buffett. He recalled: "It's true that Warren had a touch of brain block from working under Ben Graham and making a ton of money. It's hard to switch from something that has worked so well. But if Charlie Munger had never lived, the Buffett record would still be pretty much what it is."[19]

However, the fact remains that See's Candies turned out to be a pivotal investment for Berkshire Hathaway—even though Buffett was tentative about it at the time—and the idea came from Munger. Here is Buffett describing the education he gained through that experience:

> My misguided caution could have scuttled a terrific purchase. But luckily, the sellers decided to take our $25 million bid. To date, See's has earned $1.9 billion pre-tax, with its growth having required added investment of only $40 million. See's has thus been able to distribute huge sums that have helped Berkshire buy other businesses that, in turn, have themselves produced large distributable profits. (Envision rabbits breeding.) Additionally, through watching See's in action, I gained a business education about the value of powerful brands that opened my eyes to many other profitable investments.[20]

Joining Berkshire Hathaway Full Time

In 1978, Munger joined Buffett full time and was named vice chair of Berkshire Hathaway. He has remained in that role ever since. From their first meeting at that Omaha dinner party in 1959, the Buffett-Munger partnership has stood the test of time. The two men share a sense of humor and intellectual curiosity. Their example underscores the crucial importance, for success in any entrepreneurial venture, of having the right partners. It is particularly valuable when the leaders' differences complement one another. As Buffett has quipped: "When we differ, Charlie usually ends the conversation by saying: 'Warren, think it over and you'll agree with me because you're smart, and I'm right.' "[21]

Shareholders witness this banter at Berkshire Hathaway's annual meetings: Munger tosses off humorous comments while Buffett waxes wise. Both men, now well into their nineties, have acknowledged that this jocular tone may change after they are gone. But for now, they concentrate on the present. Munger observed: "We just do what works as long as it works. And when it stops working or indicates it is going to stop working, we will stop. I think there is more wise-assery in our meeting than would be appropriate forever. Now, I am the principal wise-ass."[22]

MUNGER'S VIEWS ON INVESTING

"Sit on Your Ass Investing"

Munger is known for his self-taught, multidisciplinary approach to investing. Like Buffett, he looks askance at the narrow-mindedness of traditional methods of business education; instead, he draws ideas from fields as varied as chemistry, physics, and psychology to lead him toward wise investment decisions. Both Munger and Buffett are suspicious of all of the fancy formulas used in academia and insist that you do not need all of these fancy formulas to be a successful investor. Munger insists that his success springs mainly from insights gained through reading widely and extensively.

Officially, Munger's method is called "Focus Investing." But he's given it a snappier title: "Sit on Your Ass Investing." Here is Munger explaining this approach during the 2000 Berkshire Hathaway shareholders' meeting:

> Well, I agree that all intelligent investing is value investing. You have to acquire more than you really pay for, and that is a value judgment. But you can look for more than you are paying for in a lot of different ways. You can use filters to sift the investment universe. And if you stick with stocks that can't possibly be wonderful to just put away in your safe deposit box for forty years, but are underpriced, then you have to keep moving around all the time. As they get closer to what you think the real value is, you've got to sell them, and then find others. And so, it is an active kind of investing. The investing where you find a few great companies and just sit on your ass because you've correctly predicted the future, that is what it's very nice to be good at.[23]

In addition, Buffett and Munger criticize investment philosophies that emphasize portfolio diversification. Instead, they invest most of their capital in a few well-run companies that meet their criteria for an investment, rather than trying to predict the future based on fads. Munger puts it this way: "People have always had this craving to have someone tell them the future. Long ago, kings would hire people to read sheep guts. There's always been a market for people who pretend to know the future. Listening to today's forecasters is just as crazy as when the king hired the guy to look at the sheep guts."[24]

Simplicity

Value investing is easy to describe: Invest in assets that are undervalued and be patient. But it takes real discipline to implement. The core of it, as far as Buffett and Munger are concerned, is to keep the process simple. They use the same approach in their management of Berkshire Hathaway itself, assiduously avoiding bureaucracy. Their corporate office in Omaha counts just twenty-five employees. In Berkshire's equity portfolio, Apple alone comprised 50 percent of its size or 25 percent of its overall market capitalization. The top five holdings constituted over 75 percent of the equity portfolio, even though Berkshire owned over forty stocks.

And though they have purchased sixty-two operating companies, comprising more than 360,000 employees, they allow their subsidiaries to continue operating as independent entities under the umbrella of Berkshire Hathaway. This provides Munger and Buffett the freedom to focus on what they do well, which is allocate capital. The two have been known to complete billion-dollar business deals in a single day by writing out very short contracts.

Their investment process avoids complex algorithms and sophisticated models, even though Munger excels in mathematics. Munger says, "Neither Warren nor I have ever used any fancy math in business, and neither did Ben Graham, who taught Buffett. Everything I have ever done in business could be done with the simplest algebra and geometry and addition, multiplication, and so forth. I never used calculus for any practical work in my whole damn life."[25]

Munger further observes: "I can't think of a single example in my whole life where keeping it simple has worked against us. We made mistakes, but they were not because we kept it simple . . . I would say that the chief advantage that Berkshire's had in accumulating a good record is that we have avoided the pompous bureaucratic systems. We've tried to give power to very talented people and let them make very quick decisions."[26]

To keep their investment portfolio focused on a relative handful of great companies, Munger emphasizes the concentration of risk as key to success: "Now at a place like Berkshire Hathaway or even the *Daily Journal*, we've done better than average. And now there's a question, why has that happened? And the answer is pretty simple: We tried to do less. We never had the illusion we could just hire a bunch of bright young people and they would know more than anybody about canned soup and aerospace and utilities and so on and so on and so on. We never had that dream."[27]

Surplus Cash and Repurchasing Shares

Munger and Buffett have worked to avoid the pitfalls of herd mentality investing. But they are entirely willing to move quickly when an opportunity pops up that they like. Munger describes their thinking in his typically forthright style: "I don't think we have a master plan of knowing where the opportunities are. We are trying to find intelligent things to do with a torrent of surplus cash. And we've always had a torrent of surplus cash. And we're always looking for intelligent things to do with it. And if we find things that are intelligent to do, we do it. And if we don't find anything, we'll let the cash build up. What the hell is wrong with that?"[28]

Necessary for this kind of restraint is an adjustment in expectations. "Slow and steady" could be the Berkshire motto. But Munger puts it in saucier terms: "Well generally speaking, I think the professional investors have to accept less than they were used to getting under different conditions. Just as an old man expects less out of his sex life than he had when he was 20."[29]

If Buffett feels that shares of Berkshire Hathaway itself are undervalued, he will authorize a repurchase. Munger notes: "Of course, that ought to be done. If you had a partnership with three of your crippled relatives, and one of them needed some money, wouldn't you buy out the crippled relative with the company's money? It's just simple morality. But I do think it's being overdone by some people. And it undoubtedly is being done to prop up values, which I regard as an improper use of the share repurchasing technique."[30]

While Munger understands people's desire to plunge into the market and start trading stocks the way he does, he is adamant about warning beginners away: "If you take the modern world where people are trying to teach you how to come in and trade actively in stocks, well, I regard that as roughly equivalent to trying to induce a bunch of young people to start off on heroin. It is really stupid."[31]

Psychology and Mental Models

None of the tactics that Munger uses would be worth anything without rigorous intellectual preparation. Both Munger and Buffett are known for reading at least 500 pages a day. They then apply their acquired knowledge to investing—but not in a haphazard manner. Munger in particular emphasizes a mental model that addresses faults in human thought processes that lead to poor decisions. Much of his thinking on this was anchored by the work of Robert Cialdini, PhD, and his book *Influence*. Munger referenced it during one of his best-known speeches, "The Psychology of Human Misjudgment,"[32] which he delivered at Harvard University in 1995. In his talk, Munger summarized specific biases that cause blind spots and get people into trouble.[33]

For example, Munger talked about bias from envy/jealousy. He and Buffett agree that it's not greed that drives the world, but envy. This, in turn, causes bad decision-making. Bias from deprival super-reaction syndrome, including bias caused by present or threatened scarcity, threatened removal of something almost possessed, but never actually possessed,[34] is pretty common in today's investment world. For example, traders will bid up a stock that you may have been looking at purchasing all day. Then, at the end of the day, traders make a big push up or down and you get a sense of missing out. I will address more of these biases in chapter 7.

Despite his avid entrepreneurial appetite, Munger's overall approach—to both investing and life—is based on limiting potential downsides by avoiding mistakes, rather than chasing moonshot strokes of brilliance. No matter how brilliant you are, his theory says, all humans have blind spots, and if you are doing things that expose you to harm, you will eventually run out of luck.[35]

Lollapalooza

Once all the right mental models are in place and their user identifies possible cognitive biases, Munger believes rigorous preparation is essential for helping an investor know precisely when to take advantage of the Lollapalooza Effect—something he describes as the point "when anywhere from two to four forces all are driving the investment in the same direction."[36] The Lollapalooza Effect, a term Munger coined in his 1995 Harvard speech on human psychology and misjudgment, occurs when multiple tendencies and mental models combine to push a person to act in a certain way.[37]

This makes the Lollapalooza Effect an especially powerful driver of behavior, and it can lead to both positive and negative results. Open auctions are a great example, as the value investing website GuruFocus describes: "Participants are pushed to bid by reciprocity ('I should buy because I was invited to the auction'), consistency ('I have been on record saying that I like this, so I must buy it'), commitment tendency ('I am already bidding, so I must continue'), and social proof ('I know that buying is good because my peers are doing it').[38]

While the field of psychology has been helpful for identifying biases, Munger says, it is not as good at explaining how these biases might interact and manifest in the real world, partly because of the difficulty in running controlled experiments.[39] But the purchase of Berkshire Hathaway itself, when Buffett was already committed to owning 7 percent of the company, was an example of commitment tendency, a behavioral bias toward acquiring. The death of Buffett's father during the same period might also have influenced his judgment, Munger believes.

While capitalizing on the Lollapalooza Effect can bring success akin to that of Berkshire Hathaway, a misjudgment can lead to disastrous results, such as when herd mentality goads investors toward mistakenly following trends that reflect irrationality in the market. This happened during the 2007–2009 global financial crisis. This herd mentality is every investor's worst enemy. After all, if you sell when everyone else is selling, then you are probably eating huge losses. If you do the opposite and buy when everyone else is selling, then you are likely getting bargain prices for your shares. Thus, before you make an investment, it is wise to think about how various psychological factors might be causing an irrational reaction in the market.[40]

Although it is often viewed in negative terms, the Lollapalooza Effect can be beneficial too. For instance, Munger points out that alcoholics who participate in Alcoholics Anonymous (AA) have a greater-than-expected chance of success because people follow the herd, which in this case is full of people also trying to get sober, and they stick to their own commitment to sobriety as a result. Munger saw AA as a system that makes clever use of human psychology.[41]

MUNGER'S KEYS TO SUCCESS

Munger and Buffett attribute their success to being able to recognize a profitable moment and act on it quickly. And they credit this ability to deep preparation, in the form of reading and thinking and discussing ideas for hours on end—intellectual study, rather than mere profit/loss analyses. Indeed, Munger has likened his role at Berkshire to being a colleague of Einstein's. He observes:

> Practically everybody works better when not in extreme isolation. . . . If Einstein had worked in total isolation, he would not have been as productive as he was. He didn't need a great deal of contact with other colleagues, but he needed some.[42]

What follows are some habits of mind that Munger considers keys to success.

1. Always Keep Learning

> Wisdom acquisition is a moral duty. And there is a corollary to that proposition, which is very important, it means that you are hooked for lifetime learning, and without lifetime learning you are not going to do very well. You are not going to get very far in life based on what you already know.[43]

> I constantly see people rise in life who are not the smartest, sometimes not even the most diligent, but they are learning machines. They go to bed every night a little wiser than when they got up, and boy, does that help, particularly when you have a long run ahead of you.[44]

> I think the right strategy for the mass of humanity is to specialize. . . . Nobody wants to go to a doctor that's half proctologist and half dentist, you know? So, the ordinary way to succeed is to narrowly specialize . . . Warren and I didn't do that.[45]

2. Deserve What You Want

> The safest way to try and get what you want is to try and deserve what you want. It's such a simple idea. It's the Golden Rule, so to speak. You want to deliver to the world what you would buy if you were on the other end.[46]

3. Know the Edge of Your Own Competency Munger advocates learning as much as you can, as well as knowing where your learning ends. Do not go beyond that boundary:

> It's a hugely important thing, knowing the edge. It is hardly a competence if you don't know the edge of it. You know, if you have a misapprehension regarding your own competency that means you lack competence, you are going to make terrible mistakes. I think you've got to constantly measure what you achieve against other people of achievement, and you have to keep being determinedly rational and avoiding a lot of self-delusion. But after a lifetime of observing it, I think the tendency to be pretty rational about one's own competency is largely genetic. I think people like Warren and I were just born this way. Now it took a lot of education. But I think we were born with the right temperament to do what we did.[47]

4. Be a Survivor

> It's not my nature—when you get little surprises because of human nature—to spend much time feeling betrayed. I have always wanted to put my head down and adjust, so I do not allow myself to spend much time ever with any feelings of betrayal. If some flickering idea like that came to me, I would get rid of it quickly. I do not like any feeling of being victimized. I think that is a counterproductive way to think as a human being. I am not a victim. I am a survivor.[48]

5. Understand What You Are Doing

Of course, I want the guy who understands his limitations instead of the guy who does not. On the other hand, I have learned something terribly important in life. I learned that from Howard Ahmanson. You know what he used to say? Never underestimate the man who overestimates himself. These weird guys who overestimate themselves occasionally knock it right out of the park. And that is a very unhappy part of modern life. But I've learned to adjust to it. I have no alternative. It happens all the time. But I don't want my personal life to be a bunch of guys who are living in a state of delusion, who happen occasionally to win big. I want the prudent person. There are microeconomic ideas and gain/loss ratios and so forth that also come into play. I think time and time again, in reality, psychological notions and economic notions interplay, and the man who does not understand both is a damned fool.[49]

6. Invest in Trust

If you're unreliable it doesn't matter what your virtues are, you're going to crater immediately. So, doing what you have faithfully engaged to do should be an automatic part of your conduct. You want to avoid sloth and unreliability.[50]

A fast form which civilization can reach is a seamless web of deserved trust. Not much procedure, just totally reliable people correctly trusting one another. That's the way an operating room works at the Mayo Clinic.[51]

7. Learn Important Concepts across Multiple Disciplines

You may have noticed students who just try to remember and pound back what is remembered. Well, they fail in school and in life. You've got to hang experience on a latticework of models in your head. What are the models? Well, the first rule is that you've got to have multiple models—because if you just have one or two that you are using, the nature of human psychology is such that you'll torture reality so that it fits your models, or at least you'll think it does. . . . It's like the old saying, "To the man with only a hammer, every problem looks like a nail. . . ." That is a perfectly disastrous way to think and a perfectly disastrous way to operate in the world. So, you have got to have multiple models. And the models have to come from multiple disciplines—because all the wisdom of the world is not to be found in one little academic department. That is why poetry professors, by and large, are so unwise in a worldly sense. They don't have enough models in their heads. So, you've got to have models across a fair array of disciplines.[52]

8. Just Keep Swimming

Sometimes the tide will be with us, and sometimes it will be against us. But by and large, we don't much bother with trying to predict the tides because we plan to play the game for a long time.[53]

9. At All Costs: Avoid Self-Pity

Self-pity gets pretty close to paranoia. . . . Every time you find you're drifting into self-pity, I don't care what the cause, your child could be dying from cancer, self-pity is not going to improve the situation. . . . And when you avoid it you get a great advantage over everybody else, almost everybody else, because self-pity is a standard condition and yet you can train yourself out of it.[54]

Self-pity, Munger believes, is steeped in bias—precisely the mindset that leads a person toward making bad decisions.

[You start] rationalizing all these ridiculous conclusions based on the subconscious tendency to serve oneself. It is a terribly inaccurate way to think, and of course you want to drive that out of yourself because you want to be wise, not foolish. You also have to allow for the self-serving bias of everybody else, because most people are not gonna remove it all that successfully, the human condition being what it is. If you don't allow for self-serving bias in your conduct, again you're a fool. . . . Life will have terrible blows, horrible blows, unfair blows, it doesn't matter. . . . I think the attitude of Epictetus is the best. He thought that every mischance in life was an opportunity to behave well, every mischance in life was an opportunity to learn something, and your duty was not to be submerged in self-pity, but to utilize the terrible blow in a constructive fashion. That is a very good idea.[55]

10. Put Your Unique Talents to Use, Rather than Comparing Yourself to Others

> I am always being visited by young men who say, "I am practicing law and I don't like it. I would rather be a billionaire. How can I do it?" And I tell him, "Well, I will tell you a story. A young man goes to see Mozart. And he says, Mozart, I want to start composing symphonies. And Mozart said, how old are you? And the guy says, 22. And he says you are too young to do symphonies. And the guy says, but you were 10 years old when you were composing symphonies. And Mozart says, yes, but I wasn't running around asking other people how to do it."[56]

11. Learn How to Transform Your Mistakes

> Now there is a part of life which is, how do you scramble out of your mistakes without them costing too much? And we have done some of that too. If you look at Berkshire Hathaway, think of its founding businesses. A doomed department store, a doomed New England textile company, and a doomed trading stamp company. Out of that came Berkshire Hathaway. Now we handled those losing hands pretty well when we bought into them very cheaply. But of course, the success came from changing our ways and getting into the better businesses. It isn't that we were so good at doing things that were difficult. We were good at avoiding things that were difficult, finding things that are easy.[57]

VALUES AND HAPPINESS

Whenever Munger speaks publicly, he talks about his values and how his family instilled them—particularly the virtue of biding your time, but moving quickly, with purpose and intent, at the right moment:

> Patience combined with opportunity is a great thing to have. My grandfather taught me that opportunity is infrequent, and one has to be ready when it strikes. That's what Berkshire is. It is amazing how fast Berkshire acts when we find opportunity. You cannot be timid—and that applies to all of life. You can't be timid in marriage when you find the right spouse. It might be your only opportunity to be happy in life. Too many people do not act when they should. . . . It's in the nature of stock markets to go way down from time

> to time. There's no system to avoid bad markets. You can't do it unless you try to time the market, which is a seriously dumb thing to do. Conservative investing with steady savings, without expecting miracles, is the way to go.[58]

Without Munger's insistence on these values, it is possible, even likely, that Berkshire Hathaway would not have enjoyed the decades of stability and success for which it is known.

WEALTH

As of 2022, Munger was worth $2.4 billion. Most of his fortune comes from his 15,181 Class A Berkshire shares, which represent about 1.4 percent of the firm. The $100,000 annual salary Munger draws from Berkshire has not changed in more than thirty years. His role models, Andrew Carnegie and Cornelius Vanderbilt, similarly lived on the dividends of their enterprises. As titans of industry, they considered it a point of pride to support themselves this way.

Munger on Executive Compensation

> I think if you're wealthy and own a share of a company, and you get to decide what it does and whether it liquidates or whether it keeps going, that's a nice position to be in. And maybe you shouldn't try to grab all the money in addition.[59]

Asked why Buffett's wealth is so much greater than his own, Munger answers with his standard matter-of-fact style: "He got an earlier start. He's probably a little smarter. He works harder. There are not a lot of reasons. Why was Albert Einstein poorer than I was?"[60]

PHILANTHROPY

Famously, Munger has declined to join Buffett's Giving Pledge, a promise made among many of the country's wealthiest people to give half their wealth to charity during their lives. He says that he has already transferred so much of his wealth to his children that he would be already in violation of its tenets. Munger has made no secret of his distaste for the "folly and stupidity" of many major philanthropies, preferring to put his confidence in capitalistic ventures with more progressive labor policies, such as Costco.[61]

Giving Back

Munger has, however, donated enormous sums of money to educational programs, including more than $160 million to the University of Michigan Law School, its legal research department, lawyers' club, fellowships, and residences. He has made major gifts to Stanford University, the alma mater of his wife and daughter, as well. In 2004, Munger gave the school 500 shares of Berkshire Hathaway Class A stock, valued at $43.5 million, to build a graduate housing complex,[62] in addition to donations for improvements to the library and an endowed business professorship.

The Mungers have given money to the Marlborough School in Los Angeles, the Polytechnic School in Pasadena, and the theoretical physics department at the University of California–Santa Barbara (UCSB), where his son Charles attended.[63,64,65] In 2016, Munger donated $200 million to UCSB for state-of-the art housing.[66] In late 2018, Munger purchased the 1,800-acre Las Varas Ranch on California's Gaviota Coast for a reported $70 million and gifted it to UCSB.[67]

Ever the independent thinker, Munger prefers to be personally involved in his major gifts. Now he has begun to accelerate those efforts. He is the chair of Good Samaritan Hospital in Los Angeles and in 2018 donated $21 million.[68] He has also made major gifts to the Los Angeles YMCA and the Huntington Library.[69]

None of this would have been possible without the astounding growth of Berkshire Hathaway.

PART II

BUFFETT'S SECRET SAUCE

CHAPTER 4

BERKSHIRE'S VALUE INVESTMENT PHILOSOPHY AND ADVICE

The stock market is filled with individuals who know the price of everything, but the value of nothing.[1]

PHILIP FISHER

As I have noted previously, Warren Buffett's original approach to investing was heavily influenced by Benjamin Graham and included "buying bad companies at great prices."[2] In working with Charlie Munger and learning the investment philosophy of Philip Fisher, Buffett began to believe instead in "buying great companies at good prices,"[3] a much better long-term investment strategy. In chapter 5, I'll detail exactly *how* Buffett and Munger developed their numeric criteria for determining a company's intrinsic value through what's called the discounted cash flow (DCF) model. But first, I want to talk a bit more about the enormous role that Munger played in expanding Buffett's original, somewhat one-dimensional approach.

From the perspective of investment strategy, Munger's chief contribution to their partnership was his belief in the ideas of Fisher, who formalized the so-called scuttlebutt methodology, which is all about collecting *qualitative* information about a company rather than relying merely on a ledger sheet. (More on this below.)

After Munger became vice chair of Berkshire Hathaway in 1978, Buffett began to use both qualitative and quantitative measures for assessing potential investment opportunities, combining the approaches of Fisher and Graham.

This chapter looks at the conceptual lens that Buffett and Munger use to determine what makes a good investment, starting with Fisher's investment philosophy. That approach has provided a foundation for Berkshire's historic investment success for half a century.

FISHER'S INVESTMENT INFLUENCE

Practice Scuttlebutt Methodology

Fisher was perhaps best known for his insistence on the value of gathering knowledge about a company through personal experience (i.e., scuttlebutt methodology). That is, you learn about a company not just through numbers, but by talking with its consumers, competitors, consultants, managers, former employees, and vendors. Each can contribute a piece of the puzzle, but none should be taken in isolation. For instance, former employees can provide very helpful information, especially about a company's flaws. However, they may be biased by grievances against the company. It behooves prospective investors to guard against this possible bias by balancing the perspective of former employees with what others, including consumers and managers, say.

However, former employees can sometimes provide a much-needed antidote for rose-colored investor goggles.[4] Understand that multiple sources of information will likely contradict one another. It's only logical. To make an educated judgment, you want many perspectives. But if you solicit enough different sources of information about a company, don't expect that each piece of data will agree with all the others.

No human source will be truly objective—that is the purview of figures. But after gathering perspectives from outer-ring sources like consumers and former employees, the would-be investor should approach a company's officers. They can provide facility tours and supplements to financial statements, all of which can be helpful in a scuttlebutt investigation.[5]

Buffett used the scuttlebutt technique when he purchased American Express early in his partnership days, as outlined in chapter 2.

Stay within Your Area of Competence

Another major plank of the Fisher approach holds that investors stay within the circle of their particular areas of knowledge—in other words, invest in companies that you understand so you know when to "swing at the right pitch." For many years, this was Buffett's rationale for avoiding tech investments, particularly Microsoft and later Amazon, which he avoided until one of his co-chief investment officers recommended it in 2019 (as we will discuss further in chapter 9).

Buffett believes in investing in nonflashy[6] legacy companies like Coca-Cola, Gillette, and See's Candies, which produce popular products that have strong brand loyalty and recognition. There is less gambling involved in investing in such companies than in betting on which flashy new tech start-up will actually succeed and which will fail. Companies that have been successful for a long time are likely to remain successful into the foreseeable future, especially when they are in nontech areas and in little danger of becoming obsolete. By the time Buffett got around to investing in Apple and Amazon, these two giants were already legacy companies in their own right, and investing in them was nothing like investing in start-ups. Munger plainly states, "We don't do start-ups."[7] Buffett draws a sharp distinction between investing and speculating.[8]

Diversification Is Overrated

Fisher advised investors to hold stock in a few outstanding companies rather than many average ones. Likewise, Buffett considers the current emphasis on diversification to be overrated. If you identify an asset that appears undervalued, invest in it, Buffett says. You do not need to build a potpourri basket of stocks merely to achieve diversification.

Consider a Company's Management

Corporate culture was important to Fisher. He specifically sought to invest in companies that communicated openly and honestly with their shareholders. For him, that was part of scuttlebutt methodology. For Buffett and Munger, too, assessing company management became key to their determination of its value, as I describe a bit later in this chapter.

Hold on to Investments Indefinitely

Fisher took a long-term view on investing, and not only because the value of good companies tends to increase over time. At least as important to his strategy was minimizing capital gains taxes. Capital gains taxes come in two forms. One is short-term, the tax on selling an asset held for under a year, which is taxed as ordinary income. Long-term capital gains occur when selling an asset held for over a year. The tax rate on long-term capital gains is lower than that for ordinary income and short-term capital gains because the government wants to incentivize investors to keep their money in companies over the long haul, thereby maintaining growth and stability.

Fisher's approach minimized taxes, allowing maximum amounts to be invested. He wrote: "If the job has been correctly done when a common stock is purchased, the time to sell it is almost never."[9] Finally, Fisher urged investors to ignore the overall movement of the general stock market when making purchases—advice that has become axiomatic for Berkshire Hathaway.

THE KEY TO VALUE INVESTING: UNDERSTANDING

As mentioned in previous chapters, Buffett has never been all that impressed with business degrees, either for himself or as criteria by which to judge money managers. At times, he has outright criticized business education. Part of this antipathy comes from Buffett's distaste for a classic business school concept, the Efficient Market Hypothesis (EMH), which would make it impossible to buy companies at good prices. Under this hypothesis, the price of a stock is by definition its fair market value. Beating the market is thereby impossible, and if an investor succeeds in doing so, it is only by pure luck.[10]

This is antithetical to Buffett's belief in searching for bargains—undervalued companies trading at rates below what they "should" be. Determining this "should" makes up a great deal of Buffett and Munger's work, and it's an idea that comes directly from Buffett's original mentor, Benjamin Graham. Graham argued that an investor must figure out whether a given security is significantly overvalued or undervalued relative to its intrinsic value. Following market trends is the opposite of this approach. Investors, said Graham, need to do their own research to avoid being influenced by misleading information.

About his value-investment philosophy, Graham wrote: "Value investing is based more in philosophy than on theorems. There is no step one, step two, step three. The disciplined investor does not follow the crowd but instead searches for stocks selling for less than their intrinsic value and then waits for the market to recognize and correct the disparity."[11]

At the 2008 Berkshire Hathaway shareholder meeting, Buffett spoke to the same concept, saying, "I have no idea what the stock market is going to do. It is something that I never think about at all. But I am looking for the stock to go down so I can buy it on sale. I want the stocks to go down, way down, so I can make better buys."[12]

And he has been preaching the same message for more than thirty years. In his 1987 annual letter to Berkshire Hathaway shareholders, for instance, Buffett put it this way:

> But, like Cinderella at the ball, you must heed one warning or everything will turn into pumpkins and mice: Mr. Market is there to serve you, not to guide you. It is his pocketbook, not his wisdom, that you will find useful. If he shows up someday in a particularly foolish mood, you are free to either ignore him or to take advantage of him, but it will be disastrous if you fall under his influence. Indeed, if you aren't certain that you understand and can value your business far better than Mr. Market, you don't belong in the game. As they say in poker, "If you've been in the game 30 minutes and you don't know who the patsy is, you're the patsy."[13]

As far as business school went, Buffett believes that would-be investors need to learn to develop only two key skills: how to value companies and how to understand human behavior as it relates to financial markets.[14]

Once Berkshire Hathaway has determined that a company is trading at a discount to its intrinsic value, Berkshire buys the company's stock and then—a key strategy—prepares to hold on to it for a long time. Buffett believes that the same principle applies to individual as well as corporate investors, as he explained:

> I bought my first stock on March 11, 1942. Despite World War II and all other wars, 9/11, the Cuban Missile Crisis, recessions, 14 presidents (7 Republican), and everything else, the best thing you could have done was put your money into the S&P 500 and leave it there. Do not look at the newspaper headlines. Do not listen to the talking heads. If you put $10,000 into an index fund in 1942, it would have been worth $51 million today. The only thing you had to believe was that American business would survive and thrive.[15]

In sum, the gist of his approach is pretty straightforward: "We want businesses to be ones (a) that we can understand; (b) with favorable long-term prospects; (c) operated by honest and competent people; and (d) available at a very attractive price."[16]

The key word here is "understand." This is the essence of value investing. It is the application of judgment to produce investment returns. To make this judgment, Buffett and Munger consider the following three points before making an investment.

1. Understand a Company's Management Philosophy First, investors should understand how the senior executive team is incentivized since that generally drives decision-making and behavior. Consider, for example, managers who own minimal amounts of stock and draw their compensation primarily from salary and cash bonuses. They may make strategic decisions that protect their jobs and avoid risk. In contrast, if compensation is influenced by share price appreciation over the long term, managers may be more focused on overall company growth. Pay practices, set forth in a proxy statement, can provide insight into the character and mentality of a company's senior management.

Buffett and Munger famously draw relatively small salaries and make most of their money from Berkshire stocks.[17] Buffett's salary, excluding dividends, has been $100,000 for the past forty years.[18,19,20]

It is not uncommon for Buffett to follow the performance of a company's management team over several years before he invests.[21] At the 1994 Berkshire Hathaway shareholders meeting, he elaborated on the qualities he looks for in a management team:

> One is how well they run the business, and I think you can learn a lot about that by reading about both what they've accomplished and what their competitors have accomplished and seeing how they have allocated capital over time.
>
> You have to have some understanding of the hand they were dealt when they themselves got a chance to play the hand. . . .
>
> And then the second thing you want to figure out is how well that they treat their owners.[22]

By "owners," Buffett is referring to shareholders:

> It's interesting how often the ones that, in my view, are the poor managers also turn out to be the ones that really don't think that much about the shareholders, too. . . . The two often go hand in hand. . . .
>
> Read the proxy statements, see what they think of—see how they treat themselves versus how they treat the shareholders. Look at what they have accomplished, considering what the hand was that they were dealt when they took over compared to what's going on in the industry. And I think you can figure it out sometimes. You don't have to figure out very often.[23]

No investor makes the correct call each and every time, nor need they, Buffett notes. You must merely be right a few times.

A great example of the kind of management values in which Berkshire Hathaway invests is Nebraska Furniture Mart, which Buffett purchased for $55 million in 1983 based on a handshake and a two-page contract. At least that's the story. Look deeper, though, and you can see that the company embodied the business practices that Buffett has espoused all along.

Founded in Omaha by a Russian Jewish immigrant named Rose Blumkin in 1937, Nebraska Furniture Mart started as a used furniture store in the basement of her husband's pawnshop. Blumkin opened with a mere $500 in operating capital. Nearly fifty years later, the business had grown into the largest private furniture store in the country. Blumkin's management strategy? Undercutting her rivals by selling everything at just 10 percent above cost.

After the sale, Buffett said of Mrs. B.: "Put her up against the top graduates of the top business schools or chief executives of the Fortune 500 and, assuming an even start with the same resources, she would run rings around them."[24]

This is classic Buffett. It goes with his philosophy of whom he hires at his companies. He looks for people who are intelligent, work hard, and have integrity.

2. Understand a Company within the Context of Its Industry Both Buffett and Munger are reluctant to invest in any company or industry that they do not personally understand. Neither has ever hired a consultant to make calls on buying into unfamiliar sectors. For this reason, they decline to invest in most deals that come their way.

But when they are considering investing in a particular industry, one of Buffett's favorite self-check techniques is to use scuttlebutt methodology and to interview the chief executive officers (CEOs) of competing firms to solicit their opinions. He asks: If they could invest in any single company within the industry, which one would they choose, and why? He gains valuable information and perspective this way. It was key to Berkshire Hathaway's decision to invest in GEICO, which I detail in chapter 6.

3. Understand the Company's Sustainable Competitive Advantage, or "Moat"
Does the company have a "sustainable competitive advantage"? Buffett and Munger call this a "moat." This advantage might be a trade secret, like the formula for Coca-Cola or the herbs and spices in Kentucky Fried Chicken (KFC). It could be a combination of proprietary technology, brand names, trademarks, patents, and copyrights. These so-called "intellectual assets" are every bit as valuable, if not more so, than tangible assets like factories.

After obtaining a patent, a corporate owner has the sole right to use the idea or invention for a specific period.[25] This allows it to sustain predictable revenues and sustainable profit margins. Apple, which is Berkshire Hathaway's largest holding, was granted 2,541 patents in 2021.[26] Amazon had 1,942 patents that same year.[27] A patent, however, does not guarantee financial success.

The most prevalent types of patents are utility and design patents. A utility patent covers the functions of an invention and lasts for twenty years.[28] Examples include pharmaceuticals, machines and their parts and processes, computer hardware and software, and new chemical formulas, including those for food.[29]

Design patents protect key images associated with a brand, such as Coca-Cola's signature curved glass bottle. Design patents filed before May 13, 2015, last for fourteen years and they last for fifteen years if filed after that date.[30]

A drug company's moat is based on its patents for certain lucrative formulations. Nike's moat allows it to charge premium prices based on both its branding *and* its patents. But Amazon has all three attributes that make up a sustainable competitive advantage: a dominant brand, proprietary technology, and intellectual assets.

BUFFETT'S INVESTMENT ADVICE TO THE RETAIL INVESTOR

Over the years, Buffett has shared many insights about value investing. Here are themes that are most relevant to retail investors (i.e., individual investors).

Beware of the Wolves of Wall Street

If you do not have the time or expertise to do research on individual stocks, invest 90 percent of your money in a low-cost S&P 500 index fund and 10 percent into a short-term bond fund. If you do not work in the investment industry, you are not going to outperform the indices.[31]

During the 2017 shareholder's meeting, Buffett discussed a $1 million wager that he'd made in 2006 with Protégé Partners, a New York hedge fund. The fund managers bet that over the next decade, the cumulative returns of five hedge funds (actually "funds-of-funds")[32] picked by Protégé would outperform the S&P 500 index. Buffett bet on the S&P.

Sure enough, at the end of ten years, the S&P 500 index had gained 125.8 percent and the hedge funds grew by 36 percent.[33] The crowd at the 2017 shareholders' meeting, hearing this outcome, roared with laughter,[34] and Buffett declared victory in his letter to shareholders: "The compounded annual increase to date for the index fund is 7.1 percent, which is a return that could easily prove typical for the stock market over time . . . the five funds-of-funds delivered, through 2016, an average of only 2.2 percent, compounded annually. That means $1 million invested in those funds would have gained $220,000. The index fund would meanwhile have gained $854,000."[35]

With this anecdote, Buffett underscored his long-held belief that there are few benefits to be gained through hedge fund investment managers who actively manage others' money. That's because hedge funds and other money managers typically charge fees on a "2-and-20"[36] basis—taking 2 percent as a management fee and 20 percent of the profits. Buffett pointed out that if he operated Berkshire Hathaway with a similar arrangement, his current investment managers, Todd Combs and Ted Weschler, "would be getting $180 million each merely for breathing."[37] To sum up: Buffett believes that so-called passive investments (like an index fund) can do just as well, or better, than active ones.[38]

Buffett believes that while corporate investors like Berkshire Hathaway should spend time getting to know both a company's financials and their culture (through the scuttlebutt method), individuals should probably diversify and "buy a cross-section of America"—in other words, an index fund.[39] He explained:

> I really thought that maybe we were giving a little bit the wrong lesson, because all the questions would naturally tend toward current events. So this time I went back actually to 1942 when I bought my first stock as an illustration of all the things that have happened since 1942. We've had 14 presidents (7 Republicans, 7 Democrats), we've had world wars, we had 9/11, we had the Cuban Missile Crisis, we've had all kinds of things. The best single thing you could've done on March 11, 1942, when I bought my first stock, was just buy an index fund and never look at a headline, never think about stocks anymore, just like you would do if you bought a farm. You just buy the farm and let the tenant farmer run it for you. And I pointed out that if you put $10,000 in an index fund, and then reinvested dividends—and I paused for a moment to let the audience try and guess how much it'd amount to—and it would come to $51 million now. And the only thing you had to really believe in then is that America would win the war and that America would progress as it has ever since 1776, and that if America would move forward, American business would move forward. And you didn't have to worry about what stock to buy, you didn't have to worry what day to get in and out, you didn't need to know if the federal reserve would exist or whatever it might be and, uh, America works.[40]

This belief that "America works" guides Buffett's attitudes. He has said that we need to implement social programs that take care of "the person who's a decent citizen, doesn't have market skills,"[41] in the same way that a "rich family"[42] would take care of their own child in the same situation, but that such programs should be implemented in a way that does not kill "the goose that lays the golden eggs"—in other words, the American market economy.[43] He said, "I don't wanna do anything to the goose that lays the golden eggs. And we've had the goose that lays more and more golden eggs over the years, unbelievable in this country. So we've got something that works in terms of the market system, in terms of turning out lots of goods and services people want."[44] He also believes, as he said in an interview with my students in 2009, that "the world is not a zero-sum game,"[45] and our economy will be improved by improvements in other economies, including China's. He said, "Our standard of living in the U.S. has increased seven-fold in the twentieth century."[46] Investing in the American economy will always pay off in the long run, according to Buffett.

Leave Invested Money Alone

To be successful in value investing, you need to know the actual value of the business or stock. Then leave your investments in the market indefinitely and do not trade. Swing at the right pitch.[47] You must be right only once a year.

Buffett estimates that retail investors have lost more than $100 billion in fees over the past decade by hiring investment managers who, for the most part, cannot even beat the S&P 500 index.[48] In 2016, it was reported that only 19 percent of active large cap managers beat the Russell 1000, an index that tracks approximately 1,000 of the largest companies in the U.S. equity market.[49] The Russell 1000 comprises approximately 90 percent of the total market capitalization of all listed U.S. stocks.[50]

Bottom line: Over time, the markets tend to go up. Do not follow the daily fluctuations of stocks, and do not worry about the general economy. For every 100 years, we tend to have 15 bad years. No one can predict what will happen one day, one week, or one year from now.[51]

OTHER INVESTMENT ADVICE

Read All the Time

As I've noted before, both Buffett and Munger are avid readers, partly because as intellectually curious people, they simply enjoy learning a lot about many different fields, but also because it makes good business sense. To become a successful investor, Buffett advises a person to read upward of 500 pages a day. He will gladly spend 80 percent of a day by himself, reading. Munger, too, emphasizes the importance of reading widely:

> I don't know anyone who's wise who doesn't read a lot. But that's not enough: You have to have a temperament to grab ideas and do sensible things. Most people don't grab the right ideas or don't know what to do with them.[52]

> Warren and I do more reading and thinking and less doing than most people in business. We do that because we like that kind of a life. But we've turned that quirk into a positive outcome for ourselves. We both insist on a lot of time being available almost every day to just sit and think. That is very uncommon in American business. We read and think.[53]

Be Patient

Patience plays a significant role in the Berkshire Hathaway investment philosophy. Buffett and Munger usually wait for years for investments to yield high returns.

IQ Isn't Everything

A high IQ does not guarantee success in any field. There are many other variables that influence success, including motivation, leadership, perseverance, communication skills, and street smarts. Buffett observes: "Success in investing doesn't correlate with IQ once you're above the level of 125. Once you have ordinary intelligence, what you need is the temperament to control the urges that get other people into trouble in investing."[54,55]

Develop the Right Temperament

Investors need to cultivate a certain temperament to sustain success. Munger emphasizes passionate curiosity, the need to build up mental muscles that probe the *why* behind a trend or decision. Without a certain cast of mind, he says, even the brightest person is destined for failure:[56]

> One of the key elements to successful investing is having the right temperament—most people are too fretful; they worry too much. Success means being very patient, but aggressive when it's time. And the more hard lessons you can learn vicariously, rather than through your own hard experience, the better. . . . [But] temperament alone won't do it. You need a lot of curiosity for a long, long time.[57]

Avoid Lemmings through Independent Thinking

One of the most valuable lessons Buffett learned from Graham was how to think independently—to invest for himself based on facts and reasoning rather than following the crowd.

Munger and Buffett frequently point out that the most reliable way to reap superior returns is by purchasing investments when they are undervalued ("on sale"). Almost by definition, an undervalued investment is also unpopular (although, of course, not all unpopular investments are undervalued!). By contrast, "lemmings"[58] are investors who tend to do what everyone else is doing, when everyone else is doing it. This leads to investing when prices are inflated and falling for "bubbles." Buffett likens it to buying a hamburger.[59] Would you rather buy a hamburger for 20 percent less than its usual price? Of course you would. In the case of stocks, why would you want to buy stocks when the price is inflated? Lemming-style investors fall into a psychological trap called "herding bias," which I cover in more depth in chapter 7. Munger and Buffett seek to find good deals by being contrarians.

SUMMARY

We have now discussed *why* Buffett and Munger invest the way they do. The next chapter discusses *how* Buffett and Munger go about investing—the numbers, ratios, patterns, and models that determine a company's intrinsic value.

CHAPTER 5

BERKSHIRE'S INVESTMENT METHODOLOGY

It is better to have a part interest in the Hope Diamond than to own all of a rhinestone.[1]

WARREN BUFFETT

In the first quarter of 2022, Berkshire's Class A shares topped $500,000 each—the highest stock price of any company, ever. Berkshire also owned sixty-two other businesses and had an equity portfolio valued at around $320 billion. All this from a firm that started in 1956 with an investment of $105,000 collected by a group of seven friends and family members. Today, Buffett himself has a personal net worth of around $126 billion.

How does he do it? Is there a secret involving complex mathematics and abstract economic models? Not at all. Munger says that for quantitative measurements, he and Buffett use math that is no more advanced than high school algebra.[2] But the two use an approach that braids quantitative with qualitative metrics when determining how much a company is worth and forecasting the value that it will provide to investors. It's easier to describe than to implement, so I'll do that now.

DETERMINING THE QUALITY OF A COMPANY

Buffett often says that the three most important words in investing are "margin of safety."[3] He is referring to an investment principle preached by his original mentor, Benjamin Graham. The margin of safety is the difference between the market price and the investor's estimation of its intrinsic value.[4] Graham advised purchasing securities only in the scenario when the market price is significantly below a stock's intrinsic value. A large margin of safety does not *guarantee* that the investment will make money, but it does "provide a cushion,"[5] hedging against errors in the investor's model. This is an inherently conservative approach, and over the years, Buffett has modified it somewhat, deciding that it was better to invest in "great companies at good prices" instead of "bad companies at great prices."[6]

"What we really want to do is buy a business that's a great business,"[7] he explained during Berkshire's 2007 shareholder meeting. "So, if we buy something like—See's Candy as a business, or Coca-Cola as a stock, we don't think we need a huge margin of safety because we don't think we're going to be wrong about our assumptions in any material way."[8]

This thinking necessitated a shift from Graham's bargain-hunting approach, and it demanded that Buffett and Munger produce a more refined system to determine that a pricier investment would be worth it. Despite the rigors of their approach, the work is not precise. Buffett has described it as "part art and part science."[9] To better describe his thinking, Buffett uses a wry analogy: "When you see a great business, it's like if you see somebody walk in the door, you don't know whether they weigh 300 pounds or 325 pounds. You still know they are fat, right, you know? And so if we see something we know is fat, financially, we do not worry about being precise. And if we can come in, in that particular example, at the equivalent of 270 pounds, we'll feel good."[10]

There is also the matter of a company's past performance and its sector. Both factors affect how much weight Buffett and Munger give to its margin of safety. For a solid company in a stable field, they are likely to be more flexible about demanding a wide margin of safety.

In sum, the margin of safety concept boils down to getting more value than you are paying for. But, as Munger has noted, value comes in many different forms.

WHAT QUALITATIVE FACTORS DO BUFFETT AND MUNGER LOOK FOR IN POTENTIAL INVESTMENTS?

At the most basic level, Buffett and Munger consider prospective investments that operate within a field they understand. According to the 2019 shareholder letter, "In addition, we constantly seek to buy new businesses that meet three criteria. First, they must earn good returns on the net tangible capital required in their operation. Second, they must be run by able and honest managers. Finally, they must be available at a sensible price."[11]

They prefer to purchase whole businesses rather than smaller pieces. But when that's unlikely—say, for a worldwide brand like Coca-Cola—they will gladly purchase a portion of a great business, even if the stock is trading above bargain-basement prices. "It's better to have a part interest in the Hope Diamond than to own all of a rhinestone,"[12] Buffett quipped to investors in Berkshire's 2007 shareholder letter.

Great businesses with solid futures all possess one key thing, a "moat," to use Buffett's term for a barrier that shields a company from the threat of significant competition. A protective moat might be low-cost products that dominate the market (e.g., Costco and GEICO). Another might be powerful brand identification, as in the case of Coca-Cola, Gillette, and American Express.

Because part of the Berkshire Hathaway strategy is holding on to investments over the long term, Buffett and Munger are interested only in companies that are "enduring."[13] That means that they tend to avoid industries prone to rapid, continuous change. This is not because companies within them are inherently unprofitable, but because these fields preclude investment certainty. "A moat that must be continuously rebuilt will eventually be no moat at all,"[14] as Buffett puts it.

Another thing: Despite Buffett's insistence on good managers, he shies away from companies whose success is attributable to the genius of a particular chief executive officer (CEO). It's logical: if a business requires a superstar to produce great results, the business itself cannot be deemed great. A medical partnership led by your area's premier brain surgeon may enjoy outsized and growing earnings, but that tells little about its future. The partnership's moat will go when the surgeon goes. But you can count on the moat of the Mayo Clinic to endure, even though you can't name its CEO.[15]

Other Qualitative Factors

There are additional qualitative factors that Buffett looks for in his investment opportunities, including:

- Is the company in an industry that does not compete aggressively on price?
- Does the company have a strong customer base (e.g., Gillette, Coca-Cola, Apple)?
- Is management transparent, competent, and compensated fairly?

Buying Businesses Versus Owning Stocks

While Buffett prefers to purchase companies outright rather than investing in stocks, there are times when securities may generate better value. Part of the reason is that negotiating to buy whole companies generally costs more—especially if they're well run—so Berkshire Hathaway can often get more for its money through stocks. Buffett told his shareholders in 1994, "You're not going to buy any bargains and . . . you shouldn't even approach the idea of buying a bargain in a negotiated purchase. You want to buy it from people who are going to run it for you. You want to buy it from people who are intelligent enough to price their business properly. . . . The market doesn't do that. . . . In the stock market, you get a chance to buy businesses at foolish prices, and that is why we end up with a lot of money in marketable securities."[16]

In other words, the stock market rarely prices securities based on their true worth all the time. No wonder, then, that Buffett and Munger love to take advantage of market downturns. "Be greedy when others are fearful" is one of Buffett's favorite rules.[17] An excellent example of this strategy is Berkshire Hathaway's behavior during the Great Recession of 2007–2009, when Buffett invested in several major companies whose stock was tanking—including Goldman Sachs, General Electric (GE), Wrigley/Mars, Swiss Re, and Dow Chemical. By the time the U.S. economy was back on track as the next decade got underway, Berkshire had made more than $10 billion.

QUANTITATIVE INVESTMENT FACTORS

Although Buffett and Munger insist that the financial mathematics they use are simple, they still must use some quantitative techniques to value companies.

Looking for Companies with High Intrinsic Value

Buffett searches for stocks that the marketplace undervalues. But there is no single method for determining a company's intrinsic value. Buffett's approach differs depending on a company's industry and stage of growth. What's most important to keep in mind is that this numeric value may or may not match where the company's stock is trading at any given moment.[18]

To assess a company's potential as an investment vehicle, Buffett and Munger first focus on its financial statements and disclosure to investors. They are looking for a set of specific ratios that indicate potential for yielding high returns.

Return on Net Tangible Assets

Now for some math. Most of the duo's investments are in companies that earn "more than 20 percent" of what Buffett calls the "net tangible equity capital or net tangible assets" required to run their businesses.[19] It's probably self-evident to say, but these firms earn profits without going deeply into debt.[20]

The formula for returns on a company's net tangible assets is as follows:

Return on Net Tangible Assets = Net Income/Net Tangible Assets

And Buffett's formula to determine the denominator of net tangible assets is:

Net Tangible Assets = Total Assets - Total Liabilities - Intangible Assets (i.e., goodwill, brand recognition, and intellectual property such as patents, trademarks, and copyrights) - Par Value of Preferred Shares[21]

(In this formula, the par value of a share of preferred stock is the amount upon which the associated dividend is calculated. Thus, if the par value of the stock is $1,000 and the dividend is 5 percent, then the issuing entity must pay $50 per year for as long as the preferred stock is outstanding.)[22]

This formula seeks to determine what physical assets the company has, less any debts.[23] Net tangible assets are the book value of the company's physical assets. Intangible assets such as goodwill, intellectual property, and preferred shares are subtracted from the tangible (e.g., physical) assets to arrive at net tangible assets.

Return on Equity

Return on equity (ROE) tells how effectively the company is employing the capital invested by stockholders. The formula for ROE is as follows:[24]

$$\text{Return on Equity}\left(\text{ROE}\right)=\frac{\text{Net Income}}{\text{Average Shareholders' Equity}}$$

Shareholders' Equity = Total Assets - Total Liabilities
Total Assets = Current + Long-Term Assets

Current assets are those that can be converted to cash within a year (e.g., cash, accounts receivable, inventory). Long-term assets are those that cannot be converted to cash or consumed within a year (e.g., investments, property, plant and equipment, and intangibles, such as patents).

Total liability is the sum of near-term financial obligations and those due in more than a year, as shown below:

Total Liabilities = Current + Long-Term Liabilities, where Current Liabilities = obligations due (taxes, accounts, payable, etc.), and Long-Term Liabilities = debts due more than a year in the future (bonds payable, leases, pensions)[25]

Shareholders' equity (SE) is the residual claim of the owners (shareholders) once all debts are paid. Equity is noted on a company's balance sheet, and it is one of the most common financial metrics that analysts employ to assess financial health. SE represents the amount of money that would be returned to shareholders if all of a company's assets were liquidated and all debt paid off. This is sometimes called the "book value."[26]

Suppose, for example, that a restaurant had a net income last year of $100,000 (as seen on its income statement) and total SE (on the balance sheet) of $200,000. The ROE for that year would be 50 percent.

Profit Margins and Earnings per Share (EPS)

For a company that Buffett is considering, he reviews years of financial statements, looking for consistently increasing earnings, ideally at annual rates of at least 10 percent. He then analyzes two measures:

Profit Margins = Net Income/Net Sales
Earnings per Share = Total Net Earnings/Number of Shares of Stock Outstanding

A high profit margin indicates that the company executes its business well. Increasing margins over time usually means that management has been effective at controlling expenses, and this is often associated with a company that possesses pricing power within its sector. A prime example is See's Candies, as outlined in the subsection "Capital," later in this chapter.

Different industries have different normal ranges of profit margins and EPS. Whereas certain tech providers have very high profit margins, airlines tend to have lower profit margins. As we will discuss in chapter 9, Buffett has had a love/hate relationship with airline investments throughout his career, jokingly likening it to an unhealthy addiction and calling himself an "aeroholic."[27]

Debt-to-Equity Ratio

Buffett uses the debt-to-equity (D/E) ratio to determine how much a company is borrowing. This ratio is also known as a company's financial leverage, and it is calculated as follows:

Debt-to-Equity Ratio = Total Liabilities/Shareholders' Equity

As with profit margins and EPS, determining an ideal D/E ratio depends on the industry. However, a ratio smaller than 1.0 is generally ideal. Buffett wants to know whether the company's D/E ratio is low enough to pay its debt obligations.[28]

Free Cash Flow

Assessing a company's free cash flow (FCF) is a fundamental valuation technique. FCF measures the level of cash available to a company's investors after all required investments in working capital and fixed assets have been made.

FCF is an important measure because it allows a company to pursue opportunities that enhance shareholder value. With excess cash, a company can expand production, develop new products, make acquisitions, pay dividends, repurchase shares, and reduce debt. An increase in FCF increases the strength of the balance sheet. Negative FCF can be construed as a problem, but it also could signal that a company is making significant investments for future growth.[29] If these investments earn a high rate of return, the strategy has the potential to add value for shareholders in the long run.[30]

We can calculate FCF using the following equations:

Free Cash Flow = Cash Flow from Operating Activities – Capital Expenditures

Free Cash Flow = Net Operating Profit After Cash Taxes – Net Investment in Operating Capital (where Net Operating Profit After Taxes = Revenue – Operating Costs and Cash Taxes)

Free Cash Flow = Revenue – Operating Costs and Cash Taxes – Required Investments in Operating Capital (where Required Investments = Fixed Assets and Working Capital)

If calculated properly, with all the same inputs, all three equations should produce the same result for FCF.[31]

Capital

Buffett prefers firms that do not require extensive capital to operate. The business should have neither a prohibitive cost of operations nor other significant cash outflows. See's Candies is one of Buffett's favorite examples of this principle. He bought the company for $25 million in 1972, and it has since generated an average of $40 million annually in pretax profits. Even better, noted Buffett in 2019, See's has earned more than $2 billion in total pretax income since its purchase, money that Berkshire has used to buy other businesses.[32]

See's capital needs were modest. Buffett purchased it with the idea that Berkshire could raise the price of See's candy without investing a great deal. That formula worked. And it leads us to another consideration: Is the company free to adjust prices for inflation and still maintain profitability? In other words, does the company have pricing power such that consumers will still buy its products or services even if they cost more?

According to Markets Insider, "Buffett has praised See's outsized financial returns, modest capital needs, economic moat, quality personnel, and the chocolates themselves."[33] "During the [upcoming shareholders'] meeting, Charlie and I will each consume enough Coke, See's fudge, and See's peanut brittle to satisfy the weekly caloric needs of an NFL lineman," he joked in the 2015 Berkshire shareholders letter.[34] More important, Berkshire has seen an 8,000 percent return on See's since 1972, or more than 160 percent a year.[35] As Buffett explained: "We put $25 million into it, and it's given us over $2 billion of pretax income, well over $2 billion, and we've used it to buy other businesses."[36]

Since Buffett bought See's, its annual revenue has grown from $30 million to over $380 million, and its pretax profits of under $5 million has grown to $80 million.[37]

The $2 billion of Berkshire profits from See's required a cumulative total investment of only $40 million (including equipment).[38]

Retained Earnings

Retained earnings are another important aspect of a company's balance sheet because this statistic often signals growth. The simplest way to think of retained earnings is as reinvested profits since they represent a cumulative total of net income held by a firm that can be channeled toward new projects.

Calculated by totaling net income minus dividends, retained earnings can be used to increase production, hire new employees, invest in research and development (R&D), boost ad campaigns, acquire subsidiary companies, buy back shares, or pay off long-term debts/liabilities like pensions.

Retained earnings can also be called the "retention ratio," which is equal to 1 - the Dividend Payout Ratio. The dividend payout ratio is the amount of money that is returned to shareholders. The retention ratio is the amount of money that is reinvested in the company (retained earnings).

This can be figured as follows:[39]

$$\text{Dividend Payout Ratio}\left(\%\right) = \frac{\text{Dividends Paid}}{\text{Net Income}}$$

$$\text{Dividend Payout Ratio} = 1 - \text{Retention Ratio}$$

where

$$\text{Retention Ratio}\left(\%\right) = \frac{\text{Earnings per Share} - \text{Dividends per Share}}{\text{Earnings per Share}}$$

Any way you slice it, a company that maximizes its retained earnings is one that is positioned for economic success by investing in its own growth.

Buffett wants companies that will add value to Berkshire by growing their retained earnings. If a company cannot earn returns above the cost of capital,

Buffett prefers either to return the funds to his shareholders through dividends or buy back the company's stock (if it is undervalued). In other words, will the retaining earnings lead to an increase in the company's stock market value?

The best example of this principle is Berkshire Hathaway itself. Berkshire has never paid a dividend because Buffett thinks he can earn a better rate of return for investors by reinvesting those funds. If Buffett paid dividends, his shareholders would have to pay taxes. Instead, he can use that money to enhance Berkshire's stock value. Retaining earnings, in this case, enhances Berkshire's financial flexibility. Buffett has said that he would repurchase Berkshire stock only if it dropped under 1.2 times book value per share and he thought his shareholders would make money the very next day.[40]

CHAPTER 6
CASE STUDIES

GEICO and Apple

The most important quality for an investor is temperament, not intellect. You need a temperament that neither derives great pleasure from being with the crowd or against the crowd.[1]

WARREN BUFFETT

INTRODUCTION

This chapter describes examples of two companies that have had a significant impact on Berkshire Hathaway. The Government Employees Insurance Company (GEICO) was one of Buffett's earliest investments. By examining his decision-making about this company, we get a window into the way he assesses opportunity. The same goes for Buffett's behavior regarding Apple, Inc., which is Berkshire's largest stock position today. Here, I walk you through Buffett's rationale for purchasing these particular stocks and his assessment of their valuation, which readers can use as models for their own valuation exercises.

GEICO

Trained as an accountant, Leo Goodwin, Sr., had been working at USAA Insurance for about a decade when he had an epiphany. Goodwin believed that he would be able to offer customers auto insurance rates at 20 to 30 percent less than competing firms by targeting a specific set of consumers through the mail rather than going through an insurance agent, as was standard in the industry during the first part of the twentieth century. In 1936, with his wife, Lillian, Goodwin founded GEICO in Fort Worth, Texas, and aimed his products at government employees and top-ranking noncommissioned military personnel. He and Lillian started the business with $25,000 of their own money and a loan of $75,000 from a banker, Charles Rhea.[2]

In 1937, the couple moved their operation to Washington, D.C., and it grew quickly. By 1948, Rhea had sold most of his stock to a group of investors that included Benjamin Graham, Buffett's mentor from Columbia University, who was then operating in partnership with Jerome Newman. The Graham-Newman Corporation bought half of Rhea's stock, which was then worth $712,000.[3] In 1949, GEICO went public at $27 a share.[4]

Buffett, meanwhile, was working on his master's degree at Columbia when he discovered that Graham-Newman held a position in GEICO and Graham was the chair of GEICO's board of directors. Ever-enterprising, Buffett traveled to Washington, D.C., on a Saturday in 1951 to learn more about this company that had attracted his mentor and inspired such a large investment. He knocked on the door of its headquarters and convinced a janitor to let him in. On the sixth floor, Buffett found Lorimer "Davy" Davidson, who was then assistant to GEICO's president. He eventually became the company's chief executive officer (CEO). In a classic example of Buffett's tenacity and smarts, the twenty-year-old graduate student peppered Davidson with a series of well-informed questions about the insurance industry and GEICO's unique approach to it. The two men spoke for five hours. Buffett would later say that he learned more in that conversation than he had during his entire college career.[5]

There were two ways to make money in the insurance industry, Davidson explained. The first and most obvious was through premiums on policies. The second was via investment returns on those premiums (so-called float[6]—more on that later in this chapter). Davidson also explained that GEICO's method of selling through direct marketing gave the company a significant advantage by allowing it to charge significantly less than other firms that sold policies through insurance agents. The latter, traditional method of distribution was so ingrained into the business model that most insurers could not conceive of giving it up. His session with Davidson made Buffett more excited about GEICO than he had been about any stock, ever.[7]

Graham had advised his star pupil to wait for a pullback in the market before investing. But Buffett disregarded this advice, investing more than 50 percent of his net worth in GEICO. (This amounted to 350 shares at $29⅜ a share, at a total cost of $10,282.) By the end of 1951, his holdings were worth $13,125, a 28 percent return that accounted for more than 65 percent of Buffett's total net worth.[8]

This flush of quick success, however, prompted Buffett to make a serious mistake. In 1952, he sold his entire position in GEICO for $15,259 in order to plow that money into shares of Western Insurance Securities. Western Insurance looked like a bargain, and Graham had taught Buffett all about bargain-hunting. But over the next twenty years, Buffett would see the value of the GEICO stock he'd sold balloon to well over $1 million. He'd pulled the trigger too early. It taught Buffett a lesson that would shape his investment behavior ever after.[9]

As Buffett put it: "This act of infidelity can partially be excused by the fact that Western was selling for slightly more than one times its current earnings, a P/E ratio that for some reason caught my eye. But . . . [it] taught me a lesson about the inadvisability of selling a stake in an identifiably wonderful company."[10]

It was another two decades before Buffett (now acting through Berkshire Hathaway) found an opportunity to invest in GEICO again. But he followed the company's progress, taking note of Davidson's impact as chair of the board. One of Davidson's most important moves was expanding the company's potential target market from 15 percent of all car owners to 50 percent, done by targeting professionals outside of government who had excellent driving records. This single act increased GEICO's profits significantly.

However, fortunes at the groundbreaking insurance firm were about to take a sharp turn. Between 1972 and 1976, the stock price plummeted from a high of $61 to a low of $2. In 1975, GEICO lost $126 million and failed to pay shareholders a dividend. GEICO and other insurers had inflation challenges, problems with the number and severity of accidents involving motorists they'd insured, and no-fault laws.[11]

By 1976, the company was approaching insolvency. Desperate for a turnaround, the board fired its then-CEO, Norman Gidden, and replaced him with John Byrne, a forty-three-year-old marketing executive from the Travelers Corporation.

Buffett had kept a sharp eye on these changes and requested a meeting with Byrne. The following morning, he purchased 500,000 shares of GEICO at $2⅛ per share. Berkshire's total investment in the company would amount to $19 million, in the form of a Salomon Brothers-led convertible preferred stock issuance of $75 million, plus $4.1 million in common shares at an average price of $2.55 per share. When the stock split 5–1 in 1992, Buffett's cost basis was $1.31 a share.[12]

By 1980, Berkshire's investment in GEICO was $45 million, equivalent to 31 percent of the company. Within five years, that stake had grown to 50 percent of Berkshire's equity portfolio and was worth $596 million.[13] By 1994, Berkshire Hathaway's GEICO shares were worth more than $1 billion. And on August 25, 1995, Buffett announced that Berkshire would acquire the remaining 51 percent of GEICO stock for $2.3 billion, making GEICO a wholly owned subsidiary of Berkshire Hathaway.[14]

Under Buffett's leadership, GEICO has thrived. He named Todd Combs, a top Berkshire investor (and potential successor to Buffett), as CEO of the massive insurance firm. In 2021, GEICO employed some 40,000 people and had revenues of $37 billion and a profit of $1.26 billion.[15]

The Float

The "float," which is also known as the "available reserve," refers to the money paid in premiums to Berkshire Hathaway's insurance subsidiaries that has not been used to cover any claims. Technically, this money does not belong to the insurance company but remains available to be invested. It's a bit like receiving a loan at 0 percent interest. Berkshire's float has grown from $39 million in 1967 to $147 billion in 2022.[16]

Berkshire Hathaway's float allows it to make quick purchases of troubled companies. In 2002, for example, Berkshire bought Fruit of the Loom out of bankruptcy for $835 million after its stock dropped 97 percent.[17] Buffett predicts that Berkshire's float will increase for a few more years and then decline a bit, but never more than 3 percent in any year.[18]

An insurance company's profitability can be measured by the following financial ratio, known as the "combined ratio":

$$\text{Combined Ratio} = \frac{\text{Incurred Losses and General Business Expenses}}{\text{Earned Premiums}}$$

A combined ratio below 1 (100 percent) indicates operating profitability, while a combined ratio above 1 (100 percent) indicates operating loss. However, note that insurance companies with combined ratios higher than 1 might turn profitable overall, at least in the short term, when one accounts for investing and financing activities, as well as operating activities.[19]

GEICO QUALITATIVE INVESTMENT FACTORS

Understand the Company and Industry

From the beginning, Buffett knew that he could trust Graham's judgment. The fact that Graham was the chair of GEICO's board of directors is what drew Buffett to the company in the first place. But to understand the nitty-gritty details of the company and its operations, he also knew that he had to speak with someone in a hands-on, day-to-day management role. That's what prompted him to make his visit to Washington, where he met Davidson.

Interview Executives

Buffett's five-hour direct conversation with Davidson gave Buffett an opportunity to learn about the insurance industry and GEICO's innovative business model.

Sustainable Competitive Advantage (Moat)

Did GEICO have a sustainable competitive advantage, or "moat"? The answer is most definitely yes. Buffett learned that GEICO made its money through premiums and float. But it was the firm's direct marketing that undercut other insurance companies and created a unique advantage as a low-cost operator.

Management Team

As I said in chapter 4, Buffett follows a company's management team and performance over several years—often as long as a decade—before investing. He wants to see a stable management team with passion and the ability to think creatively. He also looks for managers who act independently without being influenced by fads. Finally, he values management that is open and honest with company shareholders. As Buffett discovered by talking with the top people at GEICO, the groundbreaking insurance company easily met these standards.

Summary

From a qualitative perspective, GEICO was a solid investment opportunity for Buffett. His confidence in his investment decision was affirmed by his initial talk with Graham, his interview with Davidson, and his diligent research. His approach also fit his strategy of acquiring great businesses that traded at a discount to their intrinsic value, and then holding them for a long time—although he learned this the hard way, by initially selling GEICO too early. Buffett wants companies that offer a product that he understands in industries he can grasp. He also seeks companies that have favorable long-term prospects, are operated by honest, competent people, and are available at attractive prices. GEICO fit the bill. The company also represents a watershed in Buffett's education about mistakes in investing: Using his early 28 percent profit from GEICO to immediately buy another stock was an error Buffett came to rue, but that provided him with a lesson he never forgot.

GEICO QUANTITATIVE INVESTMENT FACTORS

Return on Equity

Buffett prefers to see a return on equity (ROE) consistently above 10 percent, but this will depend on the economic environment. For example, when Buffett purchased 500,000 shares of GEICO in 1976, the company's ROE was actually negative.

Buffett, however, recognized this situation as a unique turnaround opportunity. He had determined that its intrinsic value was appreciably higher than the current market value of GEICO's shares. This forecast proved to be correct. By 1980, under a new CEO, GEICO's ROE was 30.8 percent, nearly double the industry average.[20]

Profitability and Retained Earnings

Buffett typically examines ten years of financial data to ensure that a company is consistently increasing earnings. He was well aware of GEICO's early success. In addition, he was further encouraged by his knowledge of the insurance industry; his belief in Byrne, the new CEO from Travelers; and his confidence in other underlying metrics (such as GEICO's moat). The stock purchase became foundational to Berkshire Hathaway's overall growth.

If you had invested $1 in GEICO in 1980, it would be worth $27.89 by 1992, for a 29.2 percent compounded annual rate of return (excluding dividends). This was much larger than the S&P 500 return of 8.9 percent.[21]

Valuation

In 1976, when Buffett invested in GEICO for the second time, the company was virtually bankrupt, and losses were mounting. Under that scenario, valuing GEICO through a traditional price-to-earnings (P/E) ratio was impossible, as GEICO had no earnings.

Remember that the P/E ratio is the market value of one share divided by earnings per share (EPS). It is particularly useful for comparing companies within industries. Higher P/E ratios tend to indicate companies with higher earnings growth.[22]

Although Buffett uses P/E ratios, he does not rely on them exclusively. It's all about context. As he put it: "There's no P/E ratio that we have in mind as being a cutoff point at all. . . . I mean, you could have some business making a sliver of money on which you would pay a very, very high P/E ratio."[23]

In the case of GEICO, Buffett knew the company's brand was worth more than what its earnings showed, which means that he understood that the company was significantly undervalued. And after he met with the new CEO, Buffett walked away confident that GEICO could be turned around.

As we know, this was the right call. By 1980, four years after his investment, the company had sales of $705 million and earnings of $60 million, of which Berkshire now owned $20 million.[24] It had been a bargain-basement find, as Buffett would later acknowledge: "To buy a similar $20 million of earning power in a business with first-class economic characteristics and bright prospects would cost a minimum of $200 million."[25]

APPLE, INC.

Buffett became well known for avoiding investments in tech. Even a friendship with Bill Gates did not change his mind. Amazon's total assets had grown every year since the early aughts, but Buffett still demurred on technology. Finally, in 2016, he made an exception and began to buy stock in Apple. There were a few reasons for this. First, he understood Apple's products. Second, he considered them "sticky." In other words, Apple made computers, smartphones, and related products that became nearly addictive to consumers; once they had purchased Apple, customers found it difficult to switch their loyalty to any other brand. Part of this was due to Apple's genius in creating a closed system of equipment, not easily interchangeable with other technology. A third reason that Buffett preferred Apple (and eventually Amazon) to other tech stocks: It was a well-established company, long past the bubblelike speculation often associated with start-ups.

Between 2016 and 2018, Berkshire Hathaway amassed a substantial position in Apple through stock buys. As of the end of 2021, Berkshire held 907,559,761 shares, representing a 5.64 percent stake in the company, with a market value of $161.15 billion.[26] Apple is Berkshire's largest equity holding. It also represents one of the largest investments of Buffett's career.[27]

In an interview with CNBC in 2017, he explained his rationale: "When I take a dozen kids, as I do on Sundays out to Dairy Queen, they're all holding their [iPhones], they barely can talk to me except if I'm ordering ice cream or something like that."[28] A classic entrepreneur's observation. Even when relaxing with his family and friends at a favorite restaurant, Buffett is always scanning for opportunities.

2016–2017

In early 2016, Berkshire purchased its first batch of Apple shares. The stock "was trading in the low $100s."[29] He considered this a moment to pounce, as Apple's stock had just dropped more than 30 percent after it peaked at $133 per share. "It was trading at just ten times earnings—well below the broad U.S. stock market valuation of seventeen times earnings—and not nearly as expensive as some other popular tech stocks."[30]

Buffett also knew that Apple was an excellent brand, with a strong management team. By the end of 2016, Berkshire had purchased 61.2 million shares at prices between $106 and $118 per share.[31]

Buffett did not make these purchases himself; they were done by Todd Combs or Ted Weschler. Both former hedge fund managers, Combs and Weschler had been hired by Buffett a few years earlier to manage a portion of Berkshire's stock portfolio.[32,33] They have had a marked influence on positioning the company for the twenty-first century.

Investing in tech was a necessary shift. Technology stocks comprise 20 percent of the S&P 500, a significant amount.[34] Apple possessed many of the attributes that Buffett usually seeks: It was a leader in its industry, carried moderate debt, held one of the world's best-known brands, and engendered unrivaled consumer loyalty. At the end of 2016, Apple also had $246 billion in cash on hand,[35] giving the company great flexibility to jump onto new investment options—much like Berkshire Hathaway itself.

By the first quarter of 2017, Berkshire had doubled its stock in Apple, and by the end of the year, Berkshire owned 3.3 percent of the company.[36]

2018–2022

Buffett's appetite for the stock did not cool. In 2018, Berkshire purchased 87 million more shares of Apple, for a total holding of 255.3 million.[37] Buffett candidly remarked to CNBC that he would buy 100 percent of Apple if he could. He was sold on the company's management, economics, and culture.[38] No surprise, then, that by the end of the following year, Berkshire owned 5.7 percent of Apple, in shares worth over $70 billion.[39,40]

Yet he was still not immune to errors in judgment. At the end of 2020, Berkshire sold $7.4 billion of Apple,[41] a surprising move considering how positive Charlie Munger had been about the stock. At the 2021 shareholder meeting a year later, Buffett admitted that this had been a mistake. However, Berkshire still owned 907.6 million shares of Apple, and by August 2022 Berkshire owned 911.4 shares or 5.7 percent of Apple worth $156.8 billion.[42]

APPLE QUALITATIVE INVESTMENT FACTORS

Understand the Company and Industry

Over its forty-five-year history, Apple has developed so much brand loyalty that consumers rarely flinch at its higher-than-average prices. This consumer loyalty, paired with Apple's closed system, which makes its products incompatible with other tech platforms, has created a consistent revenue stream requiring little capital investment. While Buffett has generally avoided tech stocks, he views

Apple as more of a consumer products company, and consumer products constitute an industry he understands.[43]

Sustainable Competitive Advantage (Moat)

Apple's moat is a direct result of its unique position within the tech sector, as noted previously: a fiercely loyal customer base, reluctant to leave Apple's interlocking system of products. That moat was key to Buffett and Munger's investment. In addition, Apple's global brand name recognition helps to support the company's pricing of its products at a premium, compared with competitors.

Management Team

Apple's founder, Steve Jobs, famously hired only A-level people, and he inspired them to achieve even beyond their ambitions. That kind of passion became integral to the company's overall culture. Managers at Apple also demonstrated creativity and independence, eschewing the fads that so often dominate consumer-facing technology. Although Jobs died in 2011, several years before Berkshire's investment, Buffett found similar qualities and values in Jobs's successor, Tim Cook.

Summary

Apple was an ideal investment opportunity for Buffett: a consistently successful company, which created products he understood, in a field with obvious long-term prospects. Highly competent people led it. And at the time Buffett bought in, Apple's shares were trading at an attractive price compared to other tech brands.

APPLE QUANTITATIVE INVESTMENT FACTORS

Profitability

As with all potential investments, Buffett first examined ten years of financial statements to see Apple's consistently strong earnings. Apple's high after-tax profits showed that it was a well-run business. Its margins meant that Apple had efficiently reduced expenses, while new customers continued to drive growing sales and the "lock in" effect from Apple's propriety ecosystem of products and services.

TABLE 6.1 Apple's after-tax profit margin

Year	2012	2013	2014	2015	2016	2017	2018	2019	2020	2021
After-tax profit margin	24.0%	22.7%	24.2%	24.2%	22.8%	22.7%	23.7%	24.2%	21.7%	26.6%

Source: Gurufocus.com.

Apple's sustained after-tax profit margin (see table 6.1), consistently above 20 percent, speaks to the moat created by its business model.

Return on Net Tangible Assets

In chapter 5, I showed that the formula for a company's net tangible assets is as follows:[44]

$$\text{Net Tangible Assets} = \text{Total Assets} - \text{Total Liabilities} \\ - \text{Intangible Assets} - \text{Par Value of Preferred Shares}$$

The return on this metric can be calculated this way:

$$\text{Return on Net Tangible Assets} = \text{Net Income/Net Tangible Assets}$$

At Apple, return on net tangible assets has seen a consistent increase of more than 30 percent annually for a decade (see table 6.2).

TABLE 6.2 Apple's return on net tangible assets

	2012	2013	2014	2015	2016	2017	2018	2019	2020	2021
Return on net tangible assets	37%	31%	38%	48%	34%	36%	56%	61%	91%	150%
Net income*	41,733	37,037	39,510	53,394	45,687	48,351	59,531	55,256	57,411	94,680
Total assets*	176,064	207,000	231,839	290,345	321,686	375,319	365,725	338,516	323,888	351,002
Total liabilities*	57,854	83,451	120,292	170,990	193,437	241,272	258,578	248,028	258,549	287,912
Intangible assets*	5,359	5,756	8,758	9,009	8,620	0	0	0	0	0
Par preferred	0	0	0	0	0	0	0	0	0	0

*Figures are in millions of U.S. dollars.
Source: Gurufocus.com.

TABLE 6.3 Apple's return on equity

Year	2012	2013	2014	2015	2016	2017	2018	2019	2020	2021
ROE	36.3%	28.9%	37.6%	42.8%	34.9%	37.4%	50.9%	60.2%	90.1%	147%

Source: Gurufocus.com.

Return on Equity

Table 6.3 shows a consistently strong ROE for the past ten years, with a notable ramp-up in the last three years at even faster rates.

Remember that Buffett prefers a consistent ROE above 12 percent, so Apple's performance is more than outstanding.

Debt-to-Equity Ratio

The debt-to-equity (D/E) ratio indicates how much a company relies on debt. Also known as "financial leverage," the formula to calculate it is as follows:[45]

$$\text{Debt-to-Equity Ratio} = \frac{\text{Total Liabilities}}{\text{Total Shareholders' Equity}}$$

where

$$\text{Total Liabilities} = \text{Short-Term Debt and Capital Lease} + \text{Long-Term Debt and Capital Lease Obligation} + \text{Other Financial Liabilities}$$

and

$$\text{Total Shareholders' Equity} = \text{Total Assets} - \text{Total Liabilities}$$

Ideal D/E ratios are different depending on the industry, but in general, a ratio smaller than one (or less than 100 percent) is preferred. The lower the D/E ratio, the more Buffett can rest assured that a company can pay off its debt obligations. Table 6.4 shows how Apple met Buffett's criteria for seven years. Financial conditions created by COVID-19, something of a black swan event, altered this trajectory.

As you can see, the D/E ratio for Apple over seven years remained steadily below 100 percent. Only recently has this measure gone above 100 percent,

TABLE 6.4 Apple's debt-to-equity ratio

Year	2012	2013	2014	2015	2016	2017	2018	2019	2020	2021
D/E ratio	0%	13.1%	26.4%	41.5%	55.6%	72.5%	87.5%	104%	151%	147%

Source: Gurufocus.com.

primarily due to interest rates being near 0 percent during the pandemic. Those conditions, however, gave Apple a terrific opportunity to sell its debt at an extremely low cost. This also coincided with Apple consistently repurchasing shares of its stock, which reduced reported retained earnings (and therefore the book value of equity). These two factors created the impression on the surface that Apple was more leveraged. This is unlikely to worry Buffett. Given the company's cash, plus its short- and long-term marketable securities, Apple is effectively net debt free.

Free Cash Flow

Buffett wants to know whether a company has sufficiently strong free cash flow (FCF) to maintain its current operations. Did the company retain earnings for future investment? And what is management's track record with those investments?

Refer to chapter 5 for an in-depth look at calculating the FCF. Table 6.5 shows Apple's FCF (in billions of dollars), along with the percentage increase/decrease year over year.

Over the past ten years, the FCF for Apple has been generally healthy. Based on these figures, the FCF at Apple has increased at an average annual compounded growth rate of 9.4 percent for the past 9 years.

TABLE 6.5 Apple's free cash flow (in billions)

	2012	2013	2014	2015	2016	2017	2018	2019	2020	2021
FCF	41.5	44.6	49.9	69.8	53.5	51.8	64.1	58.9	73.4	93
% change year over year increase (decrease)		7.5	11.9	39.9	(23.3)	(3.2)	24	(8)	24.6	26.7

Source: Gurufocus.com.

Retained Earnings

From 2012 through 2020, Apple has been reinvesting about 75 percent of its retained earnings. Through much of the last decade, it also has been buying back an enormous amount of stock, which helped lead to the stock price increase and eventual split in 2020.

Table 6.6 shows Apple's retained earnings (in billions).

Table 6.7 shows Apple's dividend payout ratio, calculated as follows:

Dividend Payout Ratio = Dividends Paid Out/Net Income

And finally, table 6.8 shows Apple's retention ratio, calculated as follows:

Retention Ratio = (1 - Dividends Payout Ratio)

Besides investing to grow its already strong consumer brand, Apple pays dividends and buys back its own stock.

TABLE 6.6 Apple's retained earnings (in billions)

	2012	2013	2014	2015	2016	2017	2018	2019	2020	2021
Retained earnings	$101.3	$104.3	$87.2	$92.3	$96.4	$98.3	$70.4	$45.9	$15	$5.6

Source: Gurufocus.com.

TABLE 6.7 Apple's steadily healthy payouts

	2012	2013	2014	2015	2016	2017	2018	2019	2020	2021
Dividend payout ratio	6%	28.7%	21.5%	21.5%	26.2%	26.1%	22.8%	25.2%	24%	15%

Source: Gurufocus.com.

TABLE 6.8 Apple's retention ratio

	2012	2013	2014	2015	2016	2017	2018	2019	2020	2021
Retention ratio	94%	71.3%	71.9%	78.5%	73.8%	73.9%	77.2%	74.8%	76%	85%

Source: Gurufocus.com.

Simplifying the Math

Munger says that "some of the worst business decisions I've ever seen came with detailed analysis."[46] The more elaborate the math one relies on, the greater the potential for a model to be misused.

Yet business school professors do not get tenure by advocating rules of thumb; their success is often predicated on advancing complex models.[47] For example, consider the misuse of a financial model that led to the disaster of the Long-Term Capital Management (LTCM) hedge fund[48] in 1998. This was a fund founded and run mostly by academics, including two Nobel Prize winners in economics. The company's complex and closely guarded mathematical models generated enviable gains in just a few years. But they left investors exposed during the 1997 Asian financial crisis and the 1998 Russian financial crisis. LTCM's value imploded, and to prevent a global financial meltdown, various banks had to bail out the fund, at an aggregate cost of $3.65 billion.[49] Although Buffett accepts the principle of discounting cash flows, he does not trust these models. Munger says that he has never seen his partner actually perform a formal discounted cash flow (DCF) analysis.[50]

At the end of this chapter, I offer a detailed analysis of how Buffett and Munger might discount future cash flows at Apple.

Intrinsic Value Projections and Interest Rates

At the 2017 shareholder meeting, a shareholder asked Buffett and Munger an interesting and pointed question: How much did they expect the intrinsic value of Berkshire Hathaway to increase over the next ten years? They answered by taking future interest rates into account:

> **BUFFETT:** If I could only pick one statistic to ask you about the future before I gave the answer, I would not ask you about GDP growth. I would not ask you about who was going to be president. I would ask you what the interest rate is going to be over the next twenty years on average, the ten-year or whatever you wanted to do. And if you assume our present interest rate structure is likely to be the average over ten or twenty years, then I would say it would be very difficult to get to 10 percent.[51]

Buffett acknowledged that predicting future interest rates was the only way to provide a solid answer to this question, and this was difficult to do. The most reliable metric, he said, was looking back at Berkshire's performance over time:

> **BUFFETT:** I would say the chances of getting a terrible result in Berkshire are probably as low as about anything you can find. The chances of getting a sensational result are also about as low as anything you can find. So, my best guess would be in the 10 percent range, but that assumes somewhat higher interest rates—not dramatically higher—but somewhat higher interest rates in the next ten or twenty years than we've experienced in the last seven years.
>
> **MUNGER:** I think we have one other advantage. A lot of other people are trying to be brilliant. And we're just trying to stay rational. And it's a big advantage. Trying to be brilliant is dangerous, particularly when you're gambling.[52]

Before I go into detail on the calculation of the valuation of Apple using DCF, please recognize that some practitioners utilize more detailed inputs. My valuation is intentionally designed for a layperson. As Munger and Buffett have acknowledged, valuation is both an art and a science, and anybody using any valuation tool should think in terms of valuation ranges.

EXAMPLE OF A DISCOUNTED FREE CASH FLOW ANALYSIS OF APPLE

How Discounted Cash Flow Works

The DCF model is used to estimate the value of a company or security based on the cash that it generates into the future, which is then discounted to its present value. The model can be used with income-producing property, investment projects or fractional ownership in a business, corporate mergers and acquisitions, bonds, or common stocks. It estimates the value of an investment today based on discounted future cash flows.

There are two primary components, described in the next sections:

Part I: Forecast period
Part II: Terminal value

Part I: Forecast Period Forecast periods can range from five to ten years.[53] The DCF method calculates expected future cash flows based on present value.[54]

To understand present value, assume that you have $100 in a savings account. You earn a 1 percent annual interest rate. After one year, you will have $101. The two amounts—$100 today and $101 a year from today—are equivalent. That is, they have the same economic value. This concept is known as the "time value of money."[55]

DCF analysis calculates a reduction (discount) of future cash flows using a discount rate.[56] An attractive investment is one where the present value of the future cash flows is higher than the investment's initial cost.[57] The discount rate is estimated by the investor and can differ depending on the situation and the perceived risk of the investment being valued.[58] DCF also becomes less effective as a predictive model the further you are looking into the future.[59]

Part II: Terminal Value The terminal value (TV) is used to make predictions about time frames past when yearly cash flows can be reasonably forecast (generally five years).[60] TV is usually calculated through one of two models: (1) perpetuity growth (Gordon growth model) or (2) exit multiple.[61] The Gordon growth model assumes a constant growth rate past the point that the DCF can reasonably project.[62] The exit multiple assumes the sale of the business.[63] The Gordon growth model is considered more academic, while the exit multiple method is used more often by practical investors.[64]

Types of Terminal Value

Perpetuity Growth Method This TV calculation estimates the value of the company after the forecast period. It assumes that free cash flow will grow at a stable rate in perpetuity, starting at some point in the future. It is figured as follows:

$$\text{Terminal Value} = \frac{FCF * (1 + g)}{(d - g)}$$

where

FCF = Free cash flow (see chapter 5) predicted for the last forecast period
g = Terminal growth rate
d = Discount rate (which is usually the weighted average cost of capital, WACC)[65]

Exit Multiple Method According to Investopedia:

> Exit multiples estimate a fair price by multiplying financial statistics, such as sales, profits, or earnings before interest, taxes, depreciation, and amortization (EBITDA) by a factor that is common for similar firms that were recently acquired. The terminal value formula using the exit multiple method is the most recent metric (i.e., sales, EBITDA, etc.) multiplied by the decided upon multiple (usually an average of recent exit multiples for other transactions).[66]

Disadvantages of Discounted Cash Flow

The primary problem with DCF is choosing which numbers to put in the model. Therefore, you need to make some assumptions. If you've estimated cash flows too high, your investments may experience turmoil, which can depress future profits. On the flip side, investors may miss opportunities by estimating cash flows too low. The correct selection of a discount rate is essential; otherwise, the model is useless.[67] Even if everything is calculated correctly, economic instability and unpredictable "black swan" events are always present as potential risks that can undermine the reliability of a DCF model.

The TV tends to be highly sensitive to the terminal growth rate. Put another way: small differences in TV inputs—specifically, the growth rate—can have a large impact on the estimate of TV, and therefore intrinsic value.[68]

Another shortcoming of traditional DCF analysis is that it fails to capture the value being created by unanticipated initiatives that are not currently producing measurable cash flows. Stated another way, there is option value associated with the franchise value of Apple's brand name. Through the application of the company's intellectual property, which is imbedded into Apple's ongoing research and development (R&D) efforts, some of these options will create future value.

So How Does Buffett Do It?

Munger says that he has never seen Buffett use a formal DCF model.[69] But Buffett does have a phenomenal intuition with numbers. When I brought a group of students to meet with him in Omaha, I asked, "How do you value a company?" Buffett replied, "The discounted cash flow method."[70] How do we square these two things—the fact that Munger says he's never seen Buffett do this, and Buffett's own acknowledgment of the method's usefulness? I think the answer is simple: he mostly does it in his head.

Buffett looks at a company's FCFs for the past ten years. He also uses the thirty-year bond rate for the discount rate and then adds whatever he feels the risk premium is for that particular investment.[71] Bottom line: You cannot rely on one valuation. You must run various scenarios, examine the potential ranges they show, and then decide.

The Process of Valuing Apple

To understand how Buffett would value Apple, I created the formula and process described here. I did only one calculation, using a conservative estimate of 10 percent growth rate for Apple's cash flows. I've based this on our previous analysis, showing that in the past ten years, the average growth rate at Apple was 10 percent. I've estimated the discount rate, also called the "hurdle rate"[72] or WACC (because it is the minimum investment return you would require in order to invest), at 10 percent in June 2022. In addition, I am using a conservative 2 percent as the terminal growth rate.

Assumptions

1. Based on the previous analysis of Apple's FCFs, we can estimate that they will grow consistently at a compound rate of 8 percent per year for the next ten years.
2. A discount rate of 10 percent per year is used to allow for the effect of inflation.

3. In year 11 and into perpetuity, we assume that the company's cash flow will increase by 2 percent per year.
4. All dollar amounts are in billions.

Disclosures: Some practitioners/academics might be inclined to make detailed adjustments to their FCF calculations. I have kept mine simpler to facilitate analysis and clarity. The discount rate is usually the WACC. Since Apple has so much cash and investments, that negates its debt. Therefore, I estimated Apple's cost of equity as my discount rate. I calculated the cost of equity using the Capital Asset Pricing Model (CAPM).

Capital Asset Pricing Model

$$Rf + Beta\,(ERm - Rf)$$

Risk-Free Rate (Rf) = 3.44%, which is the yield on 10-year U.S. Treasury bonds.
Beta = 1.21, is the measure of the volatility (systematic risk) of a security or portfolio compared to the market.
Market Risk Premium (ERm-Rf) = 5.5%, which is the historical long-term average return of the S&P 500 index above the yield on Treasury securities.
Cost of Equity = 3.4% + 1.21 * 5.5% = 10%

Part I: Forecast Period for Discounted Cash Flow

The formula for DCF is

$$DCF = \frac{FCF_1}{(1+r)^1} + \frac{FCF_2}{(1+r)^2} + \frac{FCF_n}{(1+r)^n}$$

where

FCF = the cash flow for the given year; FCF_1 is for year one, FCF_2 is for year two, and FCF_n is for additional years
r = the discount rate[73]

Present Value of Discounted Cash Flows for Years 1–10 = $841.89 (see table 6.9)

TABLE 6.9 Apple's projected free cash flows

Present value of future free cash flows												
Year	**2021**	**2022**	**2023**	**2024**	**2025**	**2026**	**2027**	**2028**	**2029**	**2030**	**2031**	**Total**
Prior year FCF (in dollars)	93	100.44	108.48	117.15	126.53	136.65	147.58	159.39	172.14	185.91	200.78	
Growth rate (%)	8	8	8	8	8	8	8	8	8	8	8	
Discount factor		0.9091	0.8264	0.7513	0.6830	0.6209	0.5645	0.5132	0.4665	0.4241	0.3855	
PV of DCF (in dollars)		91.31	89.65	88.02	86.42	84.85	83.30	81.79	80.30	78.84	77.41	$841.89

CALCULATION OF TERMINAL VALUE

Part II: Terminal Value: Perpetuity Method

The TV calculation estimates the value of the company after the forecast period. Remember that the formula to calculate TV is as follows:[74]

2022 Valuation

$$\text{Terminal value} = \frac{\left(\text{FCF} * \left(1+g\right)\right)}{\left(d-g\right)}$$

So, for Apple, we have

Terminal value = (FCF∗(1+g))/(d–g) = ($200.78∗(1+.02))/(.10–.02)
= 204.7956/.08 = $2,559.95

where

FCF = 200.78 = Free cash flow for the last forecast period
g = .02 = Terminal growth rate
d = .10 = Discount rate (which is usually the WACC)

Present Value of Terminal Value = $2,559.95 ∗ .3855 = $986.97

VALUATION OF APPLE

2022 Business Value = Present Value of Future Cash Flows + Present Value of Terminal Value

Present Value of Future Cash Flows in Years 1–10 = $841.89
Present Value of Terminal Value of 10's Terminal Value = $986.97

Intrinsic Value = $841.89 + $986.97 = $1,828.86
Shares Outstanding (billions) = 16.19
Intrinsic Value per Share = $1,828.86/16.19 = $112.96

Market Price on June 16, 2022 = $130.06
Overvalued/Undervalued = 15.1% overvalued

As stated earlier, Buffett views valuation as more of an art than a science. That's why his methods go beyond merely using the DCF. In this instance, for example, you could alter the growth rate in the FCF and/or the cost of equity to produce different valuations. I did this for the cost of equity and ran scenarios using 11 percent and 12 percent. For 11 percent, the intrinsic value per share was $99.06 or 31.3 percent overvalued. For 12 percent, the intrinsic value per share was $88.01 or 47.8 percent overvalued. Of course, if the growth rate in year 10 going forward was estimated at 4 percent rather than 2 percent, the value of the firm would be significantly higher ($134.86/share) and lead to the opposite conclusion about the current market price of Apple.

This is an example of valuing Apple given a range of inputs. In this case, only the cost of equity varied to keep the example simple. Valuation tends to be most sensitive to discount rates and growth projections.

During our lunch together, Buffett made it clear that he views the DCF as an important fundamental tool to use when valuing a company.

CHAPTER 7

HOW TO MAKE BETTER INVESTMENT DECISIONS

For a large majority of fund managers, the selection of stocks is more like rolling dice than like playing poker. . . . The successful funds in any given year are mostly lucky; they have a good roll of the dice. There is general agreement among researchers that nearly all stock pickers, whether they know it or not—and few of them do—are playing a game of chance.[1]

DANIEL KAHNEMAN

WHAT IS BEHAVIORAL FINANCE?

Warren Buffett recommends that to become a successful investor, you understand two things. The first is how to value a company, as discussed in chapter 6. The second is how to evaluate human behavior. That is what we explore next. To do so, we use the concepts arising from a relatively new field called behavioral finance.

Behavioral finance builds on the pioneering work of professors Daniel Kahneman and Amos Tversky. In 2002, Kahneman won the Nobel Memorial Prize in economic sciences, and in 2011 he published the now-famous book *Thinking Fast and Slow*,[2] which examines several heuristics and biases that influence human behavior more than we might realize. These include loss aversion, overconfidence, optimism, framing, and sunk costs.

Even if they don't use the term explicitly, Buffett and Charlie Munger practice behavioral finance every day. They know that when making investment decisions, valuing a company is not sufficient. At least as important is the habit of checking oneself for biases that might lead an investor to make mistakes.

Behavioral economics, a broader category of inquiry, rejects the classical assumption that people act in perfectly rational ways, and examines how cultural, psychological, and other factors influence economic decisions.[3] Kahneman and Tversky's work illuminated these habits of mind and showed how they can lead to irrational decisions and wrong choices. Their first major concept was called "prospect theory."[4] It is now one of the foundational theories of behavioral economics.

Behavioral finance applies the general lessons of behavioral economics to one specific class: investors. It recognizes that, like other economic actors, investors are subject to psychological biases that a classical economic perspective would regard as irrational.[5]

Investors are subject to both cognitive and emotional biases. Cognitive biases result from failures or limitations in an economic model, incomplete or inaccurate information, and other factors that are genuine errors. Emotional biases, on the other hand, are not necessarily errors, but they result when investors are guided by the pleasure or pain of certain investing activities, which influences their analyses of the potential outcomes.[6]

RICHARD THALER

One of the most notable figures in the field of behavioral finance is Richard Thaler, the Charles R. Walgreen Distinguished Service Professor of Behavioral Science and Economics at the University of Chicago. A major force in integrating psychology and economics, Thaler won the 2017 Nobel Memorial Prize in economics for his contribution to behavioral economics.[7] He is the author of several successful books about behavioral economics and is the principal at Fuller & Thaler Asset Management, where he applies his insights into behavioral finance to investment decisions. In 2015, Thaler also appeared in Hollywood's examination of the subprime loan debacle in the movie *The Big Short*. "People often make poor choices—and look back at them with bafflement!" wrote Thaler and his coauthor, Cass Sunstein, in their 2008 book *Nudge: Improving Decisions about Health, Wealth, and Happiness*. "We do this because, as human beings, we all are susceptible to a wide array of routine biases that can lead to an equally wide array of embarrassing blunders in education, personal finance, health care, mortgages and credit cards, happiness, and even the planet itself."[8]

A later work of Thaler's, *Misbehaving: The Making of Behavioral Economics*, opens with an anecdote about how his business students would prefer to get a score of 96 out of 137 than a 72 out of 100, even though the 72 is actually the higher score.[9] Similarly, students loathe getting a numerically low score, even when they know that the curve ensures that an "A" will show up on their transcripts.[10] Something about seeing those 90 or 100 scores causes happiness in students. Such "irrational" preferences would seem anathema to the classical assumptions about rational actors. The students would seem to be irrational individuals, to be "misbehaving."[11] Yet these students were possibly some of the most logical, budding young business minds in the country. Some of Thaler's students doubtless went on to become investors. By the time they got there, they may have become more sophisticated. However, irrational cognitive biases can remain nonetheless. Thaler goes on to say this about investors: "Fear of losses (and a tendency toward short-term thinking . . .) can inhibit appropriate risk-taking."[12]

Kathleen Elkins summarized Thaler's advice to safeguard yourself from these blunders: "Opt for a mix of investments, mostly stocks; only check your portfolio about once a year; and don't follow the news. Just set it and forget it."[13] For many people, that sounds a lot easier than it really is. What if you're watching TV and you see that the stock market has just fallen 3 percent? Many viewers would rush to the phone and begin selling stocks to stanch their losses—right? This is precisely the wrong thing to do, in Thaler's view. "Change channels. Turn the show off. My lazy strategy of doing very little, buying mostly stocks, and then not paying attention has served me well," he told the *Financial Times*.[14]

Buffett gave similar advice in the *2014 Berkshire Hathaway Annual Report*: "Anything can happen anytime in markets. And no advisor, economist, or TV commentator—and definitely not Charlie nor I—can tell you when chaos will occur. Market forecasters will fill your ear but will never fill your wallet."[15]

DAN ARIELY

Another leading figure in the field of behavioral finance is Dan Ariely, a professor of psychology and behavioral economics at Duke University and the founder of the Center for Advanced Hindsight.[16] His website has an equally quirky name: My Irrational Life.[17]

Ariely's research contrasts how people *actually* make financial decisions to the ways that they would perform if they operated in a completely rational manner. A few of his books are *Predictably Irrational*[18] and *The Upside of Irrationality*.[19]

Like Thaler, Ariely discourages investors from regularly checking the value of their portfolios because of the anxiety provoked by market fluctuations and the erroneous decision-making likely to result—even in finance experts. At one point during the financial crisis of 2007–2009, he purposely locked himself out of his accounts. "If we're going to look at it going up and down, we are just going to be more miserable. We're not only going to be more miserable, but act on it," he told CNBC.[20]

EXAMPLES OF FINANCIAL CRISES

COVID-19 Pandemic

A recent example of a world crisis that affected financial markets is the COVID-19 pandemic, which exploded in the United States in early 2020. As a result of the business shutdown aimed at stemming the virus's spread, the U.S. stock market plummeted 34 percent from its mid-February high to a low point on March 23, 2020—the fastest fall in history.[21] This precipitated the worst economic crisis since the Great Depression of the 1930s.

In fact, the recession itself lasted only two months, ending in April, according to economists.[22] But to many people suddenly out of work or facing reduced hours, it didn't feel that way.

As usual, when crises occur, the media turned to Buffett for financial advice. His guidance? Sit tight and make no major changes. In other words, do nothing.

Indeed, the economic situation corrected itself, with some help from Uncle Sam. The Federal Reserve began pumping more liquidity into the markets by buying various types of bonds. Within eight weeks, the Fed had pumped more liquidity into the financial system than it had during the Great Recession. This in turn boosted asset prices and shored up the economy. Buffett was correct. The best thing to do was to have faith in the American economy and not to panic.

Great Recession: 2007–2009

Prompted by the collapse of an overheated real estate market, which was aided and abetted by speculative and undisciplined lending practices among financial institutions, the Dow Jones Industrial Average lost more than half its value after peaking in August 2007. Many investors sold furiously. But the market began to recover in March 2009, and four years later, in March 2013, the Dow broke its 2007 high.[23] Once again, simply waiting the crisis out would have been the best course of action. It was the one recommended by both Buffett and the scholars of behavioral finance.

Dot-com Bubble: 2000–2002

Between 1995 and 2000, the market value of Internet companies soared. Most of these firms didn't actually have profits underpinning their surge. But the NASDAQ Composite index ballooned nonetheless, growing by more than 440 percent. In 1999, Buffett was criticized for Berkshire Hathaway's below-market performance (around 40 percent below the S&P 500).[24,25] But in hindsight, it looks like he was acting prudently, not fooled by the mirage of Internet stocks whose value was based on nothing more than market frenzy.[26,27] Indeed, between March 10, 2000, when the NASDAQ index peaked at 5,048.62, and October 4, 2002, when it dropped to 1,139.90, the market experienced a 76.81 percent fall—in other words, a crash.[28]

Buffett was thinking for himself, going against the herd, and it hurt him in the short run but paid off long term. The recovery of the NASDAQ was anemic. It took twelve years, until November 2014, for the index to make its way back to the levels of March 2000, even after taking dividends into account.

Since Berkshire Hathaway has again performed below market in recent years, we might also wonder if today's economy has bubblelike characteristics that Buffett is able to see through.[29,30]

The Great Depression

On September 3, 1929, the Dow reached a peak of 381.17. After the Great Depression, the Dow Jones did not return to this peak until November 23, 1954—more than twenty-five years later![31] Officially, this economic contraction lasted more than a decade, from the stock market crash of 1929, until America entered World War II. At the nadir, in 1933, 25 percent of all U.S. workers were unemployed.[32] The painfully slow recovery led many Americans to call for an increased role for government. This resulted in the creation of Social Security for the elderly and unemployment compensation.

Summary of Crises

As you can see, these indexes took varying amounts of time to come back to their old highs. However, it appears that we have learned how to deal with these crises over time, as we have gone from twenty-five years (the Great Depression) to fourteen years (the dot-com bubble) to four years (the Great Recession) to two months (the pandemic of 2020). It is also noteworthy that the reduction in time frames also seems to correlate positively with the amount of government involvement in the markets. This has become a subject of intense debate because of its moral hazard implications. Generally, the term "moral hazard" refers to business contracts where one party has an incentive to take unusual risks in a desperate attempt to earn a profit before the contract settles.[33] In this context—government involvement in the markets—the moral hazard concern is that investors might be more likely to take imprudent risks, believing that government will bail out markets during an economic disaster. However, a full treatment of that issue is beyond the scope of this book.

BIASES

Here are seven of the major biases that lead to bad investment decisions. Even Buffett has made a few. I examine those in chapter 8.

Herding Bias

Herding bias, as the name implies, occurs when investors follow a fad or trend in an investment without doing much analysis about its advisability. It is the strongest behavioral bias. It can occur during market crises, but it can also perpetuate those crises by contributing to a sector becoming overvalued. Munger, who calls such investors "lemmings," is particularly fascinated by the phenomenon. He talks about it at almost every annual shareholder meeting of Berkshire Hathaway.

Buffett had this to say about lemmings at the 2008 Shareholder Meeting:

> I started investing when I was eleven. I first started reading about it—I believe in reading everything in sight. And I first started reading about it when I was probably six or seven years old. But for about eight years I wandered around with technical analysis and doing all kinds of things, and then I read a book called *The Intelligent Investor*. And I did that when I was nineteen, down at the University of Nebraska.
>
> And I would say that if you absorb the lessons of *The Intelligent Investor*, mainly in—I wrote a foreword and I recommended particularly chapters 8 and 20—that you will not behave like a lemming, and you may do very well compared to the lemmings.
>
> And there's three big lessons in there which relate to your attitude towards stocks generally, which is that you think of them as parts of a business; and your attitude toward the market, which is that you use it to serve you and not to instruct you; and then the idea of a margin of safety, of always leaving some extra room and things.
>
> But the people in this room, I think, have learned that important first lesson. I mean, I think most people that own Berkshire do not see themselves as owning something with a little ticker symbol or something that may have a favorable or unfavorable earnings surprise or something of the sort, but they'd rather think of themselves as owning a group of those businesses that are out there in the other room.
>
> And that's the way to look at stocks. You'll never be a lemming if you do that.[34]

According to Buffett, it seems that approaching stocks as an owner rather than a speculator is a great way for an investor to avoid herding bias.

A recent example of herding bias has been the surge in 2020 of the so-called FAANG stocks—Facebook, Amazon, Apple, Netflix, and Google. Similarly, in 2019, 39 percent of new investments went into a mere 10 percent of mutual funds that performed best in the prior year.[35] Given that past performance is no guarantee of future performance, this suggests a herd mentality. Investors who focused their investment decision-making on past performance often do the worst.[36]

Herd Mentality in Financial Markets The basic driver of herd mentality is our tendency, as humans, to bow to group dynamics. As noted previously, few companies during the dot-com boom were generating much in the way of profits. Yet investors bought into them enthusiastically.

Even investors attuned to numbers above all else apparently find it psychologically painful to go against the crowd. Nonconformity often triggers our fears because if everyone is investing in Apple and you decide to go in another direction, you may look like a fool.[37] Psychologists have discovered that contrarian investors who buck the tide actually feel more physical pain.[38] One study compared contrarian behavior to "having your arm broken."[39]

Example of Herding Bias: ConocoPhillips (2008) Buffett himself, being human, is not immune to human frailties. In 2008, oil prices spiked to all-time highs, which led to great dividends for their shareholders, and that attracted a herd of new investors. Buffett was one of them. He jumped in and bought shares of ConocoPhillips when oil and gas prices were nearing their highs for the year. Later, in his 2008 letter to Berkshire Hathaway shareholders, he owned up to that mistake:

> Last year I made a major mistake of commission (and maybe more; this one sticks out). Without urging from Charlie [Munger] or anyone else, I bought a large amount of ConocoPhillips stock when oil and gas prices were near their peak. I in no way anticipated the dramatic fall in energy prices that occurred in the last half of the year. I still believe the odds are good that oil sells far higher in the future than the current $40–$50 price. But so far, I've been dead wrong. Even if prices should rise, moreover, the terrible timing of my purchase has cost Berkshire several billion dollars.[40]

This move may in fact have been due to a combination of both herding bias and overconfidence.

How to Overcome Herding Bias Remember Buffett's general rule of thumb: Buy when others are fearful and sell when they are greedy. Herding will often lead to losses. The most reliable way to avoid herding bias is through disciplined analysis.

Talking Heads Bias

Before I wrote this book, I followed news on the financial markets closely. I listened to CNBC and Bloomberg. I also read the *Wall Street Journal, Barron's*, the *New York Times*, and about ten other newspapers and magazines, as well as various financial newsletters. I was trying to use this information to predict the future. But what it mostly did was make me vulnerable to talking heads bias, which occurs when investors give special weight to people perceived as experts, who can in turn influence financial markets. You probably know some of them already. Some examples include Jim Cramer, Becky Quick, and the team on the CNBC program *Fast Money*. Of course, Buffett and Munger also qualify. Other examples include Stanley Druckenmiller, Bill Miller, Carl Icahn, George Soros, Seth Klarman, Howard Marks, Paul Tudor Jones, and academics who specialize in investments, like Jeremy Siegel.

No matter how much of their expertise I absorbed, it didn't make me feel more confident in my knowledge, just overwhelmed with information. Worse, it was causing me to make irrational investment decisions at fragile times in the markets. I should have remembered one of Buffett's prime directives: Do not try to predict the future.

My Problem But then came the COVID-19 pandemic. Not only was everyone in the country worried about their mortality, but we were also suddenly watching the financial markets go haywire. As usual, CNBC asked Buffett what advice he'd give to people about handling their investments. Stay the course, he said. Buffett had lived through the Great Depression, world wars, recessions, bear markets, September 11, and many other crises. True, he had never experienced a pandemic. But that didn't change his basic game plan for the future. Hang on, he advised. Don't make any major changes.

This was hard advice to hear. The S&P 500 had closed down 3 percent the day before Buffett spoke on CNBC. It fell by 3 percent again the next day. It looked like the pandemic was going to significantly curtail the value of my investments, so I disregarded Buffett's advice and quickly shifted from a 70 percent stock and 30 percent bond position to a 15 percent stock and 85 percent bond position.

Now I was ahead of the market by more than 20 percent; I thought I was a genius. But now that I'd mostly left the market, I had a new problem: When should I get back in? And furthermore, what should I invest in when I did?

As I watched, the Fed pumped more money into the markets, and eventually stocks rose. Again, I changed my mix, increasing investment in equities to the point that I had 50 percent of my portfolio in stocks. Buffett's advice of doing nothing was probably the correct thing to do. But listening and doing are very different things.

How to Overcome Talking Heads Bias Do not assume that any advice you receive from any expert is true. As Munger would say, do not be a lemming—think for yourself. Ask yourself questions about the people giving advice. Who are they? For whom do they work, and what might be their motivation for sharing their opinions with you? How trustworthy are those opinions? What's their track record? What is their reputation, and what information sources are touting their views? How independent are these sources? Create your own way of researching information before you decide.

Loss Aversion Bias

Kahneman and Tversky developed the concept of loss aversion, also known as "prospect theory."[41] The basic concept is that the fear of loss looms larger than the possibility of gain. It turns out that, within human psychology, a loss hurts roughly twice as much as an equivalent gain gives pleasure. For this reason, people will avoid even rational risks in an attempt to minimize any danger of loss, even if that means forgoing large amounts of potential gain, thereby incurring opportunity loss in the process. They will even engage in great risk to avoid losing resources they already have.[42] As Munger put it, "Huge insanities can come from just subconsciously overweighing the importance of what you're losing or almost getting and not getting."[43]

Loss aversion is, according to Thaler, the single most powerful weapon in the behavioral economist's arsenal: "There are many failings that get us into trouble financially. . . . The first is loss aversion. . . . For example, investing in the stock market has historically provided much higher returns than investing in bonds or savings accounts, but stock prices fluctuate more, producing a greater risk of loss in the short-term. Loss aversion can prevent investors from taking advantage of the long-term opportunities in stocks."[44]

Examples of Loss Aversion Bias Counterintuitively, our dislike of loss can drive us to take on more risk. People tend to be risk averse when it comes to gains but risk-seeking if they are facing a loss. This can have unnerving consequences. For example, a fund manager may take more risks in the last quarter of the year if their fund is trailing the benchmark.[45]

Here's another example: I had been canny enough to see problems ahead as the subprime mortgage market began to heat up, so I was completely in cash during the majority of the Great Recession. However, as the economy began to rebound, I was still in cash. I did not want to risk losing any money, even though the market was going up. Loss aversion became a form of paralysis. Not until my wife and I switched financial planners in July 2009 did we go back into the markets. And even then, it was only because our new financial planner had advised it.

How to Overcome Loss Aversion Bias How do you guard against the paralysis of loss aversion? One practical way is to always use firm stop-loss orders to minimize your potential loss in any trade. A stop-loss order guarantees that you will get out at a certain price. For example, let's say you purchased a share of Apple for $100. You then put on a stop-loss order at $90. This means that if your share of Apple goes down 10 percent, or to $90 a share, it will automatically be sold on the open market. This strategy limits your risk of the downside, especially the tendency to fall into a bottomless loss-aversion trap.[46]

Other ways to overcome loss aversion bias are:

- Hedging, which means purchasing a security that is an inverse to your initial investment, such as purchasing a bond after buying a stock, since they tend to go in opposite directions.
- Invest in insurance products, which have a guaranteed rate of return. This money can be used to assist with your retirement or other expenses. Most annuities will guarantee you income for three to ten years.
- Invest in securities that have less volatility (e.g., government bonds, annuities, CDs).
- Be aware of the bias in your decision-making.
- Perform an analysis on any company you want to invest in, and seek out firms that continuously have strong balance sheets and cash flows.[47]

The Solution Requires Two Portfolios Some financial planners use two portfolios, with one being comparatively high risk (and high reward), and the other being more stable. This strategy comes from an exercise devised by Kahneman. He asked investors to think about how they would feel if they lost 10 percent, 20 percent, or 30 percent. Then he asked them what they might do in each instance. "The question was, at what point do you think that you would want to bail out? That you would want to change your mind?"[48] Kahneman learned that almost everyone had a loss tolerance of no more than 10 percent.[49]

To overcome this loss aversion, Kahneman asked his team of researchers to create two portfolios, one risky and one safer, based on the "regret propensity" for each individual investor. The two portfolios were managed and reported separately. In general, one of them would always be doing better than market. Having two established a psychological buffer for investors, which allowed them to *feel* safer, even though both were part of a single overall portfolio. It turned out that this approach helped insulate investors from feelings of panic and regret when the market went sideways. According to Kahneman, even the exercise of imagining how it will feel to have the value of your investments plunge is valuable for staving off the hysteria that can arise around the prospect of loss.[50]

Recency Bias

Recency bias, or availability bias, is the mental shortcut of relying on immediate examples that come to mind when evaluating a topic, concept, method, or decision. For example, the odds of a shark attack are 1 in 3,748,067.[51] However, when there is a shark attack in the news, people overestimate the likelihood that another attack will occur, so they tend to avoid the beach.

Ariely observes:

> We look at the most recent evidence, take it too seriously, and expect that things will continue in that way. If you think about the creation of asset bubbles, that's always what happens. Things go up and up and up, and we start thinking it has to always go up. . . . It's very hard for us to deal with lots and lots of information. Of course, today we're getting lots and lots of information, so what do we do when we get too much information? We simplify. We use heuristics. We rely on only part of the information. On the most salient information. And that, of course, means that the most salient information is

> probably the information everybody else knows, as well; so, we become less independent in our opinions from other investors. If everybody is in information overload, and we all do simplifications, then what happens is that we follow the simplest source of information, which is probably common to everybody.[52]

Investors' buying decisions seemed to be swayed by recent past returns on investments rather than on the recent underperformance of a stock. That was the conclusion of a study that examined the trading decisions of individual investors at a large national discount broker.[53] Although these investments "outperformed the market by 40 percent" in the prior year,[54] the investors' strategy was ultimately unsuccessful, as the stocks they sold went on to do better than the stocks they purchased later.[55]

Examples of Recency Bias The same study, which examined recency bias during the Great Recession, discovered that the fresher the information investors received, the greater the number of trades they engaged in, presumably because they were attempting to buy when prices were low. Yet, far from mitigating the impact of the downturn, this strategy actually led investors to even greater losses than would have been expected based on the market alone. During normal times, high numbers of trades among investors were also found to have a negative correlation with portfolio performance (underscoring the "set it and forget it" approach that Thaler advises).[56]

Even Buffett has been vulnerable to recency bias. Although he had purchased preferred stock in US Airways during the late 1980s, and later acknowledged that investment as a mistake, he bought shares in four major airlines between 2016 and 2020: American Airlines, United Continental, Delta Airlines, and Southwest Airlines (perhaps with the nudging of one or both of his co–chief investment officers).[57] Then the pandemic hit, and he sold his entire position of airline stocks for a loss of around $5 billion.[58]

Buffett's decision seems to have been influenced by recency bias—specifically, the airlines' increasing profitability due to consolidation. He also appears to have emphasized the high barriers to entry that airlines have. These include high start-up costs (e.g., new planes, fuel), competition for landing slots at airports, strict regulations (especially to protect passengers), brand loyalty, and economies of scale. These barriers to entry were attractive to

Buffett, and he viewed them as sustainable, which would lead to attractive returns to shareholders.

How to Overcome Recency Bias To avoid recency bias, investors need to examine long-term historical trends. They also must set goals, identify their risk tolerance, and have a financial plan that they stick to.

Confirmation Bias

As humans, we are drawn to evidence that confirms rather than disproves our views. We emphasize information that agrees with our existing beliefs—forming a point of view and then seeking data that makes us look right. It's human nature; our inborn tendency is to listen to people who agree with us. It's appealing. But it's not necessarily the smartest thing to do as an investor.

Assume that you notice that Apple's stock price has just corrected by 20 percent. You are interested in possibly purchasing it because of the decline, but you are concerned that it may go down further. You seek confirmation that it would be a good investment today. You go online and read investment articles and watch television shows with talking heads saying that it's a good time to purchase Apple. So you go ahead and purchase Apple.[59] That's confirmation bias in action.

More often, though, confirmation bias contributes to overconfidence. Suppose, for example, that most analysts anticipate that the price of Apple stock will increase 30 percent next year. This view is echoed by media coverage of Apple (which is, of course, influenced by what these analysts say). This echo chamber effect will nudge many investors into purchasing Apple shares. Meanwhile, there are also articles about the potentially devastating effects to Apple of a trade war with China. But if investors are already enthusiastic about Apple stock, they will likely ignore the bad news and focus only on what conforms to the rosy predictions.

How to Overcome Confirmation Bias Confirmation bias, which affects perceptions and decision-making in all aspects of life, often causes investors to make less-than-optimal choices. To avoid this, investors should seek out as many alternative opinions as possible.[60] Actively solicit perspectives that you disagree with and listen to them fully. Argue with yourself, and allow others to challenge you as well. This is part of the reason that Buffett wants Munger to play devil's advocate. Weaker leaders would demand that their subordinates agree with their every opinion and take any disagreement as a sign of insubordination. Buffett, on the other hand, sought out a partner who would bring up counterpoints in a good-faith attempt to lead the partnership to the best investment decisions overall.

Hindsight Bias

Hindsight bias occurs when, after the fact, you think "I knew it!" Chances are that you considered several potential outcomes, including ones that were wrong. However, because you also considered the possibility that turned out to be right, you convince yourself that you can predict the future.[61] A common failing among investors, hindsight bias is a popular area of study in behavioral economics because it often leads to overconfidence.[62] Hindsight bias can even distort our memories of what we knew or believed before an event occurred.

Examples of Hindsight Bias Buffett has talked about hindsight bias in a few of his potential investments: Google and Amazon. Buffett and Munger have said that they made a huge mistake in not investing in Google. Google founders Sergey Brin and Larry Page pitched their company to Buffett and Munger early in Google's life for an investment infusion, but they passed. Looking back on their mistake, they stated that they should have known because GEICO was getting such great traction through their advertising on Google.[63]

Another mistake was not investing in Amazon earlier. It was not until 2019 that they started to invest in that company. Buffett called Jeff Bezos, the founder of Amazon, "the most remarkable business person of our age."[64]

Both of these mistakes were probably due to Buffett's aversion to technology companies.

How to Overcome Hindsight Bias To limit hindsight bias, I created a spreadsheet of all my investments and the dates I purchased them. I track them over time to challenge my thinking. For example, let's say that I have a great idea on investing in a company (e.g., Apple). Just like Buffett, before I pull the trigger, I want to follow a company for a while. As Buffett has said, sometimes he waits up to ten years before he'll purchase a stock. I do my homework and purchase the stock at a valuation that I am comfortable with.

Mental Accounting Bias

When we talk about mental accounting, we mean how people value money. This concept was developed by Thaler in 1999 to explain that people classify various types of cash holdings differently, and irrationally, leading to errors and bad financial decisions.[65] For instance, some people may put their money in low-yield savings accounts rather than paying off debts that have a high rate of interest. Yet the latter move would actually benefit their wallet more.

Mental accounting focuses on the budgeting and categorization of expenditures. For example, some people will break down their funds into two accounts: one for home expenses (e.g., saving for a home or home repairs) and one for other outlays (e.g., gas money, clothing, utilities).[66] People often have several mental accounts for the same resource, like someone who uses one monthly budget for groceries and another for restaurant meals. Many people will constrain one type of purchase when its budget has run out, while giving free rein to the other, even though both are drawing on the same fungible resource (income).[67]

Mental accounting assumes that most people operate with two categories of spending: one bucket of money that they spend freely, such as unearned cash from gifts, bonuses, or casino winnings; and another bucket with money earned from work. Some may also think in terms of an account for money that they can "afford to lose" and another account for money that they "cannot afford to lose."[68] This can lead people to take too many risks with the "afford to lose" account, leading to inordinate losses.[69]

But in fact, "all money is the same."[70] To avoid mental accounting bias, investors must treat all money the same way, whatever "account" it may sit in.[71]

Examples of Mental Accounting Bias Kahneman and Tversky saw mental accounting bias at work in their groundbreaking theory on loss aversion. Here's an example of how they interrelate: An investor owns two stocks, a loser with a loss and a winner with a gain (both on paper). The investor needs cash, so he must sell one of his stocks. The loss aversion effect and mental accounting bias say that the investor will sell the winner. However, that's the wrong decision! Selling the loser would provide tax benefits. It would also offload a bad investment and allow the investor to keep a good one.[72] The investor sells the winner because he cannot bear the pain of the loss. This demonstrates the way that loss aversion can lead to irrational decisions.[73]

Another example is someone who spends money won at a casino to buy a new sports car instead of paying off bills.

How to Overcome Mental Accounting Bias There are several things you can do to overcome mental accounting bias. First, realize that money is money, whether it comes in the form of a gift, casino winnings, a tax refund, or wages. Try not to separate your money into different "categories." Wherever it comes from, money needs to be spent intelligently and logically to maximize gain and minimize loss. I keep track of all my accounts in one spreadsheet. This way, I see all my money as one resource, which helps with decision-making.

Summary

There are numerous behavioral biases that investors need to be aware of. This chapter reviewed seven of the most prevalent that occur when investing. Buffett and Munger both emphasize the importance of having the right temperament when investing. Understanding your biases will assist you in getting better control of your own temperament.

PART III

THE HISTORY OF BERKSHIRE HATHAWAY

CHAPTER 8

BERKSHIRE HATHAWAY: 1967–2009

Be fearful when others are greedy and be greedy when others are fearful.[1]

WARREN BUFFETT

CORPORATE VENTURING

Dr. Donald F. Kuratko, the Jack M. Gill Distinguished Chair of Entrepreneurship at Indiana University, said this about Buffett and entrepreneurship: "I would say that Buffett exhibited many of the classic characteristics and skills of an entrepreneur. However, as he grew Berkshire Hathaway and worked to purchase deals, he became more of a corporate entrepreneur through corporate venturing."[2]

There is no doubt that in addition to being a classic entrepreneur, Buffett is a corporate entrepreneur. He does this by using Berkshire's resources and his uncanny ability to value and evaluate companies to purchase businesses, invest in stocks, and make other deals. I will describe this in the context of the history of Berkshire in this chapter and the next.

One form of corporate entrepreneurship that Buffett uses is by being his own activist. He did this when he would make a substantial investment in a company and, at the same time, often take a seat on the board of directors (e.g., Coca-Cola, Salomon Brothers). Unlike current activists, who usually seek the sale of the company (or at least a major restructuring), Buffett was a patient, collaborative, and supportive board member—one who was also actively protecting the value of his investment through his influence on the board.

In addition, Buffett has demonstrated a willingness to take on thorny, controversial, and risky situations, as was the case when he made an investment in Salomon Brothers and assumed the chairman and chief executive officer (CEO) title (this topic will be discussed over the next few chapters). Again, this was a form of corporate entrepreneurship and activism, long before it became fashionable. What distinguishes Buffett is his reputation for candor and transparency, unlike other corporate entrepreneurs/activists who are more identified with combativeness and coercion, not to mention a short time horizon.

While Berkshire's decentralized and lean corporate philosophy is valid and has served shareholders well, I would also argue that Buffett's active involvement in some of the company's larger investments has also made a difference.

OVERVIEW OF BERKSHIRE

Buffett currently oversees the multinational Berkshire Hathaway, based in Omaha, with a corporate staff of a mere twenty-five people. One might imagine that with the company having a market value of $754 billion and wielding an economic influence larger than that of many medium-sized nations, the corporate headquarters would look like those of a worldwide empire. But in fact, the multinational business remains anchored in the same Omaha building, in Kiewit Plaza, that Buffett moved into in 1962, a few minutes' drive from his home.

Berkshire's office occupies just one floor in the Peter Kiewit building. As the *Financial Times* described this hotbed of investment wizardry: "Its drop ceilings, narrow hallways and tired carpets would suit the administration of a community college better than a multibillion-dollar empire. The staff of 25 dress casually. Every desk is covered with family photos, greeting cards and tchotchkes (trinkets or souvenirs). A sign hangs over the door from the anteroom: 'Invest like a champion today!'"[3]

Buffett's business-management philosophy has always been to hire the best people and give them the freedom to excel. Top talent does not want to be micromanaged, and Buffett understands this. He also understands that freedom is a huge motivator for entrepreneurs. While outsiders may view Berkshire Hathaway merely as an investment house rather than an entrepreneurial hotbed, Buffett has always approached his work from an entrepreneurial mindset. That means putting a premium on creativity and innovation, allowing employees free rein to do what they do best.

Of course, this small corporate office is no reflection of Berkshire's footprint in the world. Counting all sixty-two businesses it owns, Berkshire Hathaway has around 360,000 affiliated employees. In the third quarter of 2021, these businesses reported annual total sales of $268.7 billion and net profits of $85.9 billion. Berkshire's equity portfolio was valued at around $330 billion. The company also held about $150 billion in cash and short-term investments. Buffett maintains 30.7 percent of the voting power in the company.

A word about valuation: In 2018, a new generally accepted accounting principles (GAAP) rule, as written by the Financial Accounting Standards Board (FASB), required all companies to value their securities based on the amount of money they would receive if they were to sell the assets or be alleviated of their liabilities at the present moment. This is known as "fair market value accounting." Prior accounting rules allowed companies to list their assets and liabilities at historical cost, a convention that many criticized for distorting the reported assets and liabilities of a company.

Buffett, however, believes that the new accounting methods distort the picture of Berkshire's overall health as a company, mainly because companies are now required to adjust the reported values of their securities every quarter. That up-to-the-minute approach stands in contrast to Buffett's long-term investment mentality. Furthermore, so-called mark-to-market accounting points to a key belief that guides Buffett's approach to investing: Understanding the economics of a business is far more important than understanding where it is trading in any given quarter.[4]

Table 8.1 shows the public companies in which Berkshire Hathaway has the largest stock positions, their values, their industries, and the percentage stakes within those companies.

Throughout the years, Berkshire Hathaway has grown and divided its portfolio into four categories:

1. Insurance
2. Energy and utilities
3. Manufacturing, service, and retail
4. Finance and financial products

TABLE 8.1 Berkshire Hathaway largest stock holdings as of June 17, 2022

No.	Ticker	Company	Industry	Stake (%)	Holdings (shares)	Value (in billions)
1	AAPL	Apple Inc.	Consumer electronics	5.6	911,347,617	131.6
2	BAC	Bank of America Corporation	Banks—global	12.8	1,032,852,006	33
3	KO	Coca-Cola Co.	Beverages—soft drinks	9.2	400,000,000	23.8
4	CVX	Chevron Corporation	Oil and gas integrated	8.1	159,178,117	23.6
5	AXP	American Express Co.	Credit services	20.1	151,610,700	21.9
6	KHC	The Kraft Heinz Co.	Packaged foods	26.6	325,634,818	11.6
7	OXY	Occidental Petroleum Corp.	Oil and gas exploration and production	16.3	152,713,846	8.8
8	BYDDF	BYD Co. Ltd.	Electronic auto	7.7	225,000,000	8.4
9	USB	US Bancorp	Banks—regional—US	9.7	144,046,330	6.5
10	MCO	Moody's Corporation	Capital markets	13.4	24,669,778	6.3

Source: CNBC Berkshire Hathaway Portfolio Tracker (data from Securities and Exchange Commission filings).

Its method of growth includes acquisitions, common and preferred stock purchases, and other investments. At times, Buffett has been extremely entrepreneurial in going after these deals. What follows are some highlights.

BERKSHIRE HATHAWAY: 1967–2006

As outlined in chapter 2, Buffett opened his investment house in 1956, at the age of twenty-five. He called it Buffett Associates, Ltd. and worked with money contributed by six friends and family members. The seventh original partner was Homer Dodge, a physics professor from Vermont who drove all the way to

Omaha to give his family's life savings to Buffett, solely on word of the young man's talent. Between 1957 and 1961, the partnership gained 251 percent versus the Dow's 75 percent.[5] In financial circles, what happened next has become the stuff of legend.

1967: National Indemnity Company and National Fire & Marine Insurance Company

In March 1967, Berkshire purchased National Indemnity Company and National Fire & Marine Insurance Company for $8.6 million. National Indemnity is still part of Berkshire today, and in 2004, Buffett told his shareholders that the insurance company had been foundational to his success: "If I had not bought National Indemnity Company, Berkshire would be lucky to be worth half of what it is today."[6]

At the time of his purchase of National Indemnity, the company had a tangible net worth (Total Assets – Total Liabilities – Intangible Assets) of $6.7 million. Buffett, hewing to his belief in the importance of long-term spreadsheets, was willing to pay a $1.9 million premium for the insurance business because it typically saw underwriting profits.[7]

Today, Berkshire Hathaway has a hand in insurance and reinsurance businesses conducted through more than seventy domestic and foreign-based companies.

HIGHLIGHTS FROM 1970–1998

Between 1970 and 1998, Berkshire Hathaway experienced extraordinary growth, much of it generated through purchasing companies, notably See's Candies, Nebraska Furniture Mart, Borsheims, and the *Washington Post*.

1970–1983: Blue Chip Stamps

Blue Chip Stamps was a loyalty program similar to the credit card and airline miles rewards programs of today. Customers spent a certain amount of money and received stamps that could be redeemed for rewards in the form of products such as dining room tables, lawn furniture, and other items depending on the participating stores. In 1970, Berkshire Hathaway began investing in Blue Chip

Stamps. Berkshire increased its holdings from 36.5 percent of the company in 1977 to 60 percent in 1979. Blue Chip finally merged in a stock swap in 1983.[8] In acquiring Blue Chip Stamps, Berkshire also famously acquired interest in See's Candies, as well as Wesco Financial Corporation.

1972: See's Candies

On January 3, 1972, Blue Chip Stamps obtained a controlling interest in See's Candy Shops. Blue Chip later acquired 100 percent of See's for an overall price of $25 million. At the time, See's had pretax profits of $4 million. As noted previously, See's is one of Buffett's favorite investments because of its strong brand, cash flow, lack of requirement for new capital, and ability to raise prices with inflation. These attributes have created a moat around See's, which is what Buffett prizes. The candies are high-quality products, with their own outlet stores that can command premium prices. In business, we call this a "differentiation strategy."

Buffett and Charlie Munger have constantly praised See's Candies as one of their all-time best acquisitions. At the 2019 Annual Berkshire Hathaway Shareholder's Meeting, Buffett stated, "We put $25 million into it, and it's given us over $2 billion of pretax income, well over $2 billion."[9]

Buffett and Munger munch on the company's peanut brittle at every annual shareholder meeting. See's has become an unofficial mascot brand for Berkshire, a focal point of the supposed cult surrounding Buffett and Munger, and a symbol of their wholesome image.

1973: The Washington Post

Buffett was once fond of the newspaper industry. As discussed in chapter 1, his parents met while working at the University of Nebraska–Lincoln student paper, his mother's parents owned a print shop, and as a kid, he delivered newspapers door to door.

In adulthood, Buffett wanted to be a publisher. So, in 1973, he began to buy shares in the Washington Post Company. His initial stake of $10.6 million had grown to $221 million by the end of 1985,[10] with an annual rate of return of 16.8 percent.

In 1977, Buffett also purchased the *Buffalo News*. The newspaper industry itself remained a small part of Berkshire's overall holdings until 2012, when Buffett bought sixty-three local newspapers[11] and corralled them within a newly formed company that he called the BH Media Group.

But Buffett soon saw that the industry was undergoing business contractions that were so severe that even his childhood love of news and information could not be sustained—at least financially. In 2014, Buffett sold Berkshire Hathaway's 28 percent stake in the Washington Post Company (which had by then changed its name to Graham Holdings).[12] In 2019, he spoke about this with some wistfulness: "In towns and cities where there is a strong sense of community, there is no more important institution than the local paper."[13,14] But the balance sheets were undeniable. "The newspaper business is a declining business," he said in 2019. "That is not where we will make real money."

Meanwhile, Jeff Bezos had purchased the *Washington Post* for $250 million in cash,[15] and the newspaper appears to be stronger than ever. No wonder Buffett has called the Amazon founder the best manager in history.

In 2020, Buffett sold all his assets in the newspaper industry for $140 million in cash to Lee Enterprises because of lack of advertising revenue.

1976: GEICO

As detailed in chapter 6, Buffett had recognized the Government Employees Insurance Company (GEICO) as a great company early in his career, but he made the mistake of selling it too early. He waited another twenty-five years before finding the right moment to jump back in.

GEICO, nearing insolvency in the mid-1970s, hired a dynamic new CEO, John Byrne, in 1976. Byrne was a forty-three-year-old marketing executive from the Travelers Corporation, and this move attracted Buffett's attention. He requested a meeting with Byrne, and the following morning, he purchased 500,000 shares of GEICO stock at $2⅛ a share. His total investment in the company would amount to $19 million.

Buffett continued to acquire stock in GEICO, and by 1980, Berkshire owned 33 percent of the company.[16] Within five years, that stake was worth $596 million, and a decade later, in August 1995, Buffett bought the company outright for $2.3 billion,[17] making GEICO a wholly owned subsidiary of Berkshire Hathaway.

1979: Capital Cities/ABC

Buffett often emphasizes the value of hanging around people who are smarter than you. Tom Murphy, the former chair of the board and CEO of Capital Cities/ABC, and Murphy's longtime business partner Dan Burke, are two of the people Buffett puts on his smarter-than-me list. Look through the management insights developed by Murphy and Burke, and you'll notice their obvious influence on Buffett:

- Keep decision-making decentralized.
- Hire the best people possible and give them autonomy.
- Impose rigorous cost controls.
- Stay out of the public eye.
- Spend years developing relationships with potential prospects.
- Do not finance with equity. Finance with internally generated cash or debt that can be paid off within three years.
- Deal directly with the owners and do not partake in any hostile takeovers or purchase through an auction.
- Return requirements: double-digit after-tax return over ten years, without leverage.
- Let the owners make their best price offer, make a quick counteroffer, and move on if you cannot come to an agreement quickly.[18]

In 1979, Berkshire Hathaway began to acquire stock in American Broadcasting Corporation (ABC). In 1985, Buffett provided Capital Cities with $550 million of the $3.2 billion that it needed to purchase ABC.[19] In 1996, when Burke retired, Murphy sold Capital Cities to Disney—a deal Buffett had suggested. Berkshire also sold its stake in Capital Cities, a $2.5 billion deal.[20]

Murphy, now ninety-six years old, resigned from the board of directors of Berkshire Hathaway in 2022.[21]

1983: Wesco Financial Corporation

Wesco Financial Corporation was a diversified financial corporation headquartered in Pasadena, California, largely owned by Blue Chip Stamps. Berkshire acquired Wesco in 1983 when it bought Blue Chip, and Munger served as chair and CEO of the firm from 1984 to 2011. Wesco is still a part of Berkshire.

1983: Nebraska Furniture Mart

By 1983, Berkshire's stock price had grown to more than $1,000 a share. That year, Berkshire purchased 80 percent of Nebraska Furniture Mart, the largest private furniture store in the country, based on a handshake and a contract of less than two pages. The price was $55 million.[22] The business had been founded in Omaha forty-six years earlier by Rose Blumkin, a Russian-Jewish immigrant who could neither read nor write.

The Nebraska Furniture Mart deal exemplifies several pillars key to Buffett's financial strategy: Understand the business you are investing in (in this case, retail), and invest only if you are confident in the honesty of its managers.

Mrs. B., as Blumkin was known, had never attended school, as she'd worked in her mother's grocery store, in Minsk, Belarus, since age six. Ten years later, at sixteen, she was managing six men.

Mrs. B. emigrated to the United States at twenty-three to be with her husband, who had fled the country to escape conscription. With neither a passport nor a ticket, she managed to get herself aboard the Trans-Siberian Railroad. She escaped through the Russia-China border by telling the border agent that she would bring him brandy when she came back. But she never came back . . .

Mrs. B. instead found her way to Iowa, where her husband was living, and the couple moved to Nebraska. There, she resold clothes, raised four children, and sent her remaining family back home money so they could escape to the United States too.[23]

In 1937, at age forty-three, Mrs. B. opened a used-furniture store with only $500 cash and $2,000 in merchandise from the basement of her husband's pawnshop. Mrs. B.'s main strategy, other than working seventy hours a week, was to undercut her rivals. This provoked boycotts and lawsuits accusing her of violating fair-trade laws. During one trial, she explained that she turned a profit by selling everything at 10 percent above cost. The judge acquitted her—and bought $1,400 worth of Nebraska Furniture Mart carpet the following day.[24]

1987: Salomon Brothers

By 1986, Buffett had a personal net worth of $1.4 billion. And in 1987, Berkshire Hathaway acquired 12 percent of Salomon Brothers, a New York City investment bank, for $700 million. Both Buffett and Munger served on Salomon's board of directors.[25]

In 1990, Buffett received a call about illegal trading at Salomon Brothers. A trader had submitted bids for more Treasury bonds than the U.S. Department of Treasury rules allowed. The then-CEO, John Gutfreund, failed to discipline the trader.[26]

The U.S. government threatened to ban Salomon from participating directly in auctions of Treasury securities, which would have crippled the firm. Buffett spoke with the Treasury Department, which agreed to reverse the ban (though not without fining Salomon $290 million). Even with that penalty, Berkshire Hathaway saw the value of its stake more than double when the firm was sold to Travelers in 1997.

This event had a significant impact on Buffett, who had stepped in briefly to run the bank and forced Gutfreund's resignation. He famously told Salomon's employees: "Lose money for the firm and I will be understanding; lose a shred of reputation for the firm, and I will be ruthless."[27]

He said the same in testimony before Congress. Every year at Berkshire Hathaway's shareholder meeting, this clip is played for the audience, eliciting a roar of applause.

1988: Coca-Cola

On Monday, October 9, 1987, the Dow Jones Industrial Average fell 22.6 percent in one day, then the largest one-day percentage drop in the history of the stock market. It was known as "Black Monday."

Buffett went into overdrive. He'd always embraced the idea, "Be fearful when others are greedy. Be greedy when others are fearful,"[28] and here he put that into practice. Between 1988 and 1989, Berkshire purchased 23 million shares of Coca-Cola.[29] By 1994, Berkshire owned 100 million shares of the international soda company. Today, Berkshire holds 400 million split-adjusted shares, or 9.4 percent, of Coca-Cola. Buffett has never sold a single share of the company.[30]

Buffett had altered Benjamin Graham's old advice about buying bad companies at great prices.[31] The new strategy was aimed at "buying great companies at good prices."[32]

1989: Borsheims Fine Jewelry

Borsheims Fine Jewelry store was founded in 1870, in downtown Omaha, by Louis Borsheim. With an inventory of more than 100,000 watches and pieces of jewelry, sold out of a 62,500-square-foot facility, Borsheims is the largest private jewelry store in the country.[33]

In 1989, Berkshire purchased 80 percent of the company, leaving 20 percent of the stock behind in order to motivate its employees.

In 2009, Karen Goracke, who became president and CEO of the company in 2013,[34] gave a tour and a speech to my students who came to Omaha to visit Buffett. She attributed her success as a manager to the practice of volunteering for unfamiliar jobs within the business. This broadened her exposure and expertise, and it falls right in line with Buffett's philosophy about the benefits of hands-on experience.

1991: Bill Gates

Although Buffett and Bill Gates had been among the world's wealthiest men for many years, the two did not meet in person until a dinner party in 1991. Buffett, who had long eschewed technology stocks, was immediately taken by Gates's intelligence and humor. But he remained wary of tech and declined to invest in Microsoft, despite its phenomenal success.

To Buffett, the reasons were simple:

1. He only invests in things he understands.
2. He did not want his friendship with Gates to suggest that he was getting inside information.

Later, Buffett would admit that not investing in Microsoft was one of the biggest mistakes of his career. But in the early 1990s, that wasn't at all apparent.

By November 1992, Berkshire's stock price had surpassed $10,000 per share. The market value of the company reached $14.9 billion.

1996: Class B (Baby Berkshires)

By 1996, Buffett had amassed so much wealth through Berkshire Hathaway's investments that his personal net worth was $15 billion. In February of that year, he allowed stockholders to convert each of their high-priced Class A shares into thirty shares of a new class of common stock, Class B (affectionally known as "Baby Berkshires").

In his 1996 letter to shareholders, Buffett wrote: "As I have told you before, we made this sale in response to the threatened creation of unit trusts that would have marketed themselves as Berkshire look-alikes. In the process, they would have used our past, and definitely nonrepeatable, record to entice naive small investors and would have charged these innocents high fees and commissions."[35,36]

Buffett was concerned that shareholders through such trusts would have been unhappy and eventually hurt the reputation of Berkshire. The trusts could replicate the purchases of Berkshire and then charge high fees to naive investors.

In May, the Class B shares began trading at $1,100 a share. By January 1998, the Class A shares topped $50,000 for the first time, with a market capitalization of $76.4 billion.

1998: Dairy Queen

Founded in 1940 in Joliet, Illinois, International Dairy Queen, Inc. (IDQ) is one of Buffett's favorite places to eat. He regularly takes his grandchildren there. Dairy Queen was the first place to sell soft-serve ice cream, and today it has more than 7,000 stores worldwide.[37]

Dairy Queen operates under a franchise model, like McDonald's, in which the company collects royalties from its franchise owners. This model provides a revenue stream with minimal capital requirements.

In 1998, Berkshire bought Dairy Queen for $585 million. Today, IDQ also owns Orange Julius and Karmelkorn.[38]

1998: NetJets

Founded in 1964 as Executive Jet Airways, NetJets Inc. is an American company that sells shares (renting space on a plane, called "fractional ownership") of private business jets.[39] In 1987, the NetJets program was officially announced, becoming the first fractional aircraft ownership format in history. One of the first quarter-share owners was Berkshire Hathaway, in 1995.[40] Buffett quickly saw the potential of fractional ownership in private aviation, and in 1998, Berkshire Hathaway purchased the company for $725 million.[41]

By June 2020, NetJets, including NetJets Europe and Executive Jet Management, had over 750 aircraft. This figure represented just under 3.5 percent of all active private jets worldwide.[42] Private jets performed much better during the pandemic because they reduce the risk of COVID due to passengers not having to deal with packed planes and airports.

1998: General Re Corporation

The same year that Berkshire bought NetJets and Dairy Queen, it also purchased the reinsurance company General Re for $23.5 billion in stock.[43] General Re offers life, accident, and health insurance, as well as international property and casualty reinsurance. One of the advantages of this purchase for Berkshire was its role in increasing the investment firm's float, a concept discussed in chapter 6.

Today, General Re Corporation is the holding company for an array of global reinsurance and related operations. In addition, the insurance, reinsurance, and investment management companies in the General Re group include Gen Re Intermediaries, GR-NEAM, General Star, Genesis, U.S. Gold Corp. (better known as USAU), and Faraday.[44] This acquisition will be further analyzed in chapter 10.

1999: Berkshire Hathaway Energy

Berkshire Hathaway Energy (known as MidAmerican Energy Holdings Company until 2014) is a holding company that is 90 percent owned by Berkshire Hathaway and run by Greg Abel. In 1999, Berkshire Hathaway purchased the company in partnership with MidAmerican's Chairman and CEO David Sokol and its largest stockholder, Walter Scott, after the share price dropped 21 percent.[45] Buffett observed at the time: "We buy good companies with outstanding management and good growth potential at a fair price, and we are willing to wait longer than some investors for that potential to be realized."[46]

In this case, Berkshire waited to see a return on this investment. But that movement was encouraging enough to keep Berkshire in energy. Berkshire Hathaway Energy now owns MidAmerica Energy Company, PacificCorp, Northern Powergrid, CalEnergy Generation, HomeServices of America, BYD Company, and NV Energy.

2001: Shaw Industries Group, Inc.

Buffett has long been comfortable with retail and manufacturing, as demonstrated by his purchase of Borsheims, National Furniture Mart, and See's. On

January 4, 2001, Berkshire Hathaway bought the carpet maker Shaw Industries Group, Inc., for $2.1 billion.[47] Today, Shaw Industries is one of the world's largest carpet manufacturers, with more than $6 billion in annual sales and about 22,300 employees worldwide.[48]

2002: Fruit of the Loom

Sometimes a company's problematic balance sheets are outweighed by the strength of their brand. Such was the case with Fruit of the Loom, which Berkshire bought out of bankruptcy for a mere $835 million in cash after the company's stock plunged 97 percent in 2002.[49]

Buffett said there were actually two main reasons: "the strength of the brand and the managerial talent of [chief executive officer] John Holland."[50] That instinct proved correct. Today, Fruit of the Loom, which also sells the brands Russell Athletic and Spalding, has 32,400 employees.

2003: Clayton Homes

Clayton Homes, headquartered in Maryville, Tennessee, is the nation's largest builder of manufactured housing and modular homes.[51] While Buffett knew a bit about the company, he became much more interested after a group of finance students from the University of Tennessee in Knoxville presented him with an autobiography of the company's founder, Jim Clayton, a UT alumnus.

As Buffett told his shareholders, after reading Clayton's book and speaking with his son Kevin, who was the firm's CEO, Buffett reviewed Clayton's financials and bought the company for $1.7 billion.[52] At the time of this acquisition, in 2003, Clayton's average pretax margin for the previous five years was 19.2 percent—significantly higher than Berkshire's 11.2 percent.

In 2015, the company was accused of predatory lending toward minority customers and tolerating racism in its corporate culture. Clayton released a statement saying it "categorically and adamantly" denied those allegations.[53] And at Berkshire's 2015 shareholders meeting, Buffett backed the firm, saying he would make "no apologies whatsoever" for Clayton's lending practices.[54] The company paid $38,000 in fines and $700,000 in refunds. Nonetheless, Clayton is still going strong. In 2018, Clayton Homes's estimated revenue was $3.6 billion.[55]

2006: Brooks Sports, Inc.

Brooks Sports, Inc., also known as Brooks Running, is an American company headquartered in Seattle that designs and markets high-performance men's and women's running shoes, clothing, and accessories. Brooks products are available in sixty countries.[56]

Founded in 1914, Brooks originally manufactured a wide range of sports shoes. The company was successful through the 1970s, but then production and quality control issues caused the firm to file for Chapter 11 bankruptcy protection in 1981.[57,58]

In 2001, a new CEO, Jim Weber, was brought in to turn the company's fortunes around. He cut the product line by more than 50 percent to focus almost entirely on reengineering the brand's running shoes. Brooks emphasized design innovations to enhance athletic performance.

By 2004, the company was acquired by Russell Athletic (which itself was purchased by Fruit of the Loom in 2006, as previously mentioned). Consequently, Brooks became a subsidiary of Fruit of the Loom's parent company, Berkshire Hathaway. And in 2011, with Brooks Running the top-selling brand in the specialty running shoe market:[59,60]

> In 2012, Warren Buffett . . . recognized the potential in Brooks, which was then a subsidiary of Fruit of the Loom, owned by Berkshire Hathaway, and he personally established Brooks as a standalone company. Now, Weber reports directly to Buffett . . . He has never felt more trust from someone he's worked for, and he has also never felt more responsibility.[61]

I interviewed Jim Weber and asked him about his relationship with Buffett. He said that "when you talk to him in person, Warren listens attentively . . . there were no phones, TV, computers, or any interruptions. The last time we met at his office for three hours and then we went out to lunch in Omaha. He was warm, generous, curious, and enthusiastic."[62]

Since Weber took over in 2001, Brooks has grown every year. The way Buffett manages Brooks and his other businesses has a lot to do with his success. He gives the businesses autonomy but also holds them accountable. The structure of decentralization that Berkshire created a long time ago is very entrepreneurial. It empowers managers to be more creative by giving them more freedom.

Weber stated the following about Buffett:

> During my MBA at Dartmouth, I started to discover and devour the letters of Warren Buffett. I began to understand not only how to be a leader but what kind of leader I wanted to be. Buffett taught me that anyone can cut prices and sell a cheap product, but the challenge was to build a business to last—a business that has not only great brand strength and loyal customers but high returns on capital as well. I often tell people I have the best job in Seattle. I have the best job in this industry. I'm just having a blast.[63]

2006: ISCAR Metalworking Companies

ISCAR Metalworking Companies (IMC Group) was founded by Stef Wertheimer in his backyard in Nahariya, Israel, in 1952. Wertheimer, a refugee from Nazi Germany,[64] originally became famous for making the precision blades for jet engines. Today, ISCAR companies supply a comprehensive line of "precision carbide metalworking tools" aimed at engineering and manufacturing for major industries throughout the world.[65]

In May 2006, Berkshire Hathaway purchased 80 percent of ISCAR for $4 billion.[66] Buffett bought the rest for $2.05 billion in 2013. As of 2021, Wertheimer was the second-richest Israeli, with a net worth of $6.2 billion, and his company is a world leader in the automotive, aerospace, and die and mold industries, with more than 13,000 employees in sixty-five countries.[67]

2007: Marmon Holdings, Inc.

In 2007, Berkshire Hathaway paid $4.5 billion for 60 percent of Marmon Holdings, Inc., a global industrial organization founded by Jay and Robert Pritzker in 1953.[68] Marmon consists of thirteen business sectors, including food service technologies, water technologies, intermodal containers, and electrical products. Marmon also has more than 100 autonomous manufacturing and service businesses and employs 19,000 people around the world.[69]

Between 2011 and 2013, Berkshire purchased the remaining 40 percent of Marmon.[70] In 2021, the company generated more than $10 billion in revenue.

BERKSHIRE HATHAWAY AND THE GREAT RECESSION

Buffett and Corporate Entrepreneurship (Venturing)

Buffett's entrepreneurial side became obvious during the Great Recession. While most people were afraid to do anything, Buffett saw opportunity—a key attribute of entrepreneurs. What follows are some examples of how Buffett created opportunities for Berkshire during the crisis.

The Great Recession

According to the National Bureau of Economic Research (NBER), the Great Recession stretched from December 2007 to June 2009.[71,72] In the United States, this period represented the worst economic downturn since the Great Depression. The financial crisis was caused in part by the misuse of financial transactions known as "derivatives," which allowed buyers and sellers to bet on the extent of home loan defaults. In 2007, the U.S. home market was valued at more than $20 trillion, with almost half of that value supported by mortgage financing of one sort or another. However, more than twenty-five subprime lenders (which gave out higher-interest loans to people with higher credit risk) went bankrupt. Many subprime mortgages defaulted. As a result, the S&P 500 dropped 57 percent, the average U.S. family lost 40 percent of its net worth, and unemployment reached 10 percent.

At the lowest point of the financial crisis, Berkshire Hathaway, which had peaked at $149,200 per share on December 10, 2007, lost 51 percent of its value.[73] It bottomed out at $73,195 per share on March 9, 2009. At the time, Berkshire companies employed more than 223,000 people.

Berkshire's Investments during the Crisis

Despite the crisis, Buffett found ways to make money from it. This is no surprise, really, since a major plank of his investment strategy is to buy when everyone else is selling. "Buy American. I am," he wrote in a column that ran in the *New York Times* on October 15, 2008, when the year-to-date S&P 500 had dropped by 38 percent:

> A simple rule dictates my buying: Be fearful when others are greedy and be greedy when others are fearful. And most certainly, fear is now widespread, gripping even seasoned investors. To be sure, investors are right to be wary of highly leveraged entities or businesses in weak competitive positions. But fears regarding the long-term prosperity of the nation's many sound companies make no sense. These businesses will indeed suffer earnings hiccups, as they always have. But most major companies will be setting new profit records 5, 10 and 20 years from now.[74]

Buffett said that there was no way to predict where stocks would be in a month or a year, but he was certain that prices would recover substantially well before the overall economy turned around. For that reason, he added, his personal account, which had been invested entirely in government bonds, would soon be 100 percent in U.S. equities if prices continued on their downward trajectory. As it turns out, Buffett was several months early in identifying the market bottom, which finally arrived in March 2009. However, his statement did have a positive, if brief, impact on market sentiment.

His strategy once again proved correct. During the financial crisis, Buffett's entrepreneurial instincts made Berkshire more than $10 billion through investments in companies such as Goldman Sachs, General Electric (GE), Wrigley/Mars, Swiss Re, and Dow Chemical.

The following subsections describe Buffett's major investment moves during the Great Recession. Berkshire's cash reserves, combined with the firm's prestige, gave it a strong position from which to bargain.

2008: Goldman Sachs Buffett invested $5 billion into Goldman Sachs after Lehman Brothers collapsed. This massive boost indicated his confidence in the bank, and its stock price went up. Berkshire bought $5 billion in perpetual preferred shares that paid an annual dividend of 10 percent. It also "received warrants to purchase an additional $5 billion of common stock with a strike price of $115 per share,"[75] as well as a five-year period in which to exercise those warrants.[76]

In March 2011, Goldman redeemed Berkshire's preferred shares, paying $5.65 billion.[77] By 2013, Goldman's shares were trading above $160, and Buffett wanted to exercise his warrants. But Goldman renegotiated before Buffett could pull the trigger, giving Berkshire 13.1 million shares and $2 billion in cash.[78] Instead of taking it in all Goldman stock, Buffett agreed to this arrangement, as Berkshire's portfolio was already above its target allocation for banking shares. In the end, he would make more than $3 billion in profit for Berkshire on this investment: a $500 million premium for the preferred stock, plus $1.2 billion in dividends, and at least $1.4 billion when he sold most of the stock in 2020.[79]

2008: General Electric After GE shares fell 42 percent in 2008, Berkshire Hathaway decided to invest $3 billion in newly issued GE perpetual preferred stock. The stock came with a dividend of 10 percent that could be called after three years at a 10 percent premium. Berkshire also received warrants to purchase $3 billion of common stock at a strike price of $22.25 per share, exercisable at any time over a five-year period. Buffett insisted that company executives refrain from selling more than 10 percent of the common stock they held, either until the date when the preferred stock was redeemed or after three years had passed from the date of Berkshire's investment. The transaction closed on October 16, 2008, when GE was at $19.29.[80]

GE's common stock price fell over the five months following Berkshire's investment. On March 5, 2009, the stock traded at a low of $6.66. But Buffett made out handsomely in the end. The deal allowed Berkshire to get $3.3 billion paid back, plus $300 million in annual dividends, and the warrant allowed Buffett to buy $3 billion in GE stock for $22.25 a share for five years.

In 2011, GE paid off the loan by giving Berkshire $3.3 billion. The company had already shelled out three full years of dividends, at $300 million apiece. Together, this accounted for a Berkshire Hathaway profit of about $1.2 billion.

In 2013, as Buffett's warrant to buy the GE stock was set to expire, GE settled so that Berkshire would not have to shell out the $3 billion to buy the stock, which was then trading above the $22.25 exercise price. Instead, GE gave Berkshire 10.7 million shares, equal to the total amount he would receive over the $22.25 exercise price of the warrant. Buffett sold all of Berkshire's shares in GE during the second quarter of 2017. It is estimated that those shares were worth $315 million.

At the end of the day, Berkshire received approximately $1.545 billion in cash for lending GE $3 billion over three years.[81] This includes about $30 million in regular dividends paid over the time he held the shares, plus $1.2 billion in profit from 2011, making the deal with GE a profitable transaction indeed. In 2021, GE had a reverse split of 8:1 and in March 2022, GE was trading at $89/share.

2008: Wrigley/Mars Berkshire assisted Mars, Inc., in the financing of its acquisition of the number one chewing gum manufacturer, Wm Wrigley Jr. Company, for $23 billion.[82] Mars paid $11 billion itself, secured a $5.7 billion debt facility from Goldman Sachs, and asked Berkshire to provide the rest of the financing.[83]

Berkshire purchased $2.1 billion of Wrigley's preferred stock, which paid a 5 percent annual dividend. This gave Berkshire a 10 percent stake in Wrigley.[84] It also bought $4.4 billion in Wrigley bonds, with an 11.45 percent interest rate, that matured in 2018.[85] Combining gains on the bonds and shares with the interest payments and dividends, Buffett made around $6.5 billion from the Wrigley investment.[86]

2009: Swiss Re Swiss Re, an insurance giant based in Zurich, lost six billion Swiss francs in the Great Recession. This included mark-to-market losses of two billion Swiss francs for its holdings of structured credit-default swaps.[87] The losses put Swiss Re in danger of losing its AA rating.[88] The company turned to Buffett for potential financing.

Berkshire already had significant business ties with Swiss Re. In January 2008, it had entered a quota share arrangement with the firm, through which it acquired 20 percent of its new and renewed property and casualty business while simultaneously acquiring 3 percent of its shares.[89] On March 23, 2009, Berkshire invested $2.6 billion (three billion Swiss francs) and considered raising another two billion francs in equity if the market would bear it.

According to The Rational Walk:

> Although the investment carried an interest rate of 12 percent, Swiss Re had the right to defer interest payments, and could opt to pay interest using shares rather than cash. The investment provided Berkshire with conversion rights, but the conversion price was above Swiss Re's stock price at the time of the deal and Swiss Re retained the right to redeem the instrument at a premium to prevent future dilution.[90]

This became a successful investment for Berkshire. The three billion Swiss franc investment earned a "total of 4.42 billion Swiss francs in interest payments, redemption premium, and repayment of the original principal," according to The Rational Walk.[91] The estimated annualized internal rate of return was 25.8 percent when expressed in Swiss francs and 37 percent in U.S. dollars.[92]

2009: Dow Chemical Berkshire Hathaway made a significant investment in Dow Chemical, which allowed Dow to purchase the Rohm and Hass Company.

On April 1, 2009, Berkshire bought three million preferred shares of Dow, paying an annual dividend of 8.5 percent, for $3 billion.[93] Dow paid Buffett $255 million in dividends every year, adding to Berkshire's $1.8 billion in total profits from 2009 to 2015.[94]

2009: Burlington Northern Santa Fe Corporation On November 3, 2009, Berkshire announced that it had purchased Burlington Northern Santa Fe (BNSF) Corporation for $100 per share. Berkshire now owned 100 percent of the company.

In February 2010, Berkshire finalized the acquisition, paying a total of $26.5 billion in cash and stock to purchase any outstanding shares of BNSF that Berkshire did not already own.[95] The total consideration consisted of $15.9 billion in cash and $10.6 billion of newly issued Berkshire common stock.[96] Berkshire raised approximately $8 billion of debt at the corporate level to fund the cash component of the transaction, along with an equivalent amount of cash on hand.[97]

Buffett's rationale for purchasing BNSF was that the U.S. economy would continue to grow into the future, thus the demand for goods and transportation would only rise. Sweetening the deal for Buffett was BNSF's durable competitive advantage due to the high cost of entry into the market for any other firm.

At the end of 2009 when Berkshire purchased BNSF, its sales and net income were $14 billion and $1.7 billion, respectively. By 2021, it had risen to $23.3 billion and $5.99 billion.

BUFFETT IN THE SPOTLIGHT, UP-CLOSE

My first meeting with Buffett came about just after his purchase of BNSF. I'd written a case study on Berkshire Hathaway and sent it to Buffett's office, hoping that it might win me and my students an invitation to visit with Buffett. To my delight, that is exactly what happened! Buffett invited me to bring twenty-seven students to Omaha, and we spent a day with him. This happened to be the November day in 2009 that he announced the deal with BNSF. Reporters were chasing him everywhere, but Buffett kept his focus on our group. He was doing what he loves, which is teaching and spending time with young people. During our question-and-answer period, he said that he'd always wanted to own a train company because he used to have a toy train set growing up. I will talk further about our trips to visit Buffett in chapter 12.

CHAPTER 9

BERKSHIRE HATHAWAY: 2010–2020

In the world of business, the people who are most successful are those who are doing what they love. Never give up searching for the job that you are passionate about.[1]

WARREN BUFFETT

A NEW DECADE FOR BERKSHIRE

Following the management philosophy of Philip Fisher has long stood Warren Buffett in good stead. His general game plan has been to seek out the best investment talent and give those managers free rein. As the twenty-teens dawned, Buffett, at eighty, and Charlie Munger, at eighty-six, began to prepare for the future of the company they'd built—what would happen to it after their retirement. Their most important moves in that regard were the hiring of two new co–chief investment officers, Todd Combs and Ted Weschler. Both men were decades younger, of a generation that had come into adulthood with the rise of technology, and that perspective has undeniably influenced investments at Berkshire Hathaway. To wit: Before Combs and Weschler, Berkshire had shunned technology almost entirely. After those hires, Buffett invested in Amazon and said he had been an idiot for not jumping in earlier. He also made Apple one of the largest holdings in Berkshire's entire portfolio. In 2020, this trajectory continued with Berkshire's investment in a cloud-data company called Snowflake. At the initial public offering (IPO), Buffett had about $730 million in Snowflake shares.[2] By the end of the first day of trading, Berkshire had made over $800 million.[3]

I highly doubt that Buffett would have made these acquisitions on his own, and in decades to come, I expect that Berkshire will continue to add technology stocks to its portfolio.

Buffett hired Todd Combs in 2010, at age thirty-nine. Born in Sarasota, Florida, Combs earned his bachelor's degree in finance and international business from Florida State University, and then attended Buffett's alma mater, Columbia University, where he entered the prestigious Value Investing Program—the same program where Buffett had studied under Graham many years before.[4] Combs graduated with a master of business administration (MBA) in 2002.

Prior to joining Berkshire, Combs had founded a hedge fund called Castle Point Capital and might have been able to make more money if he'd continued to run it.[5] Buffett said, "Combs fit into Berkshire not only because of his ability and intelligence, but because he is a 100 percent for our 'no fuss' culture. We want a culture that is so embedded that it does not get tested when the founder is not around. Todd is perfect in that respect."[6]

Ted Weschler, hired at Berkshire two years later in 2012, was a hedge fund founder like Combs. The fifty-year-old was born in Buffalo, New York and lives in Charlottesville, Virginia today. He was such an admirer of Buffett that he'd bid $2,626,311 at a private auction for the chance to go to lunch with Buffett in 2010. (The money went to charity.) The following year, Weschler participated in the auction again and, though vying against other competitors whose top bids were lower than the previous year's,[7] Weschler raised his bid $100, to $2,626,411, to win another lunch with his would-be mentor.[8]

Weschler graduated from the Wharton School of Business at the University of Pennsylvania in 1989, with a degree in economics, and founded a hedge fund called Peninsula Capital Advisors ten years later.[9] Peninsula's $2 billion fund returned 1,236 percent before Buffett hired Weschler and he shut down the fund.[10]

Initially, Buffett gave Weschler and Combs individual $1 billion portfolios that each would manage separately. He gradually increased their portfolios as he grew more confident in their abilities. Neither needed to consult with anyone before making their investments, but Buffett followed their performance, checking in monthly. By 2020, both men were managing around $15 billion in stock holdings. Each receives 80 percent of his performance pay from his own results and 20 percent from the other's results. This is one way in which Buffett incentivizes teamwork and shared responsibility.

"They have excellent 'business minds' that grasp the economic forces likely to determine the future of a wide variety of businesses," Buffett said of his new managers in 2016. "They are aided in their thinking by an understanding of what is predictable and what is unknowable."[11]

Buffett later said that one of the best decisions he and Munger ever made was bringing those two on board. "These were the only two guys we could find who read just as much as we did," he quipped, only half in jest.[12]

The next subsections relate some of Berkshire Hathaway's most significant acquisitions from the last decade.

2011: Lubrizol Corporation

Berkshire Hathaway bought Lubrizol Corporation for $9.7 billion cash in March 2011.[13] The company was founded in 1928 in Cleveland, Ohio, and is now headquartered in nearby Wickliffe. Lubrizol specializes in producing chemicals such as engineered polymers, coatings, industrial lubricants, engine oil additives, specialty chemical products, and piping systems.

The things that made this purchase attractive to Buffett will be familiar to anyone who has read this far:

1. Return on equity (ROE) equal to 34 percent
2. A wide moat, courtesy of the company's 1,600 patents
3. Pricing power, which Buffett says is the single most important factor in evaluating a business
4. Steadily rising dividends, from $1.04 per share in 2005 to $1.39 in 2010
5. Earning two-thirds of its revenue from outside the United States
6. Low unionization
7. Reasonably priced stock (Buffett paid $135 a share, or thirteen times earnings and twelve times forecasted earnings for the next year)
8. Good, stable management[14]

2011: Bank of America

In 2011, Bank of America (BoA) was still reeling under economic fallout from the Great Recession. Not least of these crises was a $10 billion lawsuit from American International Group (AIG) for selling overvalued residential mortgage-backed securities through its Merrill Lynch unit.[15] That year, despite BoA's setbacks, Buffett invested $5 billion in the bank's preferred stock, which paid a 6 percent annual dividend. He also received warrants for 700 million shares that Berkshire could exercise at a fixed strike price of $7.14 a share through 2021. BoA had the option to buy back the preferred shares at any time for a 5 percent premium.[16]

Berkshire Hathaway exercised its warrants to buy those 700 million shares in 2017. At the $7.14 price per share, Buffett got a steep discount against that day's closing price of $23.58. Berkshire had made the purchase with its preferred shares from 2011, swapping them for a $16 billion-plus common stock holding.[17] Today, BoA is Berkshire's second-largest equity holding, behind Apple. In June 2022, Berkshire owned more than 1 billion of the bank's shares, worth around $34.3 billion.

2011: IBM

IBM's business services, with their recurring revenues and leading market position, initially attracted Buffett. But the granddaddy technology firm turned out to be one of Buffett's rare losing investments.

In 2011, Berkshire Hathaway purchased 64 million shares of IBM at an average price of $170 each (for a total of $10.7 billion).[18] Six years later, in 2017, Buffett began to express concerns about the company's future, especially compared to Apple. Less than six months later, he started to offload his shares, dumping "a reasonable amount of stock" when it got above $180 per share.[19] However, by the time he divested completely, in 2018, IBM was trading at around $140 per share.[20]

Buffett's conservative philosophy of investing only in companies he understands, a philosophy that has served him well in countless other situations, may have worked to his disadvantage here. Although IBM is one of the more understandable tech companies, it is also one that may be over the hill in its corporate life cycle. (More about this problematic investment and how it shaped Buffett's thinking will follow in chapter 10, on Buffett's mistakes).

2012: Oriental Trading Company

The Oriental Trading Company sells value-priced party goods, in addition to arts and crafts supplies, toys, novelties, and school supplies.[21] Founded in 1932 as one of the country's first wholesalers, Oriental Trading is headquartered in Omaha.

On August 24, 2010, Oriental Trading Company declared Chapter 11 bankruptcy protection via OTC Holdings Corp.[22] However, CEO Sam Taylor brought the firm out of bankruptcy and convinced Buffett to purchase it. On November 2, 2012, Berkshire Hathaway announced it would rescue the company by acquiring it for $500 million.[23] Taylor passed away in 2017 from brain cancer at age fifty-six. Today, Oriental Trading is run by Steve Mendlik, the current president and CEO.

2013: H. J. Heinz Co.

On February 14, 2013, Berkshire and 3G Capital purchased H. J. Heinz Co. for $28 billion. Heinz fits Buffett's playbook. It has a global brand recognition that rivals Coca-Cola and IBM, two companies in which Berkshire owned big stakes in 2013. In addition, Heinz's financial performance was sound. "It is our kind of company,"[24] Buffett told CNBC, indicating that he regarded the food company as a trophy asset, like Fruit of the Loom or the Burlington Northern Railroad.[25]

Buffett had paid a premium to acquire Heinz. Reportedly, "Under the terms of the deal, they paid $72.50 a share, 20 percent higher than the stock's closing price and 19 percent higher than its record high."[26]

Berkshire and 3G also paid about $4 billion in cash for Heinz, but Berkshire paid an additional $8 billion for preferred shares, which paid an annual dividend of about 9 percent.[27]

This acquisition will be examined further in chapter 10.

2014: Auto Dealerships

In 2014, Berkshire Hathaway purchased Van Tuyl Group, with seventy-eight independent dealerships and 100 franchises in ten states. It was the largest privately owned auto dealership group in the country, with $8 billion in sales.[28] Buffett renamed the company Berkshire Hathaway Automotive. This purchase was somewhat out of the norm for Berkshire, which had generally avoided the automotive industry. Berkshire paid $4.1 billion for the deal.

Originally based in Phoenix, the Van Tuyl Group relocated its headquarters to Dallas, but the existing CEO, Larry Van Tuyl, retained his leadership role and became the chair of Berkshire Hathaway Automotive. This is in keeping with Buffett's well-known pattern of retaining existing leaders and their expertise.

"Larry's got an operation that we think could be scaled up a lot from where it is," Buffett said during an interview with CNBC.[29]

2014–2016: Duracell

In 1989, Berkshire Hathaway purchased $600 million worth of Gillette convertible preferred shares. In 2005, Procter & Gamble (P&G) agreed to purchase Gillette for $54 billion. In 2014, Berkshire purchased Duracell from P&G in exchange for $4.7 billion in P&G stock that Berkshire owned due to the Gillette buyout in 2005.[30]

According to Buffett, "I have always been impressed by Duracell, as a consumer and as a long-term investor in P&G and Gillette. Duracell is a leading global brand with top quality products, and it will fit well within Berkshire Hathaway."[31] The deal fit nicely into the Berkshire portfolio, especially since Buffett used stock to purchase the company, reducing the tax bill significantly. Since he was able to sell the P&G shares in exchange for Duracell, he avoided the capital gains taxes that he would have had to pay if he had cashed them out.[32]

2015: Kraft Foods and H. J. Heinz

In 2015, Kraft Foods merged with H. J. Heinz through a deal made by 3G Capital and Berkshire Hathaway, each of which invested $10 billion. This valued Kraft at about $46 billion based on its stock price (before net debt).[33] The deal gave Heinz 51 percent ownership of Kraft, leaving the then-current stockholders 49 percent of Kraft.[34] The merger combined thirteen brands worth over $500 million each.[35]

In 2014, the newly formed megacompany had revenues of about $28 billion, though PepsiCo, the industry leader, had more than double that.[36] By February 2019, however, H. J. Heinz–Kraft Foods reported disappointing news: It was taking a $15 billion write-down on its intangible assets, essentially admitting that famous brand trademarks like Oscar Meyer and Kraft were overvalued.[37]

H. J. Heinz–Kraft Foods was also being investigated for accounting irregularities. Its stock fell 30 percent in one day, and the value of those shares was down by more than half since the 2015 merger. As a result, Berkshire Hathaway lost $4 billion. Buffett also claims that competition from private-label brands like Costco's Kirkland Signature are a major reason for the decrease in sales.[38]

Buffett now concedes that he overpaid for Kraft and may have misjudged aspects of the company. "It's still a wonderful business in that it uses about $7 billion of tangible assets and earns $6 billion pretax on that. . . . But . . . we paid $100 billion in tangible assets. So, for us, it has to earn $107 billion, not just the $7 billion that the business employs."[39]

2016: Precision Castparts Corporation

In 2016, Berkshire Hathaway bought Precision Castparts Corporation for $32.1 billion, which was Berkshire's largest deal to date.[40] Combs had begun buying stock in the Oregon-based manufacturer of airplane and aerospace parts, and soon told Buffett about it. Subsequently, Berkshire acquired the entire company.[41]

Precision Castparts was the world's premier supplier of essential aerospace components, such as fasteners and turbine blades for large aircraft, as well as pipes used by power stations and the oil-and-gas sector. Most of these components are designed to be original equipment, but spare parts are also an important part of the company's business model. Its products are often delivered under multiyear contracts, creating something of a moat.[42,43]

2016: Apple

As detailed in chapter 6, Berkshire bought $1 billion worth of Apple stock in May 2016. Less than a year after that, in February 2017, the company announced that Apple was its second-largest holding, with 133 million shares worth $17 billion (or 2.5 percent of Apple).[44]

Berkshire's interest in the high-end tech firm did not cool. By October 2019, the company had 249,589,329 shares of Apple worth more than $58.96 billion. And by the end of 2021, Apple was Berkshire's largest holding, with 907,559,761 shares worth $157.5 billion.[45]

2016–2020: Airlines

In November 2016, Berkshire invested in four major airlines: American, United, Delta, and Southwest. This move surprised many, as it seemed to go against what Buffett had learned through previous negative experiences with the commercial aviation industry.

In almost every annual shareholder letter between 1989 and 1996, Buffett had acknowledged his mistaken investment in US Airways. In 2007, he again laid out his argument against investing in airlines: "The worst sort of business is one that grows rapidly, requires significant capital to engender the growth, then earns little or no money. Think airlines. Here, a durable competitive advantage has proven elusive ever since the days of the Wright brothers. Indeed, if a farsighted capitalist had been present at Kitty Hawk, he would have done his successors a huge favor by shooting Orville down."[46]

In an interview in 2002, he similarly remarked:

> If a capitalist had been present at Kitty Hawk back in the early 1900s, he should have shot Orville Wright. He would have saved his progeny money. But seriously, the airline business has been extraordinary. It has eaten up capital over the past century like almost no other business because people seem to keep coming back to it and putting fresh money in. You've got huge fixed costs, you've got strong labor unions and you've got commodity pricing. That is not a great recipe for success. I have an 800 (free call) number now that I call if I get the urge to buy an airline stock. I call at two in the morning and I say: 'My name is Warren and I'm an aeroholic.' And then they talk me down.[47]

Still, disobeying his own advice, Buffett, Combs, and Weschler began purchasing billions of dollars in airline shares, starting in October 2019, with the following breakdown:

- 53,649,213 shares of Southwest Airlines worth $2,892,765,565
- 70,910,456 shares of Delta Airlines worth $3,754,708,645
- 43,700,000 shares of American Airlines worth $1,195,632,000
- 21,938,642 shares of United Airlines worth $1,911,952,650

Cumulatively, Berkshire's investment in airlines amounts to $9,755,058,860, or 4.5 percent of its total portfolio of $216,621,148,782.

What changed Buffett's point of view? Perhaps it was due to the influence of Combs and Weschler. Or consolidation within the industry may have suggested improved profitability. Whatever his reasons, Buffett's optimism was belied by the effects of the COVID-19 pandemic, which hit airline stocks hard. In March

2020, Berkshire began to sell its holdings in the industry. It had previously amassed an 11.1 percent ownership of Delta, but now dumped 18 percent of those shares (worth $314 million). Berkshire also had a 10.4 percent ownership stake in Southwest, but now it sold off 4 percent of those shares (worth $74 million).[48]

By the 2020 shareholder meeting, Buffett announced that the pandemic had convinced Berkshire to sell its entire position in all airlines (a total of $6.1 billion in stock). The ongoing uncertainty around air travel would result in empty seats, lowered ticket prices, and decreased profitability, he explained.

Robert Crandall, former CEO of American Airlines, has said that he enjoyed working for the airlines, but he also called it a "nasty, rotten business." He told his employees not to buy their own company's stock because airlines don't make money.[49] There are a number of factors that contribute to the impediments to the industry: high capital costs, unionized labor, fuel prices, and other unpredictable aspects.

2018: Haven

In January 2018, Buffett, with Amazon CEO Jeff Bezos and J. P. Morgan CEO Jamie Dimon, announced they were creating a new partnership called Haven, which would focus on reducing the cost of U.S. health care.

Calling the endlessly ballooning U.S. health-care costs "a tapeworm, in terms of American business and its competitiveness,"[50] Buffett said that he wanted to work with two business leaders he admired and trusted to see if there was a way the three of them could produce a new model for cost-efficient health-care delivery.

They wouldn't be starting a new health insurance company, Buffett assured investors. And his motivation for this partnership was "not primarily profit-making,"[51] he added. Beyond that, he was vague, saying only that the spike in per capita health-care spending—soaring from $170 in 1960 to more than $10,000 annually today—was a travesty.[52] "We want our employees to get better medical service at a lower cost. We're certainly not going to come up with something where we think the service that they receive is inferior to what they're getting now."[53]

The triad of their three organizations, together employing more than a million people, might be able to conceive some sort of new, cost-saving model for health-care delivery. Light on specifics, Buffett nonetheless made it clear that the group would aim to economize, in hopes that their model might be adopted more widely. "The resistance will be unbelievable, and if we fail, at least we tried."[54] That remark would prove prescient.

The ultimate aim was that Haven might inspire a new, nationally applicable model for health-care costs—a heavy lift, Buffett conceded. He was careful not to make promises; the trio hadn't even formalized their partnership agreement on paper. But Buffett could not hide his hope and ambition for their enterprise, saying, "There's a chance—nobody can quantify it—that we can do something significant. And we are positioned better than most people to try. And we've certainly got the right partners. So, we will give it a shot and see what happens."[55]

In February 2021, Haven announced that it would dissolve. The U.S. health-care industry was operating with systems too entrenched and complex to overhaul without a major social disruption.

2019: Amazon.com

On May 2, 2019, one day before Berkshire Hathaway's annual shareholder meeting, Buffett told CNBC that one of Berkshire's investment managers, either Combs or Weschler, had been purchasing Amazon shares. "I've been a fan, and I've been an idiot for not buying," he conceded, but he assured the television audience that no major personality change had occurred in the investor who had so long and famously eschewed technology.[56]

His casual take perhaps underplayed the seriousness of his interest. On that same date, Berkshire Hathaway revealed in a filing with the Securities and Exchange Commission that it owned 483,300 shares of Amazon at the end of the previous quarter. By late 2021, Berkshire's stake would be worth almost $2 billion, or 0.1 percent of Amazon's outstanding equity.

2019: Anadarko Petroleum

In recent years, Buffett has not shown much interest in oil stocks, but that changed when Berkshire Hathaway committed $10 billion to help Occidental Petroleum Corporation purchase Anadarko Petroleum. Anadarko had a leading position in the Permian Basin, located along the border between Texas and New Mexico, which is the site of one of the world's most productive oil fields. For a total of

$10 billion, Berkshire bought 100,000 preferred shares with an 8 percent annual dividend.[57] Berkshire also received warrants to purchase up to 80 million Occidental shares at $62.50.[58] Under the companies' merger agreement, Occidental Petroleum acquired "all of the outstanding shares of Anadarko for consideration consisting of $59 in cash and 0.2934 of a share of Occidental common stock per share of Anadarko common stock."[59]

In recent years, Buffett had appeared to be shifting his electricity holdings toward renewable energies like wind and hydroelectric power.[60] His investment in Occidental suggested to onlookers that he was confident about the oil industry and believed that the market was not fully appreciating the combined Occidental/Anadarko asset base and production capability.

2020: Kroger

In 2020, Berkshire paid $549 million for 19 million shares (or 2.3 percent ownership) of Kroger, the nation's largest grocery store company.[61] Although this did not make Berkshire the majority shareholder, it put Buffett's company in the top ten,[62] a bit of poetic justice for the kid who started out as a stockboy in his grandfather's grocery store. In 2022, Berkshire had 61.8 million shares of Kroger, worth $2.87 billion.

2020: Japanese Conglomerates

In 2020, Buffett announced that Berkshire had bought a $6 billion (5 percent) stake in Sumitomo, Mitsubishi, Itochu, Mitsui, and Marubeni, the five largest conglomerates (*sogo shosha*) in Japan.[63] There are a few reasons why he did this. It is part of his international diversification strategy, since the dollar has been depreciating and assets in the United States have been expensive. As a result, the value of dividends and their stock prices will translate favorably into a depreciating dollar. As of late 2021, Buffett had made a gain of over 30 percent.

Third Quarter of 2020

In the third quarter of 2020, Berkshire invested in a cloud-data company called Snowflake. At the IPO, Berkshire held roughly $730 million worth of shares. Snowflake went public at $120 a share. By the end of the first day of trading, the stock was up to $253.93 (a 111 percent increase), and Berkshire had made over $800 million.[64] As of March 2022, the stock price was $197.42.

In the third quarter of 2020, likely due to anticipated vaccine and other COVID-related profit spikes, Berkshire invested $5.7 billion in four pharmaceutical companies: AbbVie (21.3 million shares), Bristol-Myers Squibb (30 million shares), Merck (22.4 million shares), and Pfizer (3.7 million shares). Berkshire also sold its entire stake in Costco, 44 percent of its position in Barrick Gold, and $4 billion of its Apple holdings.[65]

Fourth Quarter of 2020

In the fourth quarter of 2020, Berkshire bought $4.1 billion in Chevron and $8.6 billion in Verizon. Berkshire sold all its positions in JPMorgan Chase, PNC Financial, M&T Bank, Pfizer, and Barrick Gold. It also cut its holdings in Apple by 6 percent, Wells Fargo by 59 percent, Suncor Energy by 28 percent, and General Motors (GM) by 9 percent.[66]

CHAPTER 10

BUFFETT'S INVESTING MISTAKES

The idea that you try to time purchases based on what you think business is going to do in the next year or two, I think that's the greatest mistake that investors make because it's always uncertain. People say it's a time of uncertainty. It was uncertain on September 10, 2001, people just didn't know it. It's uncertain every single day. So, take uncertainty as part of being involved in investment at all. But uncertainty can be your friend. I mean, when people are scared, they pay less for things. We try to price. We don't try to time at all.[1]

WARREN BUFFETT

INTRODUCTION

Everybody makes mistakes, even Warren Buffett. But he does not agonize over them. What separates Buffett from others who refuse to admit or examine their errors in judgment is his willingness to scrutinize his decisions and learn from those that did not turn out as he'd expected. As he put it when I visited with him in 2009, only one hitter in Major League Baseball history has hit over .400 (Ted Williams hit .406 in 1941), and even then he failed nearly 60 percent of the time. Worse than taking a swing and a miss, in Buffett's view, is the failure to recognize an opportunity.

"The most important mistakes are ones of omission—those that do not show up in statements, but rather are missed opportunities," he said. "The things I needed to do, and can do, but did not do them will constitute my biggest mistakes in life."

In this chapter, I examine some of Buffett's investing mistakes—both ill-advised purchases he made and opportunities he missed.

1942: Cities Service

At age eleven, Buffett purchased his first stock: six shares of Cities Service (a natural gas company)[2] preferred stock, for $38 per share (three for himself and three for his sister, Doris).[3] Unfortunately, the stock quickly dropped to $27, and he began to sweat because he didn't want his sister to lose any money. Fortunately, the stock rose back to $40, and he sold it, only to watch it climb to $200 a share.[4] This was Buffett's first lesson in investing in the stock market: Be patient, and don't let the whims of Mr. Market influence your behavior.

1952: Sinclair Gas Station

One of Buffett's first investment mistakes was the purchase of a Sinclair service station when he was twenty-one years old. He bought it with a friend in Omaha for $2,000, or 20 percent of his net worth at that time. He soon learned that the larger Texaco station across the street consistently outsold his station. This was due to Texaco's well-known brand and loyal customers. Buffett's opportunity cost for this deal was $6 billion in today's dollars.

The experience was an early lesson for Buffett. He learned how powerful brand name recognition is.[5] Beyond that, the experience showed Buffett the essential value of studying a company's ledger sheet before diving in. He constantly emphasizes the importance of branding, and he makes sure that all of his employees understand its importance too.

1952: GEICO

In 1951, Buffett invested more than 50 percent of his net worth in GEICO. (This amounted to 350 shares at $29⅜ a share, for a total cost of $10,281.25.) By the end of 1951, he had a 28 percent return, which was 65 percent of his total net worth. This flush of quick success, however, prompted Buffett to make a serious mistake. In 1952, he sold his entire position in GEICO to invest in Western Insurance Securities. Western Insurance looked like a bargain, and Benjamin Graham had taught Buffett all about bargain-hunting. But over the next twenty years, Buffett would see the value of the GEICO stock he'd sold balloon to well over $1 million. He'd pulled the trigger too early. It taught Buffett a lesson that would shape his investment behavior ever since. He was learning that he needed to hold on to great businesses for the long term.

1964: American Express Stock

In 1963, American Express became involved in a fraud that caused losses of $180 million, or $1.52 billion in today's dollars.[6] This caused the price of American Express stock to drop more than 50 percent.

Buffett used Philip Fisher's scuttlebutt methodology to examine the effect of this incident on the company. He realized that people were still using their American Express cards and checks to pay for restaurant meals, shopping, banking, and traveling. He also evaluated the financials of the company. As a result, in 1964 he invested 25 percent of Berkshire's partnership assets in American Express—and two years later, when he sold, the shares had doubled in value. The deal made his investors $20 million.

No doubt, this was a brilliant investment. However, if he had held on to that investment, it would be worth billions today. So again, he was learning that he needed to hold on to great businesses for the long term.

1962–1964: Berkshire Hathaway

As I mentioned in chapter 2, Buffett initially offered to sell his stake in a textile business known as Berkshire Hathaway for $11.50 a share in the 1960s. But after receiving a tender offer in the mail for $11.375 per share, he became angry enough to buy the entire company and fire its owner. Buffett then attempted to run the textile business for twenty years as it continued to lose money.

The lesson here is pretty clear: When investing, do not act out of emotion. Buffett has called the Berkshire Hathaway purchase the biggest investment mistake of his life—one that cost him billions in today's dollars. This is a prime example of his insistence that the most important skill in investing is controlling your temperament. I suspect that one reason he kept the failed company's name for his own investment operation was to be constantly reminded of this act of pique. By his estimation, if he had put the same investment into an insurance company, Berkshire Hathaway the investment firm would be $200 billion more valuable than it already is. As he put it: "When a manager with a reputation for brilliance meets up with a business with a reputation for bad economics, it is the reputation of the business that remains intact."[7]

1966: Hochschild, Kohn & Co.

Buffett's first outright purchase of a business was Hochschild, Kohn & Co., a privately owned Baltimore department store. In 1966, he and two partners, Charlie Munger and Sandy Gottesman, purchased all of the store's stock.[8] With Hochschild Kohn, they were getting (1) a business selling for less than book value, (2) a great management team, (3) a cushion of unrecorded real estate value, and (4) a cushion of significant LIFO inventory.[9] LIFO (last in, first out) understates the value of inventory on the books since only low-cost inventory from years past sticks around.

All of these things were potentially valuable attributes. But Hochschild Kohn was, first and foremost, a retailer, and retail is a notoriously challenging sector.[10] The problem is that consumer preferences and sales channels are constantly changing, making any competitive advantage difficult to maintain. Low barriers to entry in physical retail also make competitive advantage difficult to maintain.

Many investors have learned this fact through painful experience. Consider that longtime retail behemoths Sears and JCPenney are basically dead today. As I write, the impact of shutdowns due to the COVID-19 pandemic is bringing other national retail chains to bankruptcy. Add to this trend the effects of technology. The way we shop is changing radically and rapidly. Nobody, not even Jeff Bezos, was prepared for the way that Amazon and e-commerce generally would destroy traditional brick-and-mortar companies, a phenomenon that accelerated during the shutdowns. This put added pressure on the costs of excess capacity that already existed in retail, and it squeezed margins across traditional sales channels.[11]

Changing consumer preferences, suboptimal locations, low barriers to entry, and other trend changes left Hochschild Kohn in the dust. When Buffett sold his stake in the retailer three years later, he got back his initial investment—nothing more. His takeaway: It is preferable "to buy a wonderful company at a fair price than a fair company at a wonderful price."[12] Munger would emphasize this idea when he joined Berkshire Hathaway, and it soon became a core tenet of Buffett's approach to investing.

1966 and 1995: Walt Disney Company

In 1966, Berkshire put 5 percent of the partnership's money into the Walt Disney Company, amounting to $4 million.[13] Within one year, he sold the investment for $6.2 million, making a handsome $2.2 million. Unfortunately, this would turn out to be one of the biggest mistakes of his career. That sale cost Buffett's partnership $17 billion in future appreciation, plus $1 billion in dividends.[14] Think about the opportunity cost—what Buffett could have done with all of that money. At the 1998 shareholders' meeting Buffett had this to say: "Certainly the Disney sale was a huge mistake, I should have been buying."[15]

He repeated this mistake in 1995. That year, Berkshire owned shares in Capital Cities/ABC, and when Disney announced that it was purchasing Capital Cities/ABC, Berkshire suddenly had 21 million shares of Disney stock. By the end of 2000, Berkshire sold all of it. If Buffett had held on, the stock would be worth $13.9 billion today.[16]

1968: Intel Corporation

Intel was founded in 1968 by semiconductor experts Robert Noyce and Gordon Moore.[17] Intel went on to become one of the top technology companies in the world. Buffett had an opportunity to invest in the company in 1968 because he was a trustee with Noyce at Grinnell College in Iowa. Noyce convinced Buffett's good friend, Joe Rosenfield, and Grinnell College's investment fund to invest in the company (both $100,000), but Buffett refused because there was no margin of safety. This came to be one of his biggest investment mistakes. But it follows his trend of not investing in technology companies and not having a margin of safety.

1975: Waumbec Textile Company

Although he regretted the purchase of the failing textile company Berkshire Hathaway, Buffett did the same thing thirteen years later, when he purchased Waumbec Mills—another New England textile firm. He apparently had learned only part of the necessary lesson. Yes, avoid investing out of emotion. But Buffett would see that he also needed to grasp the deeper lesson about not being seduced by bargains for their own sake.

"Can you believe that in 1975 I bought Waumbec Mills—another New England textile company?" he wrote to Berkshire Hathaway shareholders in his 2014 letter. "Of course, the purchase price was a 'bargain' based on the assets we received and the projected synergies with Berkshire's existing textile business. Nevertheless—surprise, surprise—Waumbec was a disaster, with the mill having to be closed down not many years later."[18]

Finally, Buffett got it: "If at first, you don't succeed, move on to a new strategy," he told CNBC in 2017.[19] Buffett also learned the disadvantages of owning a business dependent on a product or service subject to compression of margins.

1980–1990s: Microsoft

Buffett famously missed the opportunity to invest in Microsoft. As we have seen, he only feels comfortable investing in companies or industries he understands. This rule disqualified him from investing in Microsoft in its early days. Later, when Buffett developed a friendship with Microsoft cofounder Bill Gates, he worried that investing in Gates's company would put their relationship at risk or look improper to regulators, who might wonder about the possibility of the two men sharing insider information. The opportunity cost to Buffett was billions of dollars.

In hiring Todd Combs and Ted Weschler as fund managers in 2010 and 2012, Buffett was clearly acknowledging that his ignorance of tech would cost Berkshire, and this could no longer stand.

My takeaway: Do not be afraid to educate yourself on areas outside your field of competence—or else be prepared to delegate to those with greater knowledge.

1989: US Airways

Buffett has seen consistently lackluster results investing in airlines. Yet he has repeatedly come back to the well, such that he joked in 2002 that he was an "aeroholic."[20]

His first foray into airlines came in 1989, when US Airways chief executive officer (CEO) Ed Colodny convinced Buffett to buy in as a way of protecting the airline from hostile takeover by a hedge fund. Buffett purchased $358 million in convertible preferred stock with an annual rate of return of 9.25 percent.[21] The strike price to turn his investment into stock was $60, and the price when he bought was $52. But Buffett was never able to convert his investment because the stock never hit $60. Colodny recalled Buffett cashing out as soon as he was able and walking away with his principal back, but not much more.[22]

In a 2002 interview, Buffett acknowledged his penchant for getting burned by airline stocks, observing that the industry had "eaten up capital over the past century like almost no other business because people seem to keep coming back to it and putting fresh money in."[23]

Airlines' enormous fixed costs, strong labor unions, and commodity pricing combined to make a particularly poor recipe for success, he said. And yet he did not learn his lesson with US Airways. Buffett would go on to buy stock in four other airlines between 2016 and 2020.

"I have an 800 number now that I call if I get the urge to buy an airline stock," he joked. "I call at two in the morning and I say: 'My name is Warren, and I am an aeroholic.' And then they talk me down."[24]

Buffett's decisions around airline investments seem to have been influenced by his expectation that consolidation within the industry would lead to increasing profitability. He also may have overemphasized the benefit of high barriers to entry as a sustainable means of producing attractive returns for shareholders.

1991: Salomon Brothers

One of Buffett's worst investments was Salomon Brothers. A series of scandals in the early 1990s nearly forced Salomon into bankruptcy, which prompted him to launch an emergency takeover of the firm. He already owned a $700 million stake in Salomon (12 percent of the company, which he'd acquired in 1987).[25]

One of the scandals involved a trader who submitted illegal bids for government securities in late 1990. The trader attempted to corner the market by purchasing more than the 35 percent share any single bidder was permitted to submit in an auction of U.S. Treasury securities.[26] The bank's internal investigators found two illegal bids worth $6 billion in five-year Treasury notes.[27] But when this maneuver came to light, the trader was not fired. The following year, in May 1991, Salomon repeated the maneuver, again cornering the Treasuries market. But this time the Securities and Exchange Commission caught on. Salomon was fined $290 million, and its CEO, John Gutfreund, was fired.[28] The trader responsible for both instances was sentenced to four months in a minimum-security prison for lying to regulators.[29]

All of this illegal activity compelled Buffett to testify at a congressional hearing. He began by apologizing for the illegal deeds, emphasizing that most Salomon employees were honorable people, and promising the firm's wholehearted cooperation with any federal investigation. "In the end, the spirit about compliance is as important or more so than words about compliance," he said. Then he continued:

> I want the right words, and I want the full range of internal controls. But I also have asked every Salomon employee to be his or her own compliance officer. After they first obey all rules, I then want employees to ask themselves whether they are willing to have any contemplated act appear the next day on the front page of their local paper, to be read by their spouses, children, and friends, with the reporting done by an informed and critical reporter. If they follow this test, they need not fear my other message to them: Lose money for the firm, and I will be understanding; lose a shred of reputation for the firm, and I will be ruthless.[30]

Buffett got out of the whole affair when Travelers purchased Salomon Brothers for $9 billion in 1997. Buffett's take was $1.7 billion, so he made a $1 billion profit.[31] In this purely fiscal sense, Salomon was not technically a mistake. But it left a bad taste in Buffett's mouth, which underscored his longtime focus on the importance of honesty and integrity to any brand.

1993: Dexter Shoe Company

In 1993, Buffett bought Dexter Shoe Company for $433 million in Berkshire stock.[32] At the time, Dexter was one of the most reputable shoe companies in the world. My feeling is that Buffett succumbed to overconfidence bias and failed to account for the effects of cheap labor from overseas and how they might compromise Dexter's brand-based competitive advantage.

Buffett said this in the 2015 shareholder letter: "Our once-prosperous Dexter operation folded, putting 1,600 employees in a small Maine town out of work. Many were past the point in life at which they could learn another trade. We lost our entire investment, which we could afford, but many workers lost a livelihood they could not replace."[33] The value of that stock today would be around

$9 billion.[34] More important, though, is the opportunity cost and what could have been done with that $9 billion.

1998: General Re

In 1998, Berkshire issued 272,200 shares to purchase the reinsurance company General Re, an act that increased the volume of Berkshire's shares by 21.8 percent.[35]

Two things went wrong with this deal. The company had too much exposure to financial derivatives, and it had a bad reputation. Buffett stated at the 2009 Berkshire annual meeting, "I was dead wrong, in 1998, when I bought it, in thinking that it was the Gen Re of fifteen years earlier, which had absolutely the premier reputation in the insurance world."[36]

Buffett avoided disaster due to his extensive business experience. On the derivative front, he instructed the Gen Re team to unwind as many of the company's derivatives as possible, as quickly as possible. This was Buffett acting swiftly to limit the impact of a potential disaster rather than waiting around to see if anything would get better, just as he did in early 2020 with the airline stocks.[37] He also replaced the top management team. "My error caused Berkshire shareholders to give far more than they received (a practice that—despite the Biblical endorsement—is far from blessed when you are buying businesses)," Buffett acknowledged.[38]

In plain terms, his mistake cost Berkshire shareholders $800 million in 2001. The lessons here? Always run through a worst-case-scenario analysis and determine what an action could cost you.[39] Also, if something goes wrong, it is sensible to cut your losses and get out as soon as possible. Furthermore, good managers are key to the success of a business.[40]

1998–Present: Google

Sometimes there are opportunities right under your nose.[41] Google's founders Sergey Brin and Larry Page approached Buffett in the late 2000s about investing in their company, and he passed, incorrectly viewing Google as merely another search engine rather than a powerful advertising vehicle. He should have known better, because Berkshire Hathaway was already familiar with Google's business model, having used it to advertise GEICO. Once again, Buffett and Munger missed out on a tech investment that could have netted them billions of dollars.

2003: Walmart

In the 1990s, Buffett was buying Walmart. His goal was to purchase 100 million shares at $23 a share. However, as he was buying, the stock moved up a few pennies over his ideal price, so in 2003 he quit buying.[42] At the 2004 Berkshire shareholder meeting, Buffett stated the following:

> I cost us about $10 billion. And Charlie said it didn't sound like the worst idea I ever came up with, which is—from him, I mean, it was just ungodly praise. And then, you know, we bought a little and then it moved up a little bit. And I thought, "Well, you know, maybe it will come back" or what—Who knows what I thought? I mean, you know, only my psychiatrist can tell me. And that thumb sucking, reluctance to pay a little more—the current cost is in the area of $10 billion.[43]

As of 2019, that 100 million-share position would have been worth around $12 billion, and that excludes dividends over the past two decades. The total return is substantially higher. Walmart's total annual return for shareholders is 7.5 percent since the start of 2004.[44]

The primary takeaway from this investment blunder is it's better to pay for quality if you believe in your idea. There is no perfect price. If you think a stock is undervalued, paying an extra 5 percent for it is not going to kill you.[45]

2006–2014: Tesco

Buffett bought his first shares of Tesco, the largest grocery chain in Britain, in 2006. But changes in the company's management began to take hold, and the result was a steady decrease in the company's profitability. Buffett did not heed the signs. Despite a profit warning in 2012, Buffett increased his Tesco stake to over 5 percent. The following year, when he had finally "soured" on the company's management, he sold off 114 million of his 415 million shares.

Buffett's fault here was holding on—perhaps due to loss aversion—when he should have divested completely. Tesco's problems did not improve. Instead, its market share continued to shrink, its margins were being squeezed, and accounting problems began to surface.

Buffett continued to sell Tesco shares throughout 2014, and his eventual after-tax losses totaled $444 million, or one-fifth of 1 percent of Berkshire's net worth.[46]

The lesson? Get out at the first whiff of poor management, or else replace the management.

"My leisurely pace in making sales would prove expensive. Charlie calls this sort of behavior 'thumb-sucking.' (Considering what my delay cost us, he is being kind)," Buffett would later concede. "In the world of business, bad news often surfaces serially: You see a cockroach in your kitchen; as the days go by, you meet his relatives."[47]

2008: ConocoPhillips

As I detailed in the discussion of herding bias in chapter 7, Buffett disregarded his tried-and-true rule about buying when there is blood in the streets. Instead, he let his emotions take over and purchased ConocoPhillips when oil was near its high. This move wound up costing Berkshire several billion dollars.

2011: Lubrizol Corporation

In early January 2011, David Sokol, a Berkshire executive, purchased a large amount of stock in Lubrizol and then told Buffett about the company. It would be an attractive purchase, he said. Berkshire heeded this advice and bought Lubrizol in March 2011 for around $9 billion. That deal made Sokol $3 million in increased stock value—a fact that did not go unnoticed by the media.

The executive eventually resigned.[48] But Buffett realized, too late, that he had not done enough due diligence when purchasing Lubrizol. Buffett's lesson: Your reputation is your most valuable asset. Do everything you can to protect it by asking more questions than you think are necessary.[49]

2011–2018: IBM

In 2011, Berkshire Hathaway bought 64 million shares of IBM for $10.7 billion (an average price of $170 each).[50] At the time, Buffett was more attracted to IBM's business in ancillary office services than computer hardware. It looked like business services would offer stability and growth due to IBM's dominant position in outsourcing information technology. But a few years later, cloud computing would begin its ascent, drastically undercutting IBM's position.

By 2017, Buffett was more sanguine about the future of Apple than he was about IBM, and he continued to lose confidence in Big Blue as it became increasingly clear that IBM was on the wrong side of the changes shaping the industry.

"When it got above $180, we actually sold a reasonable amount of stock,"[51] he said at the time. By May 2018, Buffett had sold all of his shares in the mid-$140 range.[52]

2013: Energy Future Holdings

Energy Future Holdings (EFH) was founded in 2007 with $8 billion in equity and a lot of debt. Its purpose was to purchase electric utilities assets in Texas. Buffett plunged into this investment by purchasing about $2 billion of EFH's debt, a move he made without consulting Munger. In his 2013 letter to shareholders, Buffett acknowledged this mistake. It underscores the importance of a core principle he had previously used to great advantage: Have someone at hand who can act as a sounding board for your ideas and isn't afraid to disagree with you. Buffett's lack of consultation with Munger likely cost Berkshire $873 million. "That was a big mistake," he told shareholders. "Next time I'll call Charlie."[53,54]

2015: Kraft Foods and H. J. Heinz Co.

On February 14, 2013, Berkshire and 3G Capital purchased H. J. Heinz Co. for $28 billion. In 2015, they invested $10 billion and merged Kraft Foods with H. J. Heinz. This valued Kraft at about $46 billion.[55]

But most of the Kraft Heinz portfolio included "center of the store" mainstays, while consumer tastes were rapidly turning toward periphery and organic products. A major part of this shift came in the form of increased competition from private-label brands, like Kirkland from Costco. Walmart, Target, Kroger, and other food retailers also have been expanding their private-label brands. For example, Kroger's Simple Truth organic food line is now a $3 billion brand.[56]

Buffett failed to anticipate this shift in consumer taste, as well as the ways that other food outlets were meeting it. The increasing competition, reduced sales, and lower profits translated into a $15.4 billion write-down for Kraft in 2019, which decreased its dividend by 36 percent, from $2.50 to $1.60 per share annually.[57]

Private labels have continued to increase their market share. Their sales made up 16 percent of the market before the start of the pandemic in 2020, up 2 percent since 2014. And while conventional product sales grew by 24 percent, private-brand sales significantly outpaced that rate, surging by 29 percent.[58]

"It's still a wonderful business, in that it uses about $7 billion of tangible assets and earns $6 billion pretax on that," Buffett told CNBC. But he admitted in hindsight that he had overpaid for Kraft: "We paid $100 billion in tangible assets. So, for us, it has to earn $107 billion, not just the $7 billion that the business employs."[59]

2015–2016: Precision Castparts Corporation

Berkshire Hathaway purchased Precision Castparts Corporation for $32.1 billion in 2016.[60] The company was the world's premier supplier of key aerospace components, such as fasteners and turbine blades for large aircraft, as well as pipes for power stations and the oil-and-gas sector.

One of the firms that Precision Castparts owned was a German company, Schultz Holding, which it had purchased for $870 million in 2017. But after closing the deal, Precision Castparts discovered that Schultz had grossly inflated its value through fraudulent accounting maneuvers.

Arbitrators agreed. In 2020, Precision Castparts won a $696 million ruling on the matter, and Buffett admitted his misjudgment of the books: "I was wrong . . . in judging the average amount of future earnings and, consequently, wrong in my calculation of the proper price to pay for the business," he wrote. "[Precision Castparts] is far from my first error of that sort. But it's a big one. . . . I'll make more mistakes in the future—you can bet on that."[61]

2019: Amazon

Buffett failed to invest in Bezos's revolutionary company until 2019. "I have been an idiot for not buying," he told CNBC, by way of announcing that this was about to change.[62]

Berkshire began buying Amazon in 2019. As of March 2022, Berkshire owned 533,300 shares of Amazon at $2,910 a share, equal to $1.55 billion. Amazon recently announced a 20-for-1 stock split (pending shareholder approval). This means that for every share of Amazon you have, you would get nineteen more shares. It's the same amount—you just have more shares of a cheaper stock. This gives the opportunity for more investors to purchase Amazon. At the end of the second quarter of 2022, Berkshire owned 10,666,000 shares of Amazon. As of August 2022, it is worth $1.43 billion.

2016–2020: Airlines

As noted earlier in this chapter, as well as in chapter 9, Berkshire invested in American Airlines, United Airlines, Delta Airlines, and Southwest Airlines in

November 2016. Then, during the 2020 shareholder meeting, Buffett announced that Berkshire had sold its $6.1 billion position in airlines because of the coronavirus pandemic. This contributed to losses of $50 billion for Berkshire Hathaway in the first quarter of 2020—the largest quarterly loss in the investment firm's history.

Some may disagree with my labeling the airline stocks as one of Buffett's mistakes, considering that it was the virus, not any failure of judgment or business insight, that precipitated the airlines' severe losses. But I disagree. Buffett's prior investment experience had taught him that airlines were a bad bet, and he disregarded his own hard-earned lesson. Pandemic or not, the airline industry is highly sensitive to economic cycles. Buffett knew this and had already bemoaned its high fixed costs and unionized labor. Despite all of this data, he purchased $9,755,058,860 in airline stocks, making them 4.5 percent of Berkshire's total portfolio.

What accounts for this failure to learn from past experience? My belief is that consolidation within the industry, which created less competition between airlines on ticket prices, reassured Buffett that this era would be different and lead to attractive returns for shareholders. That might have been true. But the coronavirus showed how truly fickle the airline industry can be.

SUMMARY

"To invest successfully does not require a stratospheric IQ, unusual business insights, or inside information. What is needed is a sound intellectual framework for making decisions and the ability to keep emotions from corroding the framework," Buffett wrote in the preface to *The Intelligent Investor.*[63]

Most of Buffett's mistakes come from times when he failed to hew to his own intellectual framework for decision-making. Despite these expensive errors, Berkshire Hathaway's track record still boasts some of the highest investment returns ever recorded. Buffett himself believes that mistakes in investing are unavoidable. The key is to learn from them and avoid repeating them.

The most reliable way for investors to do this is to become aware of the various biases at play in decision-making. We all have them—even Buffett. But if you keep track of your mistakes, it is possible to identify blind spots and correct for them.

PART IV

WARREN BUFFETT

The Person

CHAPTER 11

SHAREHOLDER MEETINGS, LIFE ADVICE, AND PHILANTHROPY

I measure success by how many people love me. And the best way to be loved is to be lovable.[1]

WARREN BUFFETT

Buffett has said that he has as much fun now as when he had $10,000. Personal satisfaction in life does not come with money, but in what you are doing with what you have, he believes. For this reason, Buffett counsels students never to take a job just for the money; the primary driver must be that it is something you love. The man who has enough money to go anywhere and do anything he wants says that the engine of his happiness is relationships—with family, loved ones, and a job that he considers a "vacation every day." He noted to a writer from the *Financial Times* in 2019. "I can't buy time, I can't buy love, but I can do anything else with money, pretty much. And why do I get up every day and jump out of bed and am excited? It is because I love what I do and love the people I do it with."[2]

Money and Happiness

I have already alluded to Buffett's famed frugality and disdain for corporate trappings. He dislikes schedules, meetings, company rituals, and managing people. His office has been situated in the simple Kiewit Plaza building for more than sixty years. The billionaire investor does not believe in the current trend of astronomically high salaries for corporate chief executive officers (CEOs).

When I visited with him and a group of students in 2009, he compared this practice to sports. Paying a .400 hitter was understandable, he said, but not a .240 hitter, and there were far too many .240-hitters making slugger salaries.

Since 1980, he has drawn a salary of $100,000 annually from Berkshire Hathaway, plus $289,000 in other compensation. This amount, which was less than twice the median pay at Berkshire in 2018,[3] is more than enough for him to live on, Buffett observes. He regularly speaks out against the ways that ballooning management salaries have contributed to the growing wealth gap in the United States. He also has never cashed in a share of Berkshire stock for personal use.

"If you think you are going to be a lot happier with 2*x* instead of *x*, you are probably making a big mistake; you will get in trouble if you think that making 10*x* or 20*x* will make you happy because then you will do things you should not do, like cut corners," Buffett told my students when we visited him in 2009. He emphasized that people do best when they work at jobs they love: "If I could make $100 million with some guy that made my stomach churn, I would say no."[4]

Buffett lives in the same home that he purchased in Omaha in 1957, for $31,500.[5] In 1971, he and his first wife, Susan, bought a second house, overlooking the ocean in Laguna Beach, California, for $150,000. After her death, Buffett sold it for $7.5 million.

For many years, until Buffett's daughter Susie drew the line, he drove a Lincoln Town Car with license plates that said THRIFTY.[6] Today, Buffett drives a 2014 Cadillac XTS. But other than this one extravagance, Buffett lives simplicity as a core value. He does not believe in owning lots of houses, cars, boats, or other toys. They only make life more complicated than it needs to be, he has said. "My suits are old, my wallet's old, my car's old, and I have lived in the same house since 1957, so I hang on to things."[7]

BERKSHIRE HATHAWAY ANNUAL SHAREHOLDERS' MEETINGS

For all Buffett's frugality, the annual Berkshire Hathaway shareholders' meeting has traditionally been a lavish party. I have been to twelve of these events, and they always have an atmosphere somewhere between a rock show and a religious revival (though Buffett himself is agnostic).

The very first Berkshire Hathaway shareholders' meeting was held in a cafeteria with a dozen people, in 1965. Nowadays, these events routinely draw more than 40,000 attendees. Hotel rooms are booked years in advance. The Omaha airport fills with private jets. Buffett calls these gatherings "Woodstock for capitalists" because people think nothing of standing (or sleeping) in line overnight so they can nab the best seats possible when the CHI Health Center building opens to them at 7 a.m. The meetings attract shareholders from across the world, who come to celebrate Berkshire's successes and hear its two leading minds, Buffett and Charlie Munger, discuss their views about business and life.

The meetings were livestreamed during the COVID-19 pandemic, and while that provided access to many more people, it necessarily nixed one of my favorite parts of the experience: talking to financially savvy folks from around the world. While waiting to get in, I have spoken over the years with investors, grandmothers, lawyers, brokers, and students. One of my most memorable talks was with another student of Buffett like myself, who mentioned a great new stock called Google. This was in 2016, when shares of the world's most powerful search engine were selling for around $700. Today, Google stock goes for around $3,000 a share. Indeed, the best part of going to a Buffett shareholder meeting is hobnobbing with and learning from the people in attendance.

The Mad Dash

When the doors opened at 7 a.m., I sprinted toward the front as the Pink Floyd song "Money" blasted all around me. Berkshire's board of directors was present, including Microsoft cofounder Bill Gates. And before launching into the day's agenda, we attendees could nibble on a complimentary continental breakfast and/or visit an exhibit hall featuring some twenty Berkshire Hathaway companies like See's Candies, Brooks Brothers, Fruit of the Loom, Pampered Chef, and Borsheims, all selling their products. All attendees received a 20 percent discount.

At the accompanying book fair, several entrepreneurs who had written about Buffett signed their books and spoke with guests. In 2010, Bill Gates, Sr., father of the Microsoft cofounder, was signing the book he wrote, *Showing Up for Life: Thoughts on the Gifts of a Lifetime*.

Highlighting the carnival-like feeling was a newspaper-throwing competition, in honor of Buffett's childhood paper route. Whoever threw a newspaper closest to the door of a Clayton mobile home stationed in the hall won a prize—though they had to beat Buffett first.

The Movie

The meeting usually kicks off with an hour-long movie—part comedy, part business—in which Buffett touches on whatever life lessons are on his mind. Munger is almost always in the film, often accompanied by such celebrities as Arnold Schwarzenegger, Jimmy Buffett (no relation), Susan Lucci, and Ernie Banks. One year, LeBron James turned up. Other surprise appearances have featured such businesspeople as Bob Iger, Susan Decker, and Kathy Ireland.

To cap it off, cheerleaders from the University of Nebraska often make an appearance, waving their pompoms to get the crowd revved up.

Question-and-Answer Session

Then comes the main event—a five-hour question-and-answer session with shareholders. Munger and Buffett sit at the middle of a table, facing their board of directors, and answer questions from CNBC journalists, experts in insurance, railroads, and energy, and Berkshire Hathaway shareholders, who line up at thirteen microphones to see if they can shake loose a few nuggets of wisdom from the famed "Oracle of Omaha."

Buffett and Munger do their usual comedy routine throughout these sessions, bantering with one another as they answer questions and scarf down enormous quantities of chocolate fudge and peanut brittle made by See's Candies, washing it down with bottles of Coca-Cola.

Despite the tens of thousands of people in the arena, there is total silence when Buffett and Munger speak, with attendees straining to hear every word. In 2016, the audience included 3,000 people who'd flown in from China and sat in a separate room with their interpreters.

"What would you have done differently in life in your search for happiness?" one person asked.

Buffett responded, "Earlier in life, I decided that my favorite employer was myself. So, nothing." With his simple, straightforward response, he revealed himself to be, at heart, an entrepreneur.

Other questions have touched on everything from business and economics to personal growth, Buffett's and Munger's thoughts on success, and how to live a fulfilling life.

BUFFETT'S VALUES AND KEYS TO SUCCESS

Buffett has long attributed much of his success to his first wife, Susan (Susie) Thompson Buffett. Her influence turned him from a Republican into a Democrat and increased his awareness of the importance of human rights, equity, and diversity. He has said that she made him a whole person.

Yet when the two met in 1950, Susie thought that Warren was a jerk. Her father sat Susie down and explained that the young financier with the prodigious intellect was not like other people. She might have a hard time talking to him about certain topics, but he had a heart of gold. Susie listened to her father, marrying Warren in 1952 in Omaha at the Dundee Presbyterian Church, not far from where Buffett grew up.

Although the Buffetts separated as a couple in 1977, Susie and Warren remained legally married until her death from oral cancer in 2004. In 2006, Buffett married his second wife, Astrid Menks, who had been a good friend of Susie. He has always emphasized Susie's positive influence. She filled a void in him, he said.

Howard Buffett's Values

Values have been both an essential component of Buffett's belief system and key to his overall appeal—his brand, if you will. Initially, he emulated the values he'd learned from his father, Howard, who measured himself by means of two scorecards. The first monitored his inner life: "Am I being a good person? Am I doing the right things? Am I treating people correctly? Am I honest?" Howard asked himself constantly.

The second, outer scorecard, measured such things as "How big is my house? How nice are my car and my clothes? How much money do I make? What do people think of me?"[8]

For Howard Buffett, the inner scorecard always mattered more.

Parenting amid Wealth

Each of Buffett's three children attended public schools in Omaha. And as they grew up, it became increasingly important to Buffett that the family's enormous wealth did not hinder his kids.

The perfect inheritance to leave one's children, he said, was "enough money so that they would feel they could do anything, but not so much that they could do nothing."[9] He felt it was essential to instill in them the drive to become successful.

For example, in 1977, Buffett's youngest son, Peter, was a first-year student at Stanford University. Buffett had just given the nineteen-year-old $90,000 in Berkshire stock, with the stipulation that this would be the only inheritance Peter would receive. The $90,000 (equivalent to $421,360 in today's dollars, not counting stock appreciation) came from the sale of his grandfather's farm, which Warren had converted to Berkshire Hathaway stock.[10]

Peter had always intended to become a musician and music producer, so after much consideration, he dropped out of Stanford, bought some equipment, and devoted himself to perfecting his art. Peter could have gone to work for his father and become vastly wealthy. But he says that he has never regretted his choice: "I used my nest egg to buy something infinitely more valuable than money: I used it to buy time."[11]

Peter had learned from his father the importance of pursuing what you love, and he understood that his ability to do so was an unusual privilege, "a gift I had not earned," as he put it in his memoir, *Life Is What You Make of It: Find Your Own Path to Fulfillment*.[12] "There are many people who are privileged, either in terms of money, emotional support or some sort of unique talent or opportunity. But they fail to understand the value of time," he wrote. "Without those hundreds of unpaid hours spent fiddling with my recording gear, I would not have found my sound or approach."[13]

Even though Peter had enough money to build the foundation for a life in music, it was not so much that he would never have to work. "I learned more in those difficult times about myself and my resiliency than I ever would have if I had a pile of money and glided through life," he says. "I honestly feel that my father's refusal [to let me take the easy way out] was an act of love—as if to say, I believe in you, and you do not need my help."[14]

Despite Buffett's obvious concern for his children, they recall him as a somewhat distant parent—physically present, but always preoccupied with his thoughts, or else reading. It was difficult to get his attention. "You're Warren Buffett's son? But you seem so normal!" people often said to Peter. He wrote, "I have always taken it as a compliment—a compliment not to me, but to my family. . . . Why? Because what we mean by 'normal' really comes down to this: that a person can function effectively and find acceptance among other human beings. To put it another way, it means that a person has been given the best possible chance to make the most of his or her own life."[15]

Peter Buffett believes that the values he absorbed at home are fundamental to his ability to function as a normal person. At the top of the list of these values was a sense of trust, a belief that the world and its people are essentially good and worth fighting to improve. As he put it, "People assume an easy life of money and privilege. But the support, the privilege, really comes from having two parents that said and believed that I could do anything. That support did not come in the form of a check. That support came in the form of love and nurturing and respect for us finding our way, falling, figuring out how to get up ourselves."[16]

Buffett's two other children, Howard and Susie, followed paths that more closely tracked with their father's. More on them below.

Integrity and Character

When making any new hire at Berkshire Hathaway, Buffett says he considers character the most important attribute of any candidate. Buffett himself lives his values regarding integrity by never participating in a hostile takeover of any company. He insists that it is better to proceed honestly, even if it means making less profit, rather than acting in a manner that can be questioned. This characteristic has led to Buffett becoming a sought-after voice on critical economic issues.

Anyone Buffett hires, he trusts. And he empowers his employees to make decisions without seeking his signoff or permission. But if there is bad news, Buffett expects his staff to tell him immediately and never try to hide it.

There are more than 360,000 employees in the sixty-five companies owned by Berkshire Hathaway, so many people that someone, somewhere, is likely to be doing something illegal, Buffett has acknowledged. He cannot stop this, but he does have safeguards.

First among them is Berkshire's five-page Code of Conduct and Ethics, which addresses insider trading, protection and proper use of assets, conflicts of interest, confidentiality, compliance with laws, rules and regulations, timely and truthful public disclosure, and accounting irregularities, and emphasizes the importance of the firm's reputation above all else.

When in doubt, Buffett says, remember this rule of thumb: "I want employees to ask themselves whether they are willing to have any contemplated act appear the next day on the front page of their local paper—to be read by their spouses, children, and friends—with the reporting done by an informed and critical reporter."[17]

The Value of Communication and Creative Thinking

When asked late in life about the qualities he viewed as important for building a successful career in business, Buffett emphasized persistence, creativity, and thinking "way outside of the box."[18] Other characteristics that he admires are generosity, sharing credit with others, and strong leadership abilities. Buffett also believes that if you admire someone, you should emulate that person's behavior.

But during a visit with my students, he highlighted something else: "I recommend that you improve your oral and written communication skills. This will improve your pay by at least 50 percent. They will not teach you this in business schools. Good communication of good ideas gets you much further in life." When trying to fill jobs at Berkshire Hathaway, Buffett added, "80 percent of the people that I run into need to improve their ability at explaining their ideas."[19]

Wealth Inequality

Like many other observers of the U.S. economy, businesspeople have become increasingly concerned about the nation's widening wealth gap. Buffett says that he is particularly sensitive to this problem and he is willing to pay more taxes to address it.

In 2011, when a student asked him about his views on the Occupy Wall Street movement, Buffett implied that he could understand where the anger came from. U.S. tax laws have indisputably "tilted toward the wealthy," he said. "In 1992, the top 400 incomes averaged $40 million a year. By 2011, the average was $220 million; a 5-fold increase since 1992. Since then, the tax rate has dropped by 7 percent. I pay less percentage of taxes now than 40–50 years ago."

But he does not believe that giving workers money, such as through a Universal Basic Income program, is the answer to what he sees as a structural problem. Buffett believes that the rich should take more responsibility in taking care of people who cannot take care of themselves.

Unless something is done, Buffett believes, the wealth gap will continue to widen to levels that are unsustainable. While suggesting that part of the answer is worker retraining, which will allow more people to take part in a tech-driven global economy, Buffett has cautioned against doing anything extreme. "The question is, what happens to the person who is a decent citizen, doesn't have market skills? And we can solve that," he told CNBC in 2019. "A rich family can handle if they've got six children and one of them is not as good in the market, is just good in every other personal quality. They take care of him. And we've got $60,000 of GDP per capita in the United States. That's six times what it was when I was born in real terms. So, we can take care of people and we should. But we shouldn't screw up the market system."[20]

BUFFETT, INHERITANCE, AND PHILANTHROPY

Buffett has said that his children will not inherit a significant portion of his wealth, and that he is against dynastic fortunes. Instead, almost all of his money will go to philanthropy. He put it this way:

> I do not have a problem with guilt about money. The way I see it is that my money represents an enormous number of claim checks on society. It is like I have these little pieces of paper that I can turn into consumption. If I wanted to, I could hire 10,000 people to do nothing but paint my picture every day for the rest of my life. And the GNP would go up. But the utility of the product would be zilch, and I would be keeping those 10,000 people from doing AIDS research, or teaching, or nursing. I do not do that though. I do not use very many of those claim checks. There is nothing material I want very much. And I am going to give virtually all those claim checks to charity when my wife and I die.[21]

Originally, Buffett had no intention of being involved in the doling out of his net worth. He assumed that his wife, Susie, would outlive him, and she would oversee philanthropic activities with the money he left her. But life did not turn out that way; Susie died before her husband, and by that time, they had been separated for decades.

So, Buffett was pushed to confront his values within the realm of charitable giving. His humility prevailed as usual; Buffett does not believe in putting his name on buildings.[22] "I have more respect for the housekeeper who gives money on Sunday to charity than the person who puts their name on a building," he said to me and my students in 2009.

However, he has decided to give away all of his money. In 2018 and 2019, he began to make good on this commitment in a significant way by donating a total of $7 billion in Berkshire stock to five charities. The Bill and Melinda Gates Foundation, the largest recipient, received $36 billion from Buffett in 2006. Buffett also gave to charities run by his children: they include the Susan Thompson Buffett Foundation, the Sherwood Foundation, the Howard G. Buffett Foundation, and the NoVo Foundation.

When Buffett explained his decision to give 80 percent of his stock to the Gates Foundation, he told Berkshire shareholders that he believes in donating excess wealth to people who are smart, hardworking, and energized.[23] Buffett has given money to charities every year since 2006 and continues to give money every year. As of 2022, Buffett has donated a total of $46.1 billion to various charities.[24] By the time of his passing, Buffett will have contributed more than 99 percent of his fortune to charity.[25]

Bill and Melinda Gates Foundation

Buffett's $36 billion gift to the Bill and Melinda Gates Foundation in 2006 made history as the largest charitable donation ever made by an individual. The Gates Foundation works to eradicate global poverty by funding health-care and education initiatives, especially those targeted toward girls.

Susan Thompson Buffett and Sherwood Foundations

Buffett's daughter, Susie, runs the Susan Thompson Buffett Foundation and the Sherwood Foundation, both based in Omaha. The Susan Thompson Buffett Foundation, which was created in 1964, focuses on education by giving out 4,000 college scholarships to high school graduates in Nebraska who pursue undergraduate studies at any of Nebraska's public institutions of higher education. The Sherwood Foundation is committed to improving child and family welfare through community investment in public education, human services, and social justice. Susie is also a director on the Berkshire Hathaway board.

During my interview with Susie, I thanked her for giving out the scholarships and said that one of my friends got one. I told her that my friend had five kids, and it really helped him. It gave Susie such joy to hear that. She mentioned that people always come up to her and thank her for that. It seems that one of her biggest joys in life is helping others.

Howard G. Buffett Foundation

Howard, Buffett's elder son, is the chair of the Howard G. Buffett Foundation, which focuses on agriculture, nutrition, conservation, and humanitarian conflict issues. Howard is also a director on the Berkshire Hathaway board.

NoVo Foundation

Peter, Buffett's youngest child, was on *Barron's* list of the most effective philanthropists in 2009 and 2010. He directs the NoVo Foundation, which supports the prevention of violence against women, social and emotional learning, adolescent girls' rights, and indigenous communities in North America.

Glide Foundation

Buffett has donated to other charities in smaller amounts, including the Glide Foundation, which focuses on the homeless and otherwise needy in San Francisco. Every year, Buffett auctions off a lunch with himself to support Glide. In 2019, the winning bid was $4.6 million, made by a twenty-eight-year-old cryptocurrency entrepreneur. In 2022, Buffett announced that this year would be his last for these private luncheons. An anonymous person won with a bid of $19,000,100.[26]

The Giving Pledge

Buffett has urged other billionaires to follow his lead, joining him and Bill Gates in pledging to donate almost all of their fortunes to charity through the Giving Pledge. This effort was initiated by Buffett and Gates in 2010, and to date, it has succeeded in getting more than 231 billionaires from around the world to pledge $600 billion in donations. Some of the more famous sign-ons include Larry Ellison, Michael Bloomberg, Mark Zuckerberg and Priscilla Chan, Carl Icahn, Ray Dalio, Elon Musk, John Doerr, Leon Cooperman, Walter Scott

Jr., David Rockefeller, Barron Hilton, Ted Turner, Sheryl Sandberg, Seth Klarman, Sara Blakely, and T. Boone Pickens.

What is most striking about this group, beyond their immense wealth, is the diversity of political affiliations they represent—from liberal Democrats like Turner to fierce right wingers like Pickens, and every gradation in between—a testament to Buffett's integrity and the strength of his perseverance.

Girls, Inc. of Omaha

In 2015, Buffett donated his 2006 Cadillac DTS, with 20,310 miles on the odometer, to a charity auction. It sold for $122,500, more than ten times its $12,000 *Blue Book* value. The proceeds went to Girls, Inc. of Omaha, a charity long favored by the Buffett family.[27] Girls, Inc. supports the empowerment of Omaha girls through education and fitness programs that teach such skills as robotics, public speaking, financial literacy, and yoga.[28]

Foundation Goals

The idea behind all of Buffett's philanthropy is simple, but not easy: he is looking for swing-for-the-fences efforts that are important to society but do not have natural funding sources. He says of his trustees, "If they start giving half a million to this hospital and a million to that college, I will come back and haunt them."[29]

BUFFETT AND HAPPINESS

Luck, quite clearly, plays an enormous role in every life, and Buffett acknowledges this. He recognizes his own good fortune in being born into a stable family that valued education. But he also believes fiercely in the American value system, which says that any person can rise through persistence, no matter the circumstances at the beginning.

The fact is, most people in the United States are born into families that are middle-to-lower-middle class. The common denominator we share is that America still rewards hard work and does not place a cap on how far its citizens can advance.

With these values as his foundation, Buffett continues to preach the importance of striving to do work that you love rather than chasing wealth for its own sake. He insists that he has been happiest when giving, teaching, or otherwise helping others. I believe that these values are a major reason for Buffett's historic success.

Second only to Buffett's fame for enormous wealth is his renown for aphorisms on how to live a fulfilling life. I have included a few of them here.

Hang Around with People Who Are Better Than You

Buffett and Munger both emphasize that it is important to cultivate the company of people who are more successful or skillful than you, whatever your field of endeavor. Work for someone you admire, someone who will both challenge and teach you, someone whose presence inspires you to push beyond what you have done before. Seek out people who make you want to jump out of bed in the morning.[30]

The Most Important Decision You Will Make in Life

Buffett has repeatedly said the most pivotal decision in a person's life is not what school they attend, nor what career they choose. During talks with students from several universities in 2009, 2011, and 2018, he made the same interesting statement: "The most important decision you will make in your life is who you marry."[31]

One of the Worst Mistakes You Can Make in Life

The converse, then, is also true. According to Buffett, one of the worst mistakes you can make in life is not understanding people as well as you thought. He based this view on his own first marriage, after his wife, Susie, left him in 1977 to live in San Francisco and pursue her own career. However, this did not diminish Buffett's respect for her. They never divorced and were seen together at public events until her death in 2004.

When asked about the keys to happiness, Buffett has never mentioned a single possession or experience that can be purchased. He speaks only of the importance of surrounding yourself with people who love you. He calls himself the luckiest person in the world because he loves what he does for a living and is surrounded by people who love him. He describes this unconditional love as the most powerful force in life.

BUFFETT'S RECIPE FOR BECOMING LOVABLE

Love yourself and others unconditionally.
Maintain a positive attitude; be compassionate and understanding.
Show kindness to everyone and have integrity.
Smile; look people in the eye and be a good listener.
Be the kind of friend that you would want; help others.
Be real/vulnerable.
Cultivate gratitude.
Allow yourself to be imperfect and laugh at yourself.
Enjoy your life (people are attracted to others that are having fun).
Spend time with friends.
Try to enjoy your job.[32]

In short: Love what you do. Happiness is not about making money, although money is always nice to have.[33]

CHAPTER 12

A DAY WITH WARREN BUFFETT

The difference between successful people and really successful people is that really successful people say no to almost everything.[1]

WARREN BUFFETT

VISITS TO MEET WARREN BUFFETT IN OMAHA

For much of his career, Buffett routinely traveled the world, giving talks at universities about his business ideas, values, and overall approach to life. But in 2005, he decided it would be more efficient to invite groups of students from several schools to come to Omaha and visit with him.

I had the honor of attending three of these meetings, along with my students, in 2009, 2011, and 2018. I'd heard about the opportunity from a cousin of mine who lives in Omaha, but the first time I applied, in 2007, I was rejected. Furthermore, Buffett's secretary told me that the waiting list was so long I could not even get on it.

I was not deterred. I had a burning desire to learn as much as possible about the "Oracle of Omaha," one of the most prolific business minds of all time. But how was I going to get myself noticed among the hordes of other people who apparently felt the same way? I needed a project, a campaign, something that would set me apart. So, from 2008 to 2009, I wrote a case study examining how Buffett and Berkshire Hathaway had handled the Great Recession. It was accepted for publication by a respected academic journal, and I sent a copy to Buffett's office with a note requesting a visit.

2009 INVITATION

Within ten days, I received a letter from Buffett himself, informing me that my school, the University of Akron, had been moved to the top of the list for his session in November 2009 and I could bring twenty-seven students. This felt especially significant coming so soon after the Great Recession. We would have an opportunity to learn from Buffett about his view of what had happened and what the future held. We were one of six schools that got the nod for that day. (Buffett met with 162 students per day for six or seven days spread throughout the school year.)

We flew in to Omaha on a Thursday evening. The following morning, we began with a tour of Buffett's beloved Nebraska Furniture Mart. The tour was led by a grandson of the company's legendary founder, Mrs. B. Next, it was off to the main event—our two-hour question-and-answer session with the Oracle himself. That first year, we met with him in Berkshire's corporate office.

Along with us, there were business students from the University of Illinois, Texas Christian University, Boston College, University of Toronto, and the University of South Dakota. Mostly, they asked questions about the economy, Buffett's investment methodology, and his values. But they also probed his heart, including the reasons why he was inviting them to Omaha. Buffett told us that the most successful businesspeople he'd ever met were rarely those with Ivy League degrees, but rather people with the most business experience, tenacity, and willingness to pursue ideas seen as disruptive to the status quo.

We were prohibited from taking pictures or recordings, although everyone made detailed notes and shared them with me. What follow are a few examples of questions and answers from the session. (For a more complete record of that event, please see appendix 4.)

When surveying companies, what are the red flags that stand out when you look at a company?

> If you like 100 shares of a company, you should be willing to buy the entire company. I look at companies that I understand. I like to see track records over the past ten years, and I like to know where the company is going in the next ten to twenty years. I also like to focus on a limited number of areas.

I approach investing like recruiting for a basketball team. I look for seven-footers. Not only do I look for seven-footers, but they also must handle the ball. I like durable competitive advantage (moats). For example, Wrigley's was founded in 1891, and Coke in 1886. Today, Coke sells 1.6 billion eight-ounce servings in the world every day. If you add one penny to that, that is $16 million a day, or $6 billion a year.

I want things that are not going to change a lot. I also want a quality management team that has passion and is ethical. Finally, I must buy it when the price is right.

The problem that Berkshire has is that it is too big. There are not that many good ideas for companies our size.

I recently went on Amazon.com and bought a 1951 edition of Moody's. How many people do you know that do that? I started to look through the pages for companies that I might be interested in buying/investing. This is exactly what I did when I started investing. I would look at earnings growth, price per share, and industry, among other things, and if they passed that test, I would interview management to determine if they were honest.

Give us an example of a right pitch that you are waiting to swing at.

An example of the right pitch was when I bought 6 percent of Coke in 1988. Nothing bad could have happened. Sales were up every year. The company needed little capital. Coke only makes the syrup. You do not need a lot of ideas to get rich. You only need five good ideas.

Why do you choose to invite students to Omaha? What do you expect to get out of it?

I graduated from the University of Nebraska–Lincoln at age nineteen in 1950. I then applied to Harvard to get an MBA, and they rejected me. That was a mistake for them and their development office. I then read a book by Benjamin Graham called *The Intelligent Investor*, and I knew that I wanted to study under him at Columbia. So, I wrote to him and got accepted at Columbia.

Graham was a role model of mine and a professor at Columbia. He taught one class at Columbia and donated the money back to the school. Graham did this to volunteer his time and give back to society. He mentored me. So, I chose to do the same. If I can help 5–10 percent of the students, I am happy to do this. I love to do this.

After the question-and-answer session, Buffett took us out to lunch, choosing four young people who would ride with him in his old Cadillac with the license plate that said "THRIFTY." Due to luck (or, more likely assertiveness), one of my own students was seated right next to Buffett in the front. At lunch, I jumped on a similar opportunity. Seated directly across from Buffett, I asked, "How do you value a company?"

"The discounted cash flow method," he said simply, implying that anyone could do the same.

Buffett had brought us to one of his favorite restaurants, a place called Piccolo Pete's in South Omaha. His famed frugality was as evident around food as it is in any other arena. Buffett's typical breakfast is a $3 McDonald's breakfast sandwich. (He chooses his version of the Egg McMuffin—with sausage or without—based on how the stock market is doing.) Buffett is something of a fiend for McDonald's, actually, eating Chicken McNuggets at least three times a week.[2] So I suppose we were fortunate to be eating at an actual restaurant, where we were served chicken parmesan.

Our luncheon happened to fall on the day it was announced that Buffett was purchasing the Burlington Northern Santa Fe Railroad. Reporters and camera operators were chasing him everywhere. But to my surprise, Buffett seemed to want nothing to do with the media. His attention was solely on the visiting students. As the afternoon wrapped up, a waitress brought out dessert—root beer floats. Ours were the usual style, six to eight inches tall. But then came Buffett's. It was enormous—well over a foot high! He guzzled it down with a huge grin. Afterward, he took a few hours to take individual and group pictures with all of the students.

Throughout the day, one of my students, a communications major, slyly videotaped as much of the visit as he could, while another student interviewed Buffett. No one else was taking that kind of initiative. It was classical entrepreneurial behavior, in that entrepreneurs do not wait for others to tell them what to do—they just do it. Buffett was clearly impressed, so much so that he asked for the interviewer's résumé.

2011 INVITATION

Two years later, I had a new job, at Gonzaga University. I was trying to figure out how to get invited back to visit Buffett. Buffett admires persistence and humility, but I'd already caught his eye once. I knew I would need to produce something truly creative to win a second invitation. With Buffett, you must earn an audience. After all, in June 2011, someone had just paid $2.6 million just to have lunch with him, and here was our school, asking for a whole day. I knew that we'd need to come up with something unique, a project that would showcase my students' creativity and entrepreneurial abilities. "Conceive a new product," I told them, "something that you think Buffett would like. I'll send it to him as a pitch."

I set no limits on what they could create, only that it be legal, ethical, and reflective of Gonzaga's values. Other than that, they had free rein. Their project could be a video of some sort (such as a movie, documentary, or advertisement), a paper (perhaps an analysis of a company, or an investment recommendation), a song, or even a play.

At heart, the assignment was designed to encourage students to think and act like entrepreneurs by creating something new and trying to sell it. But maybe, I thought, it also would earn us another invitation to Omaha.

By semester's end, I had five products designed by five teams of students. I selected the three that I felt were the most innovative and squarely aimed at the tastes of their customer.

Warren Buffett Pinball Machine

The Warren Buffett Pinball Machine tickled me immediately. I thought it was a brilliant idea, as Buffett had owned a pinball machine company while still in high school. The idea for this new iteration came from a team made up of one religious studies major, one would-be electrical engineer, and a business student.

The team planned to buy a used pinball machine and redesign and rebuild it with a series of obstacles and bonuses that would mirror Buffett's life. They imagined someday scoring licensing rights to make and market this idea.

I advised them to act like a start-up—that is, create promotional material, raise funds, and purchase and design their prototype. Given that this was a one-semester class, the team had neither the time nor the resources to do all that I'd suggested and had to content itself with detailed diagrams documenting their design. But conceiving the product had been a valuable exercise.

Buffett in the Boardroom with a Bat

The second product I sent to Omaha was a parody of the game Clue, with Buffett as one of the possible murder suspects instead of Mrs. White or Colonel Mustard, and various spots on Gonzaga's campus as the location of the imagined crime. My students created a prototype, an actual game board featuring pictures of campus buildings.

Video Illustrating the Mission and Values of Gonzaga

The final product I sent Buffett was a DVD highlighting the various aspects of our university, with special attention to the culture at Gonzaga and the entrepreneurship program. The video was created by a variety of students from around the campus since our entrepreneurship program is open to all students at the university.

I stood in line at the Spokane post office with my package for Buffett, imagining his reaction when he opened it. Based on my intuition, I thought we had about a 60 percent probability of winning an invitation. In less than a week, I heard from Buffett's secretary. He liked all three products and wanted us to come to Omaha.

As before, while my students enjoyed their tour of some flagship Berkshire Hathaway businesses, the question-and-answer session with Buffett was the highlight of the trip. One exchange, on the value of education, stood out:

What part should cost play in college? Is college worth it? Could you please comment on the massive student loan debt?

> I did not want to go to college. I thought that I could get just as good of an education reading something than just going to school. My father made me go to school. I do not know what my degrees were, but they mean a lot when you are seeking a job. There is a lot of value in education. 99 percent of companies value education. At Berkshire Hathaway, we value it at 50 percent.

When you have high demand, you can increase prices at schools. When I was in school, I learned a lot from a few courses. A few people inspired me and got me excited about doing things. Benjamin Graham had a huge influence on me. If you have a few teachers that have an influence on you, you are a lucky person.

2018 INVITATION

The 2018 invitation came about in a very similar way as in 2009. I wrote two case studies on Buffett and Berkshire Hathaway, got them published, and sent them to him. He responded by inviting me and twenty students to Omaha. This time, I brought my wife and two professors.

Buffett's visits with students had become wildly popular on campuses around the world by this point. Now there were nine schools invited—including one from Peru—with around 200 students and professors each day. Along with the Gonzaga crew, Buffett had invited the University of Pennsylvania, Northwestern University, University of Arizona, University of Minnesota, University of Nebraska–Lincoln and University of Nebraska–Omaha, and the University of Tennessee.

The talks had become so large and ungainly that he held the question-and-answer session in the ballroom of Omaha's downtown Hilton. He was eighty-eight, and this would turn out to be the last year he invited schools to visit. But everyone could tell that he still loved teaching.

The day ended with a visit to Borsheims jewelry (students were offered a 20 percent discount on any purchase) and a tour of Buffett's most recent purchase, the Oriental Trading Company, a toy and gift firm that Berkshire had bought out of bankruptcy in 2012.

IMPACT

These trips generated significant publicity, and they remain major highlights in my professional career. There was a news story and photos on the front page of the *Wall Street Journal*. I was interviewed on WTAM 1100 in Cleveland about what my students had learned and how I had managed to win no less than three invitations to visit with Buffett. In the years since, whenever I happen upon the LinkedIn profile of a former student who went on one of these visits, I inevitably see their "Day with Warren Buffett" featured prominently under "Relevant Experience." Several have their pictures with him posted. Despite their myriad successes postcollege, almost every one of them says their biggest takeaway from Buffett was his advice on how to live a fulfilling life.

It is my sincerest hope that others will follow suit, integrating Buffett's values on the true meaning of success: having a passion for the work you do, living with integrity, respecting everyone you meet, and surrounding yourself with people who love you unconditionally.

CHAPTER 13
BERKSHIRE HATHAWAY LOOKING FORWARD

If you aren't willing to own a stock for ten years, don't even think about owning it for ten minutes.[1]

WARREN BUFFETT

BERKSHIRE AND THE FUTURE WORLD OF FINANCE

For years, Warren Buffett was criticized for not investing in technology companies. Investors ridiculed his focus on traditional, old-economy corporations like Coca-Cola and Dairy Queen, which looked distinctly unsexy in the early 2000s compared with the high-flying tech stocks. When the dot-com bubble burst, he got the last laugh. But judging by more recent moves at Berkshire Hathaway, it seems clear that Buffett has acknowledged that economies are changing; that technology and future-finance models will become increasingly important; and that he'd better get on board, or else delegate to others more comfortable swimming in these fast-moving new waters.

Over the past decade, Berkshire's stock portfolio has gradually shifted from an emphasis on staid companies such as Wells Fargo, IBM, and ConocoPhillips to cutting-edge, tech-based firms like Apple, Davita, Charter, and Verisign. Old standbys American Express, Coca-Cola, and Kraft Foods remain among Berkshire's holdings, but their weight has reduced dramatically. Apple alone now represents 45 percent of Berkshire's portfolio.[2] If you include its fractional positions in such companies as the cloud-computing firm Snowflake, the Brazilian-based digital bank Nubank, and Amazon, the e-commerce giant, Berkshire's exposure to technology/e-commerce now comprises about 50 percent of its holdings. In short, technology stocks have reoriented a fifty-year tradition at Berkshire.

These investments are surely due to the influence of Todd Combs and Ted Weschler, brought in as portfolio managers in 2010 and 2012. Just as Charlie Munger helped to broaden Buffett's approach to investing when he joined Berkshire in 1978, Combs and Weschler have taken the baton and guided Berkshire into the future. But heritage remains important to Buffett. Notice how many of Berkshire's more recent investments continue the firm's longtime focus on financial services, while incorporating the growing influence of technology.

FINTECH

In 2017, academics came up with the name "fintech" to apply to the confluence of financial services and technology, a growing sector that, in hindsight, was inevitable. Fintech firms have been around since at least 2008. If you log into your bank on a smartphone, you are using fintech. The same goes if you make trades online. Any companies developing software to process transactions or help people manage money are fintech companies.[3] These companies use automation, including artificial intelligence, to process transactions and data accurately and instantaneously.[4] Global investment in fintech firms soared more than 12,000 percent between 2008 and 2020. In 2021, global fintech funding was $131.5 billion.[5]

CRYPTOCURRENCY AND BLOCKCHAIN

Fintech includes a variety of applications of technology to traditional banking and finance. However, it also includes one of the most controversial areas in future finance: cryptocurrency. The term "cryptocurrency" refers to cryptography-secured digital currency. Counterfeiting it is almost impossible.[6] It exists only in electronic form, via digital tokens. This should not be confused with simply paying online (online transactions involve fintech, but usually not cryptocurrency). As Jake Frankenfield of *Investopedia* puts it, all cryptocurrencies are digital currencies, but not all digital currencies are cryptocurrencies.[7]

The primary distinction between them is the province from which they derive their value. Fiat currencies, which can be digital (e.g., U.S. dollar, euro, yen), also exist in physical form. They derive from a centralized economy and are distributed by a specific bank or government agency.[8] Cryptocurrencies, such as Bitcoin and Ethereum, are examples of decentralized digital currency systems.[9] They are distributed across many networked computers, reducing the possibility of a single hack or even government interference causing problems for the flow of the currency.[10]

Cryptocurrencies function using encryption and a technology called "blockchain,"[11] which allows people participating in the network to confirm their transactions without going through any central authority.[12] Blockchain data is entered permanently and unchangeably. According to Adam Hayes, "For Bitcoin, this means that transactions are permanently recorded and viewable to anyone."[13] Blockchain technology also could theoretically be used for noncrypto transactions and even have nonfinancial applications, such as voting[14] and smart contracts.[15] Smart contracts can function like self-fulfilling contracts, with the performance of one portion of the contracted workflow initiating payment or another contracted portion of the workflow.[16]

The billionaire entrepreneur Mark Cuban says that he wasn't terribly excited about Bitcoin and cryptocurrencies in general—until he grasped the value of smart contracts:

> Being somebody who looks at technology and trying to find new ways to apply it . . . what really gets me excited is what you can do with smart contracts in terms of applications because that's what leads to game changers. And when you get game changers, that's what leads to industries changing how they do business. And when industries change how they do business, to integrate smart contracts and other blockchain-based applications, then the world changes.[17]

Evan Conrad, a Silicon Valley cryptoentrepreneur, acknowledged the Wild West flavor of this sector, telling me that no one person truly knows what is happening within cryptofinance at any given moment. "Crypto moves so quickly that by the time the information has moved from the builder types [of people] to the writer types, the on-the-ground information has changed. So almost everything you read about crypto, that isn't literally source code, is out of date."[18]

According to Frankenfield, "Experts believe that blockchain and related technology will disrupt many industries, including finance and law. The advantages of cryptocurrencies include cheaper and faster money transfers and decentralized systems that do not collapse at a single point of failure. The disadvantages of cryptocurrencies include their price volatility, high energy consumption for mining activities, and use in criminal activity."[19] In the context of cryptocurrency, "mining" refers not to the physical extraction of a natural resource, but rather to complex computer algorithms that individuals solve using expensive computer "rigs" in order to yield new cryptocurrency.

Buffett, Munger, and Cryptocurrency

In 2018, Buffett declared his dislike of Bitcoin in particular, likening it to "rat poison squared."[20] Munger echoed those feelings in his typically colorful language: "I certainly didn't invest in crypto," he said in 2022. "I'm proud of the fact I've avoided it. It's like a venereal disease or something. I just regard it as beneath contempt."[21] He has said that cryptocurrencies should be banned outright, praising the Chinese for doing so.[22] Other countries that have banned cryptocurrencies include Qatar, Nepal, Tunisia, Turkey, Bangladesh, Egypt, Morocco, and Iraq.[23]

Despite the duo's disdain for cryptocurrencies, Berkshire is exposed to the sector through its investment in Nubank, which allows cryptocurrency transactions.[24,25] And Munger has acknowledged the potential usefulness of blockchain technology. Even Berkshire's traditional bank investments have forced it to face the brave new world of fintech.

Berkshire and Fintech

In October 2018, Berkshire purchased an 11 percent stake at the initial public offering (IPO) of the Brazilian e-commerce company StoneCo (STNE),[26] at $24 per share. At the time, it was worth $340 million.[27] The same year, Berkshire invested $356 million in One97 Communications Ltd., the parent company of Paytm, to get a 3 percent stake.[28] Paytm, an e-commerce platform, went public in November 2021 and was one more fintech firm brought into the Berkshire portfolio by Todd Combs. Paytm was also Berkshire's first investment in an Indian company. In addition, Berkshire sunk $250 million into the data warehousing company Snowflake (SNOW) in 2020, at the IPO price of $120 per share.[29] Snowflake's Financial Services Data Cloud is used by various industries, including insurance, banking, investment, and fintech itself.[30] Berkshire then purchased an additional 4.04 million shares from another stockholder.[31] In terms of dollar amounts, these investments were extremely small, given Berkshire's market capitalization.

The incursion into future finance continued. In June 2021, Berkshire invested $500 million in Nubank and added to those holdings with another $1 billion in shares in the fourth quarter. Nubank (NU) went public at $9 a share in December 2021.[32]

It is no accident that digital banking is a growing sector in Latin America. Cristina Junqueira, a cofounder of Nubank, said that the region's history of being underserved by traditional banking systems made it naturally fertile ground for this aspect of fintech. "There is so much opportunity in [Latin America]," she said, pointing to a surging population, high fees associated with traditional banking, and its "horrible" customer experiences. "Worldwide there is no place that is better suited in terms of having a great opportunity for fintech companies to tackle."[33]

CENTRAL BANK DIGITAL CURRENCIES

While global cryptocurrencies like Bitcoin increase in popularity, individual nations are seeking ways to preserve key aspects of their traditional financial systems through central bank digital currencies (CBDCs).[34] These are regulated currencies, issued by a country's central bank, but they exist only in the digital sphere.[35] A CBDC can supplement or replace traditional fiat currencies.[36]

The Bahamas was the first country to adopt a CBDC. Others that have followed include Nigeria and the Eastern Caribbean Union (composed of Antigua and Barbuda, Dominica, Grenada, Montserrat, St. Kitts and Nevis, St. Lucia, and St. Vincent and the Grenadines).[37]

Compared with cryptocurrencies, CBDCs are more stable and, like traditional currencies, can be accepted globally. Cryptocurrencies, by contrast, are more volatile, unregulated, and vulnerable to fraud. Also, its digital tokens are not widely accepted.[38] Yet cryptocurrencies are publicly viewable on a decentralized ledger, whereas CBDC transactions are only known to the sender, the receiver, and the bank.[39]

CHINA'S CENTRAL BANK DIGITAL CURRENCY

China is the first major country to use a digital currency.[40] At work on this innovation since 2014, China now uses the renminbi (RMB), of which the digital yuan (e-CNY) is a subunit. The two are used interchangeably, and may ultimately replace all cash and coins in circulation.[41] The financial technology expert Richard Turrin believes that this move, to a digital currency that can be used both domestically and internationally, positions China to mount a significant challenge to the U.S. dollar in international trade over the next decade. It may also allow other nations to reduce their dependence on the dollar.[42] "China is the largest trading country and you're going to see digital yuan slowly supplant the dollar when buying things from China," Turrin told CNBC in 2022. "What you're going to see in the future is a rollback, a risk management exercise that seeks to slowly and maybe just slightly reduce the dependence on dollar, from 100 percent down to 80 percent, 85 percent."[43]

The centralization of the digital yuan means that China could freeze or close accounts at will, while keeping tabs on every move its people make with their money. It would also give the Chinese government increased control over technology companies like Tencent and Ant Group.[44] And with the digital yuan overtaking electronic payment systems such as Alipay and WeChat Pay,[45] China could put a leash on the economic power wielded by its largest tech firms.[46] This presents serious implications for those companies' shareholders. But the ultimate aim for China, Turrin believes, is to position the digital yuan as a "sanction-buster."[47]

Although its economy is still smaller than that of the United States, China is already well ahead in pioneering the use of financial technology. The United States would need another five years, at least, just to get out of planning and trials for a potential digital dollar, Turrin says.[48]

U.S. CENTRAL BANK DIGITAL CURRENCY

The Federal Reserve (Fed) has steadfastly refused to take a stance on CBDCs. But President Joe Biden signed an executive order on March 9, 2022, directing the U.S. Treasury, the Commerce Department, and other key agencies to assess the risks and benefits of creating a central bank digital dollar, among other cryptocurrency issues.[49] Biden noted that a digital dollar system might benefit Americans who lack access to traditional bank accounts. This way, they would have direct access to funds going in and out of an electronic account.

But clearly, the main motivation behind his concept, known as Project Hamilton, is assessing the necessary infrastructure for such a shift.[50] As a result, researchers at the MIT Digital Currency Initiative[51] are at work examining the privacy, speed, safety, auditability, programmability, and interoperability of a central bank digital dollar.[52] Shortly after the president's executive order, Bank of America issued a note calling a CBDC in the United States "inevitable."[53]

Of course, cultural differences between the United States and China will likely affect the ways that citizens of each nation embrace digital currencies. While China is pushing its citizens to adopt the CBDC, giving the government even more control over its people, for American consumers, privacy questions are sure to be a major stumbling block.

OPPORTUNITIES AND RISKS FOR BERKSHIRE

Given the evolution of global currencies from physical to digital incarnations, what opportunities and risks lie ahead for Berkshire Hathaway? I expect Berkshire to continue seeking transaction-focused companies, with a proven platform, dominant market position, and wide moat—particularly outside the United States. Under the influence of Combs and Weschler, I also anticipate that Berkshire will use smart contracts related to blockchain technology. Even Munger has conceded a potential future for blockchain, and given Berkshire's core competence in insurance products, it seems likely that the firm will look to this arena when searching for ways to jump aboard the digital currency bandwagon.

On the other hand, the digitization of money could have serious consequences for traditional banking and, by extension, for Berkshire. A U.S. CBDC, for example, could eliminate commercial banks as intermediaries. This may be why Buffett recently sold many of Berkshire's positions in financial stocks (e.g., Goldman Sachs, JPMorgan, Wells Fargo, Visa, and Mastercard). Berkshire still maintains huge holdings in Bank of America and American Express, and its stock portfolio contains 25 percent financials. Still, it was hard to miss the significance of Buffett selling off so many strongholds in traditional banking.

If people choose to bank directly with the Fed, the central bank would need to either facilitate consumer borrowing (which it might not be equipped to do) or find new ways of injecting credit. For these reasons, some experts believe that private digital currencies are preferable to a CBDC.[54]

CRITICISMS OF BUFFETT

Berkshire's Underperformance

Over the past twelve years, Berkshire's returns have not always bested the S&P 500, a noticeable change for an investment house famed for its stratospheric results. These blips have opened Buffett to criticism. In 2019–2020, for instance, Berkshire underperformed the S&P 500 by 15 to 20 percentage points. Over the longer term, too, Berkshire is slightly down, compared with the S&P 500 (see table 13.1).

There are a lot of ways to interpret these fluctuations. Investors sometimes complain about the enormous amount of money that Buffett has kept in cash.

TABLE 13.1 Berkshire vs. S&P 500 returns, 2010–2021

Year	Berkshire return (%)	S&P 500 return with dividends (%)
2010	21.4	15.1
2011	(4.7)	2.1
2012	16.8	16
2013	32.7	32.4
2014	27	13.7
2015	(12.5)	1.4
2016	23.4	12
2017	21.9	21.8
2018	2.8	(4.4)
2019	11	31.5
2020	2.4	18.4
2021	29.6	28.7
Average	**14.3**	**15.7**

But it's important to note that Berkshire's size has much to do with the slowing growth of its stock value. Put simply, the bigger Berkshire gets, the less likely it is to generate dramatic returns. Munger insists that he would still buy Berkshire over an S&P 500 fund, any day. Buffett has been less sanguine, even hinting at a recent shareholder meeting that investors seeking large returns quickly might be better served elsewhere.

However, Berkshire has done extremely well lately. As of June 2022, Berkshire's A shares were $417,202. The market value of the company was $614.1 billion, making it the seventh most valuable company in the world. Berkshire's year-to-date stock is down -7.31 percent in 2022, as opposed to the S&P 500's -17.93 percent. Despite past statements about the unseemliness of buying back shares to boost the price of stock, this is precisely what Buffett has done in recent years. And it has indeed helped. In 2020 and 2021, Berkshire bought back $24.7 billion and $27 billion worth of its stock.[55] In the first quarter of 2022, Berkshire kept up the momentum, buying back another $1.2 billion in shares.[56] Not surprisingly, between March 2021 and March 2022, Berkshire's stock has returned 33.76 percent, as opposed to the S&P 500's 13.99 percent.

Considering the advanced age of both Buffett and his partner, Munger, it is no surprise that Wall Street openly speculates about the direction of Berkshire after they have gone. It is possible—even likely—that shareholders will push Berkshire's new leaders to be more creative and less conservative. Instead of keeping $150 billion in cash on the sidelines, why not do something with all that money?

Buffett has begun to offer some answers to that question. For example, when Russia invaded Ukraine in February 2022, he immediately began buying stock in Occidental Petroleum Corporation. Berkshire bought 136,373,000 shares of Occidental,[57] at a market value of $7.7 billion. Berkshire then bought 9.6 million more shares in June, giving it a 16.3 percent stake in the company, making it Berkshire's ninth-largest holding.[58]

In March 2022, Berkshire announced that it had agreed to purchase the New York–based insurance company Alleghany Corporation for $11.6 billion, paying a premium of 25 percent above the close.[59] The acquisition was one of the five biggest in Berkshire's history.

In the first quarter of 2022, Berkshire bought $51 billion in stock.[60] Berkshire's new stock positions in the first quarter were $4.2 billion in Hewlett Packard (HP), $2.95 billion in Citigroup (C), $2.61 billion in Paramount Global (PARA), $1.13 billion in Celanese (CE), $895 million in McKesson (MCK), $620 million in

Markel (MKL), and $390 million in Ally Financial (ALLY). Berkshire also added to existing positions including $557 million in Apple (AAPL), $203 million in Chevron (CVX), $3.86 billion in Activision Blizzard (ATVI), $78.2 million in General Motors (GM), $102 million in RH (RH), $471 million in Liberty Media (FWONK), and $281 million in Floor & Décor Holdings (FND).

Could there be spinoffs of some companies under Berkshire's umbrella after Buffett and Munger are no longer with the company? Anything is possible. But this seems an unlikely scenario to me since Berkshire has performed so well overall.

What about paying dividends? Adam Mead, the author of *The Complete Financial History of Berkshire Hathaway*, has proposed that Berkshire provide a regular dividend of up to 25 percent of normalized operating earnings. Buffett has steadfastly refused to do anything of the sort, insisting that he can still get better rates of return from that money than his shareholders would. But if Berkshire decides to stop repurchasing shares or cannot find any other businesses that it wants to acquire, infrequent special dividends could be an option.[61]

Personal

It's easy to take shots at a multibillionaire and accuse such a person of being nothing more than a capitalist driven by greed. But Buffett has pledged to donate more than 99 percent of his personal wealth to charity, and he has already given away billions. He has also willed that his heirs gradually donate rather than sell any Berkshire shares that they inherit from him. "I estimate that it will take 12 to 15 years for the entirety of the Berkshire shares I hold at my death to move into the market," he forecast in 2020.[62]

Buffett's daughter, Susie, believes that many have overlooked the importance her father accords to social causes. She told me, "People don't understand how much my dad cares about social injustice, human rights, women's rights, and the civil rights movement."

The most obvious enactment of these beliefs is Buffett's involvement with the Giving Pledge. Buffett conceived of the project with his friend Bill Gates, aiming to inspire the world's wealthiest people to do as he is doing, and give at least half of their net worth to philanthropy during their lifetimes, or upon their deaths.[63] In this effort, Buffett has been fairly successful, securing pledges from fellow billionaires Larry Ellison, Sara Blakely, Michael Bloomberg, Beth and Seth Klarman, George Lucas, Paul Allen, and Patrick Soon-Shiong.

And of course, there are Buffett's beloved sessions with college students, detailed in chapter 12. I have been fortunate enough to see him in action as a teacher three times, and the experience had a significant impact on the way that I live my life. When faced with a tough decision, I often ask myself: What Would Warren Do?

BERKSHIRE AFTER BUFFETT: SUCCESSION

In 2012, Buffett announced that he had stage 1 prostate cancer.[64] At subsequent shareholder meetings, he seemed to be his usual cheerful self, insisting that the disease had not progressed to become life-threatening. At Berkshire's virtual meeting for shareholders in 2021, he took questions for hours. I don't expect that he will ever officially retire.

Still, he has clearly slowed down. And the question of succession at Berkshire looms. For some fifty years, Buffett has held three jobs at the firm, and each will need to be filled: chairman of the board of directors, chief executive officer (CEO), and chief investment officer. With the hiring of Todd Combs, in 2010, and Ted Weschler, in 2012, the chief investment officer succession question has been resolved.

As for new leadership on the board of directors, Buffett has made it clear that his son Howard (currently president of Buffett Farms and BioImages) will take over as chair. From that position, he will lead a board composed of the following members:

- Charlie Munger (vice chair)
- Greg Abel (vice chair of noninsurance businesses for Berkshire Hathaway)
- Ajit Jain (vice chair of insurance operations for Berkshire Hathaway)
- Susan "Susie" Buffett (Warren's daughter and chair of both the Susan Thompson Foundation and the Sherwood Foundation)
- Kenneth I. Chenault (former chair and CEO of American Express)
- Christopher Davis (chair of Davis Select Advisors, an investment company)
- Susan Lynne Decker (CEO of Raftr and former president of Yahoo!)
- Ronald L. Olson (partner of the law firm of Munger Tolles & Olson, LLP)

- David "Sandy" Gottesman (founded First Manhattan Co., an investment advisory firm)
- Stephen B. Burke (former head of seven companies, including NBC and Comcast)
- Charlotte M. Guyman (former Microsoft manager and cofounder of BoardReady, a not-for-profit corporation and a leader in several social organizations)
- Meryl B. Witmer (general partner of Eagle Capital Partners LP)

Susie Buffett joined Berkshire's board in 2021, as did Christopher Davis. I believe that Susie and Chris will safeguard the culture of Berkshire. Both are owner-oriented and business-savvy. I can't envision either allowing future managers, directors, or shareholders to deviate from Buffett's founding principles.[65] In 2022, Wally Weitz, the founder of Weitz Investment Management in Omaha, replaced the seat left by Tom Murphy.[66]

When examining the backgrounds of Meryl Witmer, Wally Weitz, and Christopher Davis as a whole, you have essentially three very similar profiles that likely don't add any discernibly unique dimension to the Berkshire board. This is a governance weakness. In my opinion, Berkshire needs young, innovative, fresh minds that will challenge and prod Buffett's successors, not apply a traditional value investor's mindset.

The final piece of the puzzle—and a mystery that kept people guessing for years—will be Berkshire's new CEO. At the 2020 annual shareholder meeting, Buffett tipped his hand, telling the audience that his two board vice-chairmen, Abel and Jain, would be on hand to answer questions. This was a first, and the change was noted. Then, due to the COVID-19 pandemic, Buffett cancelled the in-person gathering and instead streamed the meeting on Yahoo! But when the cameras turned on, Abel was the one on the dais talking to shareholders.

This raised eyebrows. For years, Buffett had praised Jain's contributions, and many shareholders assumed that the former McKinsey executive was Buffett's most likely successor. Jain, who emigrated to the United States from India in his twenties, earned a master of business administration (MBA) from Harvard in 1978, and by 1986, he was working at Berkshire, where he has thrived. Buffett once quipped that if he, Munger, and Jain were ever on a sinking boat, Berkshire's shareholders would do best for themselves by saving Jain first.[67] "Ajit has created tens of billions of value for Berkshire shareholders," Buffett wrote in his 2016 annual letter. "If there were ever to be another Ajit and you could swap me for him, don't hesitate. Make the trade!"[68]

But at the 2021 Berkshire shareholder meeting, Munger made the question of succession all but official, clearly indicating that Abel would become the next CEO. Buffett, while surprised at the disclosure, didn't deny it, saying, "The directors are in agreement that if something were to happen to me tonight, it would be Greg who'd take over tomorrow morning."[69]

Greg Abel

Born and educated in Canada, Abel, fifty-eight, is the vice chair of noninsurance businesses for Berkshire Hathaway. He has extensive experience with capital allocation and has overseen many of Berkshire's recent acquisitions.[70] But Abel, like Buffett, did not grow up with wealth. Raised in a working-class neighborhood of Edmonton, Abel showed himself to be entrepreneurial and independent from an early age. And his values were similar to Buffett's. As a child, he went door-to-door distributing advertisement flyers and collecting bottles for cash. Later, he worked as a laborer for a forest products company.[71] Through high school and college, Abel worked part time in a fire-extinguisher factory, which paid his way through the University of Alberta.[72]

With a degree in accounting, Abel went to work for PricewaterhouseCoopers (PwC) in San Francisco. In 1992, he was hired at CalEnergy, where he eventually rose to CEO. During this period, Berkshire bought a controlling interest in the company, which had changed its name to MidAmerican Energy Holdings Company, and in 2014, MidAmerican became Berkshire Hathaway Energy. The company has assets of more than $90 billion and owns energy-industry subsidiaries in the United States, the United Kingdom, Canada, and the Philippines.[73]

In January 2018, Abel, then chair of the board at MidAmerican Energy, was named to his current position at Berkshire and appointed to its board of directors.[74]

CONCLUSION

The worldwide fascination with Buffett arises from his enormous financial success, midwestern common sense, modest lifestyle, and self-deprecating sense of humor. People view him as a relatable model for their own potential. But against the backdrop of his vast wealth, it is Buffett's humility that stands out, his insistence on living by a moral compass. I can't think of many other billionaires who regularly insist that love is more important than material success.[75]

Still, Buffett is rightly viewed as a font of financial knowledge. So valuable is his expertise that CNBC has created a Warren Buffett Archive, with 122 hours of recordings, allowing anyone to watch Berkshire's annual meetings in their entirety, accompanied by transcripts.[76] Berkshire Hathaway, too, has begun sharing its founders' knowledge by livestreaming annual shareholder meetings.

An "investor is neither right nor wrong because others agree or disagree with him," wrote Buffett's mentor, Benjamin Graham. "He is right because his facts and analysis are right."[77] Ever focused on fundamentals, Buffett believes that these are the most important words ever written about investing.[78] And for years, this approach has made him the wealthiest man on the planet. But recently, that ranking has slipped a bit—likely because Buffett has been busily giving away his money. Since 2006, he has donated more than $41.5 billion in Berkshire stock to various philanthropies.[79] Buffett's personal wealth has been dropping relative to others. As of June 24, 2022, the Bloomberg Billionaire's Index had the following rankings (in billions):[80]

1. Elon Musk ($223)
2. Jeff Bezos ($140)
3. Bernard Arnault ($131)
4. Bill Gates ($116)
5. Larry Page ($107)
6. Sergey Brin ($102)
7. Warren Buffett ($96.8)
8. Gautam Adani ($94.9)
9. Steve Ballmer ($94.5)
10. Mukesh Ambani ($90.4)

For all the market crises that the U.S. economy has endured, and all the down years that Berkshire itself has weathered, Buffett remains the ultimate optimist. Invest in the stock market and you will come out ahead in the end, he insists, because the United States always moves forward. Its entrepreneurs always find ways to create new value.

APPENDIX 1

BERKSHIRE HATHAWAY AND SUBSIDIARIES CONSOLIDATED BALANCE SHEETS: 2016–2021

Period ending	December 31, 2021	December 31, 2020	December 31, 2019	December 31, 2018	December 31, 2017	December 31, 2016
Assets						
Insurance and other						
Cash and cash equivalents	85,319	44,714	61,151	27,749	28,673	24,109
Short-term investments in U.S. Treasury bills	58,535	90,300	63,822	81,506	84,371	58,322
Investments in fixed maturity securities	16,434	20,410	18,685	19,898	21,353	23,432
Investments in equity securities	350,719	281,170	248,027	172,757	170,540	134,835
Equity method investments	17,375	17,303	17,505	17,325	21,024	15,345 (investment in Kraft Heinz)
Loans and finance receivables	20,751	19,201	17,527	16,280	13,748	40,397 (total receivables)
Other receivables	35,388	32,310	32,418	31,564	29,392	–
Inventories	20,954	19,208	19,852	19,069	17,366	15,727
Property, plant, and equipment	20,834	21,200	21,438	20,628	19,868	19,325
Equipment held for lease	14,918	14,601	15,065	14,298	10,167	9,689 (PPE and assets held for lease)
Goodwill	47,117	47,121	57,052	56,323	56,478	55,375
Other intangible assets	28,486	29,462	31,051	31,499	32,518	33,481
Deferred charges – retroactive reinsurance	10,639	12,441	13,747	14,104	15,278	8,047
Other	15,854	14,580	13,232	9,307	9,391	12,954
Total insurance and other assets	**743,323**	**664,021**	**630,572**	**532,307**	**530,167**	**451,038**
Railroad, utilities, and energy						
Cash and cash equivalents	2,865	3,276	3,024	2,612	2,910	3,939
Receivables	4,177	3,542	3,417	3,666	3,531	-
Property, plant, and equipment	155,530	151,216	137,838	131,780	128,184	123,759
Goodwill	26,758	26,613	24,830	24,702	24,780	24,111
Regulatory assets	3,963	3,440	2,881	3,067	2,950	4,457
Other	22,168	21,621	15,167	9,660	9,573	13,550
Total railroad, utilities, and energy assets	**215,461**	**209,708**	**187,157**	**175,487**	**171,928**	**169,816**
Total assets	**958,784**	**873,729**	**817,729**	**707,794**	**702,095**	**620,854**

Note: Figures are in millions of U.S. dollars.

Source: Berkshire Hathaway, Inc., Annual Reports. Retrieved from https://www.berkshirehathaway.com/reports.html.

Period ending	December 31, 2021	December 31, 2020	December 31, 2019	December 31, 2018	December 31, 2017	December 31, 2016
Liabilities and shareholders' equity						
nsurance and other						
Unpaid losses and loss adjustment expenses	86,664	79,854	73,019	68,458	61,122	53,379
Unpaid losses and loss adjustment expenses under retroactive reinsurance contracts	38,256	40,966	42,441	41,834	42,937	24,972
Unearned premiums	23,512	21,395	19,782	18,093	16,040	14,245
Life, annuity, and health insurance benefits	22,452	21,616	20,155	18,632	17,608	15,977
Other policyholder liabilities	9,330	8,670	7,723	7,675	7,654	6,714
Accounts payable, accruals, and other liabilities	30,376	30,344	27,611	25,776	24,569	23,608
Derivative contract liabilities	–	1,065	968	2,452	2,172	2,890
Aircraft repurchase liabilities and unearned lease revenues	5,849	5,856	5,281	4,593	–	–
Notes payable and other borrowings	39,272	41,522	37,590	34,975	40,409	42,559
Total insurance and other liabilities	**255,711**	**250,223**	**234,570**	**222,488**	**212,511**	**184,344**
ailroad, utilities, and energy						
Accounts payable, accruals, and other liabilities	15,696	15,224	14,708	11,410	11,334	11,434
Regulatory liabilities	7,214	7,475	7,311	7,506	7,511	3,121
Notes payable and other borrowings	74,990	75,373	65,778	62,515	62,178	59,085
Total railroad, utilities, and energy liabilities	**97,900**	**98,072**	**87,797**	**81,431**	**81,023**	**73,640**
ncome taxes, principally deferred	90,243	74,098	66,799	51,375	56,607	77,442
Total liabilities	**443,854**	**422,393**	**389,166**	**355,294**	**350,141**	**335,426**
hareholders' equity						
Common stock	8	8	8	8	8	8
Capital in excess of par value	35,592	35,626	35,658	35,707	35,694	35,681
Accumulated other comprehensive income	(4,027)	(4,243)	(5,243)	(5,015)	58,571	37,298
Retained earnings	534,421	444,626	402,493	321,112	255,786	210,846
Treasury stock, at cost	(59,795)	(32,853)	(8,125)	(3,109)	(1,763)	(1,763)
Berkshire Hathaway shareholders' equity	506,199	443,164	424,791	348,703	348,296	282,070
Noncontrolling interests	8,731	8,172	3,772	3,797	3,658	3,358
Total shareholders' equity	**514,930**	**451,336**	**428,563**	**352,500**	**351,954**	**285,428**
otal liabilities and shareholders' equity	**958,784**	**873,729**	**817,729**	**707,794**	**702,095**	**620,854**

ote: Figures are in millions of U.S. dollars.

urce: Berkshire Hathaway, Inc., Annual Reports. Retrieved from https://www.berkshirehathaway.com/reports.html.

APPENDIX 2

BERKSHIRE HATHAWAY AND SUBSIDIARIES CONSOLIDATED STATEMENTS OF EARNINGS AND COMPREHENSIVE INCOME: 2016–2021

Period ending	December 31, 2021	December 31, 2020	December 31, 2019	December 31, 2018	December 31, 2017	December 31, 2016
Revenues						
Insurance and other						
Insurance premiums earned	69,478	63,401	61,078	57,418	60,597	45,881
Sales and service revenues	145,043	127,044	134,989	133,336	130,343	123,053
Leasing revenues	5,988	5,209	5,856	5,732	2,452	2,553
Interest, dividend, and other investment income	7,465	8,092	9,240	7,678	6,536	6,180
Total insurance and other revenues	**227,974**	**203,746**	**211,163**	**204,164**	**199,928**	**177,667**
Railroad, utilities, and energy						
Freight rail transportation revenues	23,177	20,750	23,357	23,703	21,080	19,683
Energy operating revenues	18,891	15,540	15,353	15,555	15,155	14,621
Service revenues and other income	6,052	5,474	4,743	4,415	3,770	3,143
Total railroad, utilities, and energy revenues	**48,120**	**41,764**	**43,453**	**43,673**	**40,005**	**37,447**
Total revenues	**276,094**	**245,510**	**254,616**	**247,837**	**239,933**	**215,114**
Investment and derivative contract gains	**78,542**	**40,746**	**72,607**	**(22,455)**	**2,128**	**8,304**
Costs and expenses						
Insurance and other						
Insurance losses and loss adjustment expenses	49,964	43,951	44,456	39,906	48,891	30,906
Life, annuity, and health insurance benefits	6,007	5,812	4,986	5,699	5,618	5,131
Insurance underwriting expenses	12,569	12,798	11,200	9,793	9,321	7,713
Cost of sales and services	114,138	101,091	107,041	106,083	104,343	97,867
Cost of leasing	4,201	3,520	4,003	4,061	1,455	1,335
Selling, general, and administrative expenses	18,843	19,809	19,226	17,856	19,189	17,973
Goodwill and intangible asset impairments	-	10,671	96	382	-	-
Interest expenses	1,086	1,105	1,056	1,035	1,132	1,099
Total insurance and other costs and expenses	**206,808**	**198,757**	**192,064**	**184,815**	**189,949**	**162,024**

Railroad, utilities, and energy						
Freight rail transportation expenses	14,477	13,120	15,436	16,045	14,031	13,134
Utilities and energy cost of sales and other expenses	13,959	11,638	11,296	11,641	10,772	10,471
Other expenses	5,615	4,796	4,002	3,895	3,231	2,589
Interest expenses	3,086	2,978	2,905	2,818	3,254	2,642
Total railroad, utilities, and energy costs and expenses	**37,137**	**32,532**	**33,639**	**34,399**	**31,288**	**28,836**
Total costs and expenses	**243,945**	**231,289**	**225,703**	**219,214**	**221,237**	**190,860**
Earnings before income taxes and equity method earnings (losses)	110,691	54,967	101,520	6,168	20,824	32,558
Equity method earnings (losses)	995	726	1,176	(2,167)	3,014	1,109
Earnings before income taxes	111,686	55,693	102,696	4,001	23,838	33,667
Income tax expense (benefit)	20,879	12,440	20,904	(321)	(21,515)	9,240
Net earnings	90,807	43,253	81,792	4,322	45,353	24,427
Earnings attributable to noncontrolling interests	1,012	732	375	301	413	353
Net earnings attributable to Berkshire Hathaway shareholders	89,795	42,521	81,417	4,021	44,940	24,074
Net earnings per average equivalent Class A share	59,460	26,668	49,828	2,446	27,326	14,645
Net earnings per average equivalent Class B share	39.64	17.78	33.22	1.63	18.22	9.76
Average equivalent Class A shares outstanding	1,510,180	1,594,469	1,633,946	1,643,795	1,644,615	1,643,826
Average equivalent Class B shares outstanding	2,265,269,867	2,391,703,454	2,450,919,020	2,465,692,368	2,466,923,163	2,465,739,654

Note: Figures are in millions of U.S. dollars.

Source: Berkshire Hathaway, Inc., Annual Reports. Retrieved from https://www.berkshirehathaway.com/reports.html.

Period ending	December 31, 2021	December 31, 2020	December 31, 2019	December 31, 2018	December 31, 2017	December 31, 2016
Net earnings	90,807	43,253	81,792	4,322	45,353	24,427
Other comprehensive income						
Unrealized appreciation of fixed maturity securities	(217)	74	142	(438)	29,051	7,038
Applicable income taxes	50	(19)	(31)	84	(10,076)	(2,459)
Foreign currency translation	(1,011)	1,284	323	(1,531)	2,364	(1,541)
Applicable income taxes	(6)	3	(28)	62	(95)	66
Defined benefit pension plans	1,775	(355)	(711)	(571)	225	354
Applicable income taxes	(457)	74	155	143	(45)	(187)
Other, net	100	(42)	(48)	(12)	(9)	(17)
Other comprehensive income, net	234	1,019	(198)	(2,263)	21,415	3,254
Comprehensive income	91,041	44,272	81,594	2,059	66,768	27,681
Comprehensive income attributable to noncontrolling interests	1,030	751	405	249	555	291
Comprehensive income attributable to Berkshire Hathaway shareholders	$90,011	$43,521	$81,189	$1,810	$66,213	$27,390

Note: Figures are in millions of U.S. dollars.

Source: Berkshire Hathaway, Inc., Annual Reports. Retrieved from https://www.berkshirehathaway.com/reports.html.

APPENDIX 3

BERKSHIRE HATHAWAY AND SUBSIDIARIES CONSOLIDATED STATEMENTS OF CASH FLOWS: 2016–2021

Period ending	December 31, 2021	December 31, 2020	December 31, 2019	December 31, 2018	December 31, 2017	December 31, 2016
Cash flows from operating activities						
Net earnings	90,807	43,253	81,792	4,322	45,353	24,427
Adjustments to reconcile net earnings to operating cash flows						
Investment (gains) losses	(77,576)	(40,905)	(71,123)	22,155	(1,410)	(7,553)
Depreciation and amortization	10,718	10,596	10,064	9,779	9,188	8,901
Other, including asset impairment charges	(3,397)	11,263	(1,254)	2,957	458	(161)
Changes in operating assets and liabilities						
Unpaid losses and loss adjustment expenses	4,595	4,819	6,087	3,449	25,027	4,372
Deferred charges—retroactive reinsurance	1,802	1,307	357	1,174	(7,231)	(360)
Unearned premiums	2,306	1,587	1,707	1,794	1,761	968
Receivables and originated loans	(5,834)	(1,609)	(2,303)	(3,443)	(1,990)	(3,302)
Other assets	(1,686)	(1,109)	(2,011)	(1,832)	(1,665)	(373)
Other liabilities	2,389	3,376	190	2,002	1,194	1,684
Income taxes	15,297	7,195	15,181	(4,957)	(24,957)	4,044
Net cash flows from operating activities	39,421	39,773	38,687	37,400	45,728	32,647
Cash flows from investing activities						
Purchases of equity securities	(8,448)	(30,161)	(18,642)	(43,210)	(20,326)	(16,508)
Sales of equity securities	15,849	38,756	14,336	18,783	19,512	28,464
Purchases of U.S. Treasury bills and fixed maturity securities	(152,637)	(208,429)	(136,123)	(141,844)	(158,492)	(96,568)
Sales of U.S. Treasury bills and fixed maturity securities	27,188	31,873	15,929	39,693	49,327	18,757
Redemptions and maturities of U.S. Treasury bills and fixed maturity securities	160,402	149,709	137,767	113,045	86,727	26,177
Purchases of loans and finance receivables	(88)	(772)	(75)	(1,771)	(1,435)	(307)
Collections of loans and finance receivables	561	393	345	342	1,702	490
Acquisitions of business, net of cash acquired	(456)	(2,532)	(1,683)	(3,279)	(2,708)	(31,399)
Purchases of property, plant and equipment, and equipment held for lease	(13,276)	(13,012)	(15,979)	(14,537)	(11,708)	(12,954)

Other	297	(3,582)	(1,496)	(71)	(3,608)	(377)
Net cash flows from investing activities	29,392	(37,757)	(5,621)	(32,849)	(41,009)	(84,225)
Cash flows from financing activities						
Proceeds from borrowings of insurance and other businesses	2,961	5,925	8,144	2,409	2,645	14,172
Repayments of borrowings of insurance and other businesses	(3,032)	(2,700)	(5,095)	(7,395)	(5,465)	(2,577)
Proceeds from borrowings of railroad, utilities, and energy businesses	3,959	8,445	5,400	7,019	3,013	3,077
Repayments of borrowings of railroad, utilities, and energy businesses	(4,016)	(3,761)	(2,638)	(4,213)	(3,549)	(2,123)
Changes in short-term borrowings, net	(624)	(1,118)	266	(1,943)	2,079	130
Acquisition of treasury stock	(27,061)	(24,706)	(4,850)	(1,346)	–	–
Other	(695)	(429)	(497)	(343)	(121)	112
Net cash flows from financing activities	(28,508)	(18,344)	730	(5,812)	(1,398)	12,791
Effects of foreign currency exchange rate changes	5	92	25	(140)	248	(172)
Increase (decrease) in cash and cash equivalents and restricted cash	40,310	(16,236)	33,821	(1,401)	3,569	(38,959)
Cash and cash equivalents and restricted cash at beginning of year	48,396	64,632	30,811	32,212	28,643	67,602
Cash and cash equivalents and restricted cash at end of year*	**88,706**	**48,396**	**64,632**	**30,811**	**32,212**	**28,643**
**Cash and cash equivalents and restricted cash at end of year*						
Insurance and other	85,319	44,714	61,151	27,749	28,673	24,109
Railroad, utilities, and energy	2,865	3,276	3,024	2,612	2,910	3,939
Restricted cash included in other assets	522	406	457	450	629	595
	88,706	**48,396**	**64,632**	**30,811**	**32,212**	**28,643**

Note: Figures are in millions of U.S. dollars.

Source: Berkshire Hathaway, Inc., Annual Reports. Retrieved from https://www.berkshirehathaway.com/reports.html.

APPENDIX 4

QUESTION-AND-ANSWER SESSIONS WITH WARREN BUFFETT IN 2009 AND 2011

2009

There were five other schools attending the event with us: University of Illinois, Texas Christian University, Boston College, University of Toronto, and the University of South Dakota. There was a grand total of 162 students and six professors. The question-and-answer period did not allow any pictures or recording devices in the session. However, several students took detailed notes.

Buffett on the Economy

Where do you view the U.S. compared to the rest of the world in twenty-five years? Do you believe that the U.S. will still be the leading economic country in the world, or will the emerging countries develop and overtake the U.S.? If so, which country(ies) specifically do you believe will become economic superpowers, and why?

We will still be the leading economy over the next twenty-five years, just not as much as we did in the past. Other emerging countries will catch up with us, but that is all right because the world is not a zero-sum game. We will be better off if others are better. Our standard of living in the U.S. has increased sevenfold in the twentieth century.

The U.S. is the most important market in the world and will recover very fast, but not at the same margin as ten years ago. China is finally converting to an economic system that works, and with the amount of people living there, it has great growth potential. China and other emerging economies will assist us with solving the world's problems (e.g., energy, biological, etc.).

By having more of the world better off economically, it should help with security issues, as parts of the world envy countries with the riches, which could lead to nuclear and biological attacks on the U.S.

The U.S. has a huge deficit. What will be the fate of the U.S. dollar, and how will the government deal with this?

Twenty years ago, we did not have this problem. Today, the U.S. has a $1.4 trillion deficit, of which $400 billion is the current account deficit. Who finances our debt? (1) Sell debt to U.S. citizens; (2) sell debt to other countries; and/or (3) monetize the debt, which will lead to inflation.

Over time, our dollars will buy less. We do not know how far the dollar will fall, as we have never been through anything of this magnitude before.

Cash is stupid. It is not a good asset over time. You want assets. Congress holds the destiny of the dollar. What Congress has done so far is all right, but if they continue, the value of the dollar will continue to devalue.

It must be noted that Buffett makes the assertion that cash is not a good asset over time because of inflation. While he does feel this way, there are times when the market is overvalued, and he might prefer cash over purchasing overvalued assets.

Small-business growth in the U.S. has been diminished. What does the U.S. need to do to increase small-business growth?

Buffett said that you really must love your business to be successful. If someone has a good track record, they should be able to get educational assistance and money to start or grow a small business. The Small Business Administration does this, but a new program between Berkshire and Goldman Sachs just started. It is a $500 million program to assist small businesses. Perhaps one of the more powerful statements Buffett has ever made is the following:

I do not remember the name of the study, but there was a paper written on the correlation between IQ, GPA, and school attended, with business success. The findings indicated that the best correlation with success was when the person got started in business. Experience was the most important determinant in success.

The success of my businesses is dependent on networking and partnership. Form strong partnerships with people you can trust and feel comfortable to pursue common purposes.

Buffett on Investments

Why are you switching from companies like Coke and Gillette to cash-eating companies like BNSF and utilities?

I have shifted my focus from cash-oriented businesses to utilities and regulation organizations. The reason is due in part to the fact that I do not want to run Wall Street firms. Why the new paradigms in utilities? Because little cash capital is required, and they are very profit oriented. There is the potential for growth and price flexibility.

What caused you to invest in Goldman Sachs after what happened to Salomon Brothers?

Goldman Sachs needed affirmation that they were going to survive. Goldman's fear was a run on the bank. There was the Federal Deposit Insurance Company (FDIC) for common people in banks, but not an FDIC for investment banks.

In my view, Buffett stepped up to be the equivalent of the FDIC to restore confidence in the financial system, even though Goldman Sachs really did not need the cash! This was like what J. P. Morgan did in the Great Depression when he stepped up to bring liquidity to the markets in 1929.

Buffett continued to talk about how mad he is at the big salaries on Wall Street. He said he can understand paying a .400 hitter in professional baseball, but not .240 hitters. There are too many .240 hitters making too much money!

Would you encourage us to pick individual stocks or mutual funds?

If you are willing to invest the time to select stocks, then go that route. If not, dollar-cost average in low-cost mutual funds.

Buffett said that he was at a party in September 2008 and was surrounded by a group of women who normally ignored him, but suddenly, he was very popular, and they were all worried whether their money was safe. He said NO, and they all stayed around him.

> My best year in investing was in 1954, and that was a recession. If you wait to see robins, spring will be over.

Basically, what Buffett is saying is that you should buy when the market is down. Do not wait until it goes up, when everyone else is buying. Buffett continued:

> Buying stocks when everyone is selling is the best time to be buying stocks . . . especially during a financial crisis. Why save sex for your old age?

How does global philanthropy help Third World companies and economic growth?

> I have five foundations and farm this out to people who can do a better job than me. I believe in specialization of labor, where you should focus on what you do well. I believe in the Gates Foundation. That is why I gave him so much money. The reasons why I believe in the Gates Foundation are (1) Bill Gates spends a lot of time doing this; (2) we have the same goals, which are to save every human life on Earth; and (3) he has blood in the game . . . he works with his own money!
>
> You need to give back to society because society is what helps you to become successful. It is important to note that no one human being is any more important than another.

What are the biggest mistakes/failures that you have made, and what did you learn from them?

> The biggest decision you will make in life is your spouse.

Buffett joked that you should look for someone with low expectations.

> In life, there will be mistakes, but do not agonize over those mistakes because character needs to be built out of those experiences.

Buffett noted that people's failure in life is due in part to the fact that they vacillate on their setbacks and refuse to explore further prospects that may bring solutions to their impending worries.

For example, Buffett notes he once spent $3 billion to buy a shoe company that is now worthless. He also bought 50 percent of a Sinclair station early in his career, and it went to zero. That was 20 percent of his net worth at the time. That is equivalent to an opportunity cost of $8 billion today. Buffett emphasizes:

> Do not make mistakes for the fun of it, but rather avoid mistakes if it is within your jurisdiction. You only must do a very few things right in your life so long as you do not do too many things wrong.
>
> Always be well positioned for opportunities. Do not bother with other people's successes; rather, stay within your circles of competence.

Microsoft founder Bill Gates once told him: "Buffett, you have to invest in computers. They will change the way you do everything." Buffett responded:

> Will they change the way you chew gum? Will they change whether you chew Spearmint or Juicy Fruit? Will they change whether you drink Coke or Pepsi? If not, then I will stick with my investments, and you stick with yours.

He added:

> Another mistake is working without sleep, which leads to a bad and an unproductive decision-making process.

Once we have earned an income enough to cover our subsistence needs, what is the appropriate balance between leisure, family, and work?

> Satisfaction does not come with money; just with what you have got and what you are doing. Love what you do, and you will be satisfied. It is important to recognize that happiness is not about making money, but money is a nice thing to have.
>
> Work with people and an organization you love and admire. If you do not have this, then move on.
>
> I do not let my work decisions/investments change my way of life: I do not miss a movie, a meal, a trip or event with my wife and kids. Despite my

> anticipated busy schedules in the future, I have resolved not to substitute quality time with family and friendships for my ambitions.

Buffett still lives in Omaha because all his friends and family are there. He likes the fact that his grandchildren go to the same school he attended. He has said that he would not be any happier with several houses in Los Angeles or New York than with his home in Omaha.

What is your view on charitable giving in your name?

> I do not believe in giving money to build buildings with names on it at schools. I have more respect for the cleaning lady who gives money on Sunday to charity than the person who puts their name on a building. We have needs in the U.S.: 20 percent of the households are earning $21,000 or less.
>
> I am for equality to help others and for equal rights for men and women.

2011

Buffett on Entrepreneurship, Innovation, and Job Creation

How can the U.S. encourage more entrepreneurship and innovation, so we can increase new businesses and create more jobs in today's difficult economic environment? Who should oversee this initiative? The U.S. appears to be losing a lot of the top entrepreneurial foreign students to their home countries. How can we be more accommodating to them?

> Immigration policies need to change in the U.S. They do not make any sense. Entrepreneurship and innovation have been working since 1790. Back then, the U.S. had 4 million people in 1790 and had 25 percent of the world's output. The system works. It unleashes the potential of the individual.
>
> I was born in 1930. Since 1930 the GDP per capita has increased six times. Unfortunately, the rest of the world has caught on. China has figured out a way to unleash the potential of its people. It went thousands of years without doing this and now it is. Unleashing the potential of people is more important than any government action or policy. Bill Gates wrote a book called *The Road Ahead* in 1995. Nowhere in the book does he mention anything about the

Internet. The point is we do not know where the next big idea or industry is going to come from.

Manufacturing has been declining in the U.S. and is down to 10 percent of GDP. What is going to happen to the U.S.?

They have been saying this since 1980. After 1980, we created 40 million new jobs in the next 20 years. Who would have predicted Google? Microsoft? One hundred years ago we had 32 million workers on farms. Today we only have 6 to 7 million. In 1970 we exported 5 percent of GDP. Today we export 12 percent of GDP.

I cannot tell you what the jobs will be in 10–12 years. Each person in the U.S. has an average of seven pairs of shoes. That is over 2 billion pairs of shoes. Now we produce 2 percent of the shoes in the U.S., but it has not hurt us to let the Chinese produce shoes.

What are your thoughts on inflation?

Today, $1 from 1930 has a purchasing power of 6 cents. Yet the country has done well. Over time, most currencies depreciate primarily due to inflation. To me, that means you want to own good businesses. The best thing you can do is to own a business or expertise (whether you are a doctor, lawyer, etc.). You own that talent, which is your most important asset. I would pay $100,000 for 10 percent of your future earnings.

The next ten years, we will see significant amounts of inflation. Europeans gave up their printing press. When you do this, and you get into trouble, you cannot borrow money in your currency. In the U.S., we have printed a lot of money. This will bring inflation, but it will not end the world.

Fixed-dollar investments are a mistake. It makes no sense. Money markets lose money every day because of inflation. The riskiest investment is currency. You would need to have a country where the currency is rising.

What are your predictions on the defaults of municipal bonds?

The problem is that we are making too many promises to employees. The ability to solve the problem exists; however, we may have to change the promises. We owe $48,000 per person and $120,000 per household. Readjustments will always need to be made. Massive defaults will not happen. But we may be on the cusp of them. It will get postponed due to the consequences.

Buffett on Politics

What are your thoughts about the current state of the political process in the U.S.? What role do you think the government should play? What can we do to change the current flawed system?

The politicians are doing what is right for them to get reelected and not what is right for the country. I do not care who is in office because I would be doing the same thing whether the Democrats or the Republicans were in office. We would still buy good companies at good prices. We do not look at the stock market. We buy stock in a company that an idiot can run because one day, one will.

How do you feel about Occupy Wall Street?

The tax laws over the past 10 to 20 years have tilted towards the wealthy. In 1992, the top 400 incomes averaged $40 million a year. By 2011, the average was $220 million; a fivefold increase since 1992. Since then, the tax rate has dropped by 7 percent. I pay less percentage of taxes now than 40–50 years ago.

Buffett on Education

What advice would you give me in college?

Do anything that excites you. Do what sparks your interest. Go work for a person or company that you admire.

I would recommend that you improve your oral and written communication skills. This will improve your pay by at least 50 percent. They will not teach you this in business schools. Good communication of good ideas gets you much further in life. Any investment in you is best.

Berkshire Hathaway has hired a net 5,000 jobs this year and does not have a hard time filling jobs. Eighty percent of the people that I run into need to improve their ability at explaining their ideas both orally and written. Make yourself a person that you would want to hire. We look for people with not necessarily the highest IQs, but people who have a good work ethic, are loyal, honest, and reliable.

What would you like the U.S. education system to look like? What steps do you think should be taken to improve the U.S. school system in the immediate future? What do you think that we as soon-to-be college graduates can/should do to best help society/community/economy?

If you do not have a good public school system, equality is a joke. All my children went to public schools. Today, all my friends in New York send their children to private schools. Test scores at schools correlate inversely with the number of free lunches at schools. The income level of a family is the best indicator of the achievement level of students.

We are spending $6 billion on our children and not getting any improvement on our investment. Once you lose a good public school system, you need to get it back.

Our education and health-care systems are hard to change; 4 percent of our GDP is spent on education, and 17 percent of GDP is spent on health care. The rest of the world spends an average of 10 percent of their GDP on health care. This puts the U.S. at a disadvantage.

Despite spending 17 percent of our GDP on health care, the U.S. does not have any more doctors, nurses, etc. per capita than other countries. Our education and health-care systems are the two worst problems in the country and will be in the future. The U.S. is the richest country in the world and has a lot of resources. We will be better twenty years from now. Our competitive problem starts with health-care issues in the U.S.

Buffett's Value System

Has there ever been a time when you were not positive or were there times where you were less positive and wanted to give up?

My set point has always been to be happy. My dad got elected to Congress and I did not want to move away from Omaha to Washington, D.C. Success is getting what you want, and happiness is wanting what you get.

Today, the population of the world is seven billion. The U.S. population is 311.8 million. If you were to draw a ticket out of a lottery (that included all the people in the world), the odds that you would draw a person from the U.S. are 4.45 percent. The odds that you would draw a person from the U.S. who is the same sex as you are 2.225 percent. The odds get less if you take into consideration race and social class.

The U.S. is the richest country in the world. You are lucky to be born in the U.S. Better things happen to people who are optimistic.

Buffett on Berkshire Hathaway

What Berkshire Hathaway management practices can be improved or changed?

I had the luxury of creating my own company. It is like creating your own painting. You can define what you want the company to be and how to run the company. There were no institutional barriers in terms of compensation and policies. Berkshire Hathaway does not have stock options but has other things to motivate employees. The company has a strong culture. At Notre Dame, if you work there, you buy into their culture. You buy into what they stand for and what they are about. This is the same for our company.

Why did you hire Todd Combs among several hundred portfolio managers that applied?

All the applicants had high IQs. However, I hire not just for IQs, but I also look for the following: How have they done and do things? Do they have a love for Berkshire Hathaway? They are not interested in working at other companies.

Since 1965, I cannot think of anyone that has left Berkshire Hathaway for another job. You want a self-selection process in investment and operation arenas. By working at Berkshire, they give up the opportunity to make more money. The people Berkshire hires are extraordinary human beings! Their character is essential, and our board of directors and I must feel good about the hires.

Buffett on Investments

What is the most important aspect of your selling discipline?

I do not have a selling discipline. I have a buying discipline. My philosophy is to buy a business at the right price. I have no exit strategy. All you must do is have one good decision. Buy something that you should keep for five years if the stock market closed.

How have the principles of value investing changed with tech companies?

I started in the investment arena at age seven. I read all the books on investing at the Omaha Public Library. Read chapters 8 and 20 in *The Intelligent Investor*. Those are the best chapters written on investing. I have been doing the same thing since I was nineteen years old, when I first read *The Intelligent Investor*. I learned what I could learn. Look for margin of safety, and look for stocks that are undervalued.

How do you value social ventures?

These are ventures that someone is going to subsidize for a while. Berkshire does not do this because it does not make economic sense to its shareholders. The market system will not solve social problems. That is for governments to solve. Maybe through private philanthropy of shareholders' returns can social ventures succeed.

Is it necessary to have 100 percent of the market information to outperform the market?

The stock market is an incredible place to make money, and it is liquid. I like it when farm prices go up and down in a year. That gives an investor an opportunity to buy at a low level.

In 1950, I got out of school and bought a Moody's. I read 7,000 to 8,000 pages twice. When I got to page 1433, I found the company Western Insurance Securities and noticed that it was selling at a bargain price of .5x earnings.

When people get afraid, there are investments to do. You must think differently from those around you. You will have options that do not require a lot of intelligence. You must get into a position where people do not pull the rug from underneath you.

My partner, Charlie Munger, says you get into trouble with the following three things: liquor, ladies, and leverage.

In 1998, Long Term Capital Management (LTCM) had around 200 employees with IQs in the 150s. The employees of LTCM had some of the highest IQs in the U.S. They each had 15–20 years of experience, worked with their own money, and were good people. However, they almost took down the whole financial system. They became too comfortable, and their models did not predict a hiccup like the East Asian currency crisis. Leverage got them into trouble. Stay away from emotions, the crowd, and borrowed money.

NOTES

1. WARREN E. BUFFETT'S BACKGROUND

1. James Berman, "The Three Essential Warren Buffett Quotes to Live By," *Forbes*, April 20, 2014, https://www.forbes.com/sites/jamesberman/2014/04/20/the-three-essential-warren-buffett-quotes-to-live-by/?sh=544c78aa6543.
2. Warren Buffett, 2021 Berkshire Hathaway Annual Shareholder Letter (Omaha: Berkshire Hathaway), February 26, 2022, https://www.berkshirehathaway.com/letters/2021ltr.pdf.
3. CNBC Warren Buffett Archive, "Buffett on Meeting Lorimer Davidson," April 3, 2018, https://buffett.cnbc.com/video/2018/04/03/buffett-on-meeting-lorimer-davidson.html.
4. Alice Schroeder, "FT Series Part 1: Warren Buffett," *Financial Times*, September 26, 2008.
5. Alice Schroeder, "How Warren Buffett Made His First Dime," *Parade*, Sept. 7, 2008.
6. Robert Miles, *Warren Buffett Wealth: Principles and Practical Methods Used by the World's Greatest Investor* (Hoboken, NJ: Wiley, 2004), 25.
7. Alice Schroeder, *The Snowball: Warren Buffett and the Business of Life* (New York: Bantam, 2009), 46.
8. Schroeder, *Snowball*, 20.
9. Schroeder, *Snowball*, 21.
10. Schroeder, *Snowball*, 5.
11. Todd Finkle, "Warren E. Buffett and Berkshire Hathaway, Inc.," *Journal of the International Academy of Case Studies* 16, no. 5 (2010): 70.
12. Jesse Koltes, "2016 Berkshire Hathaway Meeting Notes: Q&A w/Charlie Munger," *The Charlieton*, May 15, 2016, http://thecharlieton.com/brk2016/.
13. Schroeder, *Snowball*, 42.
14. Schroeder, *Snowball*, 42.
15. Doris Buffett, *Giving It All Away: The Doris Buffett Story* (Sag Harbor, NY: Permanent Press, 2010).
16. *Becoming Warren Buffett*, directed by Peter Kunhardt (HBO, 2017).
17. Schroeder, *Snowball*, 116.
18. Linda Childers, "Doris Buffett: Putting the Pain in Perspective," August 6, 2018, https://www.bphope.com/putting-the-pain-in-perspective/.
19. Schroeder, *Snowball*, 643.

20. Schroeder, *Snowball*, 643.
21. Schroeder, *Snowball*, 35.
22. Miles, *Warren Buffett Wealth*, 25.
23. Schroeder, *Snowball*, 33.
24. Schroeder, *Snowball*, 60.
25. Schroeder, *Snowball*, 106.
26. Doug Kass, "Kass: Warren and Me," *TheStreet*, May 1, 2013, https://www.thestreet.com/investing/kass-warren-and-me-11909459.
27. Andrew Kilpatrick, *Of Permanent Value: The Story of Warren Buffett* (Mountain Brook, AL: Andy Kilpatrick Publishing Empire, 2008), 62.
28. Brad Davis, "Buffett Still Big on Economy, Still Looking for Big Deal," *Omaha World Herald*, February 24, 2019.
29. Lorna Baldwin, "Here is Warren Buffett's First Tax Return, Filed at Age 14," June 26, 2017, https://www.pbs.org/newshour/economy/warren-buffetts-first-tax-return-filed-age-14.
30. Zack Guzman and Mary Stevens, "Here's How Warren Buffett Hustled to Make $53,000 as a Teenager," January 31, 2017, https://www.cnbc.com/2017/01/31/heres-how-warren-buffett-hustled-to-make-53000-as-a-teenager.html.
31. Joshua Kennon, "One of the Wealthiest People in America: A Chronological History of the Oracle of Omaha: 1930–2019," *The Balance*, June 25, 2019, https://www.thebalance.com/warren-buffett-timeline-356439.
32. Miles, *Warren Buffett Wealth*, 27.
33. Miles, *Warren Buffett Wealth*, 27.
34. Timothy Vick, *How to Pick Stocks Like Warren Buffett* (New York: McGraw-Hill, 2000), 10.
35. Schroeder, *Snowball*, 63.
36. Lisa Du, "Warren Buffett's High School Yearbook Totally Nailed What He Would Be When He Grew Up," *Business Insider*, June 6, 2012, https://www.businessinsider.com/warren-buffetts-high-school-yearbook-foreshadowed-his-future-career-2012-6.
37. Andrew Norman, "Peter Buffett's Roots," *Hear Nebraska*, April 25, 2011, https://hearnebraska.org/feature/peter-buffetts-roots-scoop/.
38. Steve Jordon, "Omaha Benefits Despite Buffett's Philosophy on Local Giving," *Omaha World Herald*, May 5, 2013, https://www.omaha.com/news/omaha-benefits-despite-buffett-s-philosophy-on-local-giving/article_115fa215-71af-5443-9057-987d6faba31d.html.
39. "Alibaba Founder Jack Ma: 'Harvard Rejected Me 10 Times,'" *Business Insider*, September 14, 2015, https://www.businessinsider.com/jack-ma-harvard-rejected-me-10-times-2015-9?IR=T.

2. EARLY INFLUENCES, COLLEGE, AND PARTNERSHIP YEARS

1. Dale Carnegie, *How to Win Friends and Influence People* (New York: Simon and Schuster, 1964), 106.
2. Alice Schroeder, *The Snowball: Warren Buffett and the Business of Life* (New York: Bantam, 2009), 57.
3. Carnegie, *How to Win Friends and Influence People*, 14.
4. Carnegie, *How to Win Friends and Influence People*, 14.
5. Carnegie, *How to Win Friends and Influence People*, 14.

6. Carnegie, *How to Win Friends and Influence People*, 14.
7. Carnegie, *How to Win Friends and Influence People*, 23.
8. Carnegie, *How to Win Friends and Influence People*, 34.
9. Carnegie, *How to Win Friends and Influence People*, 57.
10. Carnegie, *How to Win Friends and Influence People*, 69.
11. *Ground Report*, "More of an Equity Investor of Entrepreneurs," November 14, 2012, https://www.groundreport.com/more-of-an-equity-investor-of-entrepreneurs/.
12. *Becoming Warren Buffett*, directed by Peter Kunhardt (HBO, 2017).
13. Schroeder, *Snowball*, 74.
14. Robert Hagstrom, *The Warren Buffett Way*, 3rd ed. (Hoboken, NJ: Wiley, 2014), 22.
15. Hagstrom, *Warren Buffett Way*, 26.
16. Hagstrom, *Warren Buffett Way*, xxiii.
17. Jason Fernando, "Arbitrage," *Investopedia*, August 30, 2021, https://www.investopedia.com/terms/a/arbitrage.asp.
18. Randall Lane, "The $50 Billion Decision," *Forbes*, March 26, 2012, https://www.forbes.com/forbes-life-magazine/2012/0409/all-access-warren-buffett-omaha-graham-newman-50-billion-decision.html.
19. Lane, "$50 Billion Decision."
20. Philip Fisher, *Common Stocks and Uncommon Profits and Other Writings* (New York: Harper, 1958).
21. Fisher, *Common Stocks*, 3.
22. Robert Hagstrom, *The Essential Buffett: Timeless Principles for the New Economy* (New York: Wiley, 2007), 61.
23. *Becoming Warren Buffett*, directed by Peter Kunhardt (HBO, 2017).
24. Lane, "$50 Billion Decision."
25. Andrew Kilpatrick, *Of Permanent Value: The Story of Warren Buffett* (Mountain Brook, AL: Andy Kilpatrick Publishing Empire, 2008), 89.
26. Kilpatrick, *Permanent Value*, 88.
27. Hagstrom, *Warren Buffett Way*, 10.
28. Hagstrom, *Warren Buffett Way*, 11.
29. Todd Finkle, "Warren E. Buffett & Berkshire Hathaway, Inc.," *Journal of the International Academy for Case Studies* 16, no. 5 (2010): 61–88.
30. Martin Fridson, *How to Be a Billionaire* (New York: Wiley, 1999), 179.
31. Warren Buffett, Buffett Partnership Ltd. letter, January 22, 1969.
32. Warren Buffett, *Warren Buffett on Business: Principles from the Sage of Omaha* (Hoboken, NJ: Wiley, 2009), 198.

3. CHARLIE MUNGER

1. Charlie Munger, *Poor Charlie's Almanack: The Wit and Wisdom of Charles T. Munger*, 3rd ed., ed. Peter Kaufman (Marceline, MO: Walsworth, 2005), 6.
2. Munger, *Poor Charlie's Almanack*, ix.
3. "How Charlie Met Warren," CNBC Squawk Box video, May 5, 2014, https://www.cnbc.com/video/2014/05/05/how-charlie-met-warren.html, at 1:54.

4. Charlie Munger, "A Conversation with Charlie Munger and Michigan Ross—2017," interview by Scott DeRue, University of Michigan, YouTube video, December 20, 2017, https://www.youtube.com/watch?v=S9HgIGzOENA, at 55:39.
5. Munger, "Conversation with Charlie Munger."
6. Munger, "Conversation with Charlie Munger."
7. Munger, "Conversation with Charlie Munger."
8. Munger, "Conversation with Charlie Munger."
9. Munger, "Conversation with Charlie Munger."
10. Munger, "Conversation with Charlie Munger."
11. Charlie Munger, "Influencers Transcript: Charlie Munger, May 9, 2019," interview by Andy Serwer, Yahoo! Finance video, May 9, 2019, https://sg.finance.yahoo.com/news/influencers-transcript-charlie-munger-105001910.html.
12. Munger, "Conversation with Charlie Munger."
13. Munger, "Conversation with Charlie Munger."
14. Munger, "Conversation with Charlie Munger."
15. Warren Buffett, "The Superinvestors of Graham and Doddsville," *Columbia Business School Magazine*, 1984, https://www8.gsb.columbia.edu/sites/valueinvesting/files/files/Buffett1984.pdf.
16. Munger, "Conversation with Charlie Munger."
17. Janet Lowe, *Damn Right! Behind the Scenes with Berkshire Hathaway Billionaire Charlie Munger* (Hoboken, NJ: Wiley, 2003), 78–79.
18. Munger, "Conversation with Charlie Munger."
19. Munger, *Poor Charlie's Almanack*, vi.
20. Warren Buffett, 2014 Annual Shareholder Letter (Omaha: Berkshire Hathaway), February 27, 2015, http://www.berkshirehathaway.com/letters/2014ltr.pdf.
21. Buffett, 2014 Shareholder Letter.
22. Munger, "Influencers Transcript."
23. Warren Buffett and Charlie Munger, 2000 Annual Berkshire Hathaway Shareholders' Meeting (Omaha), CNBC Warren Buffett Archive, April 29, 2000, https://buffett.cnbc.com/video/2000/04/29/morning-session---2000-berkshire-hathaway-annual-meeting.html.
24. Morgan Housel, "8 of the Smartest Things Charlie Munger Has Ever Said," The Motley Fool, April 26, 2013, https://www.fool.com/investing/general/2013/04/26/8-of-the-smartest-things-charlie-munger-has-ever-s.aspx.
25. Munger, "Conversation with Charlie Munger."
26. Munger, "Influencers Transcript."
27. Charlie Munger, "Charlie Munger: Full Transcript of Daily Journal Annual Meeting 2019," ed. Richard Lewis, Latticework Investing, March 3, 2019, http://latticeworkinvesting.com/2019/03/03/charlie-munger-full-transcript-of-daily-journal-annual-meeting-2019/.
28. Munger, "Influencers Transcript."
29. Munger, "Daily Journal."
30. Munger, "Influencers Transcript."
31. Munger, "Daily Journal."
32. Charlie Munger, "The Psychology of Human Misjudgment" (speech, 1995), YouTube video, October 5, 2018, https://www.YouTube.com/watch?v=4ICaAKuAudQ, at 1:15:22.
33. Munger, "The Psychology of Human Misjudgment."

34. Munger, "The Psychology of Human Misjudgment."
35. The Swedish Investor, "Charlie Munger: Mental Models for the Rest of Your Life," YouTube video, June 26, 2021, https://www.youtube.com/watch?v=ywyQ_eNNCJU, at 17:53.
36. Robert Goldsborough, "Timeless Investment Lessons from Warren Buffett's Business Partner," Yahoo! Finance, May 2, 2014, https://finance.yahoo.com/news/timeless-investment-lessons-warren-buffetts-110000095.html.
37. "Charlie Munger: The Lollapalooza Effect and How It Affects the Stock Market," GuruFocus, September 13, 2019.
38. "Lollapalooza Effect," GuruFocus.
39. "Lollapalooza Effect," GuruFocus.
40. "What Is the Lollapalooza Effect?," The Motley Fool, October 19, 2016, https://www.fool.com/knowledge-center/lollapalooza-effect.aspx.
41. "Lollapalooza Effect?," Motley Fool.
42. Josh Funk, "Warren Buffett's $2 Billion Right-Hand Man," *The Post and Courier*, May 31, 2008, https://www.postandcourier.com/business/warren-buffett-s-billion-right-hand-man/article_82931669-1a19-5a89-81a1-b189cc2a8c6f.html.
43. Charlie Munger, "USC Law Commencement Speech," *Genius*, May 1, 2007, https://genius.com/Charlie-munger-usc-law-commencement-speech-annotated.
44. Munger, "USC Law Commencement Speech."
45. Adriana Belmonte, "Charlie Munger Explains the Best Career Strategy 'for the Great Mass of Humanity,' " Yahoo! Life. May 21, 2019, https://www.yahoo.com/lifestyle/career-advice-charlie-munger-buffett-155842582.html.
46. Munger, "USC Law Commencement Speech."
47. Munger, "Daily Journal."
48. Munger, "USC Law Commencement Speech."
49. Munger, "Psychology of Human Misjudgment."
50. Munger, "USC Law Commencement Speech."
51. Munger, "USC Law Commencement Speech."
52. Munger, "Psychology of Human Misjudgment."
53. Charlie Munger, "Macroeconomics," YouTube video, April 16, 2021, https://www.youtube.com/watch?v=d2yLhEsY-9Y.
54. Munger, "USC Law Commencement Speech."
55. Munger, "USC Law Commencement Speech."
56. Warren Buffett and Charlie Munger, 2019 Annual Berkshire Hathaway Shareholders' Meeting (Omaha), CNBC Warren Buffett Archive, May 4, 2019, https://buffett.cnbc.com/2019-berkshire-hathaway-annual-meeting/.
57. Munger, "Daily Journal."
58. Housel, "8 of the Smartest Things Charlie Munger Has Ever Said."
59. Julia LaRoche, "Charlie Munger Doesn't Take a Salary and Wishes Other Executives Would Do the Same," Yahoo! Finance, April 14, 2017, https://finance.yahoo.com/news/charlie-munger-doesnt-take-salary-wishes-executives-154120420.html.
60. Munger, "Daily Journal."
61. Andy Serwer, "Charlie Munger's Advice on Investing and Life Choices That Make a Person Wealthy," Yahoo! Finance, May 9, 2019, https://www.youtube.com/watch?v=RFxXl9eAWV4&t=2318s.

62. *Stanford Report*, "Mungers Donate $43.5 Million to Help Construct New Graduate Student Residence," August 26, 2004, https://news.stanford.edu/news/2004/september1/munger-91.html.
63. "Financier Munger Gives DuBridge Lecture," California Institute of Technology, January 29, 2008, https://www.caltech.edu/about/news/financier-munger-gives-dubridge-lecture-1381.
64. Michael De La Merced, "Charles Munger, Warren Buffett's Longtime Business Partner, Makes $65 Million Gift," *New York Times*, October 24, 2014, https://dealbook.nytimes.com/2014/10/24/a-billionaires-65-million-gift-to-theoretical-physics/.
65. Kelsey Brugger, "Charlie Munger to Donate $200 Million to UCSB for New Dorms," *Santa Barbara Independent*, March 24, 2016, https://web.archive.org/web/20160329041412/http://www.independent.com/news/2016/mar/24/charlie-munger-donates-200-million-ucsb-new-dorms/.
66. Keith Hamm, "UCSB Gifted Las Varas Ranch: Billionaire Charlie Munger Finances Purch of 'Coastal Jewel,' " *Santa Barbara Independent*, https://www.independent.com/2018/12/12/ucsb-gifted-las-varas-ranch/.
67. Hamm, "UCSB Gifted Las Varas Ranch."
68. "Munger Gives $21 Million to Good Samaritan Hospital," *Philanthropy News Digest*, March 12, 2018, https://philanthropynewsdigest.org/news/munger-gives-21-million-to-good-samaritan-hospital.
69. "Charlie Munger," Golden, 2020, https://golden.com/wiki/Charlie_Munger.

4. BERKSHIRE'S VALUE INVESTMENT PHILOSOPHY AND ADVICE

1. Rob Berger, "Top 100 Money Quotes of All Time," *Forbes*, April 30, 2014, https://www.forbes.com/sites/robertberger/2014/04/30/top-100-money-quotes-of-all-time/?sh=1c5541fd4998.
2. Investopedia, "Why Did Warren Buffett Invest Heavily in Coca-Cola in the Late 1980s?," January 16, 2021, https://www.investopedia.com/ask/answers/052615/why-did-warren-buffett-invest-heavily-cocacola-ko-late-1980s.asp.
3. Investopedia, "Why Did Warren Buffett Invest Heavily in Coca-Cola in the Late 1980s?"
4. Philip Fisher, *Common Stocks and Uncommon Profits and Other Writings* (Hoboken, NJ: Wiley, 1958), 46.
5. Fisher, *Common Stocks*, 46.
6. CB Insight, "28 Lessons from Warren Buffett's Annual Letters to Shareholders," March 10, 2021, https://www.cbinsights.com/research/buffett-berkshire-hathaway-shareholder-letters/.
7. Warren Buffett and Charlie Munger, 2008 Annual Berkshire Hathaway Shareholders' Meeting (Omaha), CNBC Warren Buffett Archive, May 3, 2008, https://buffett.cnbc.com/2008-berkshire-hathaway-annual-meeting/.
8. Buffett and Munger, 2008 Annual Berkshire Hathaway Shareholders' Meeting.
9. Fisher, *Common Stocks*, 113.
10. Lucas Downey, "Efficient Market Hypothesis (EMH)," Investopedia, February 5, 2020, https://www.investopedia.com/terms/e/efficientmarkethypothesis.asp.
11. Janet Lowe, *Value Investing Made Easy* (New York: McGraw-Hill, 1996), 11.

12. Buffett, 2008 Annual Berkshire Hathaway Shareholders' Meeting.
13. Warren Buffett, 1987 Berkshire Hathaway Annual Shareholder Letter (Omaha: Berkshire Hathaway), February 29, 1988, https://www.berkshirehathaway.com/letters/1987.html.
14. Warren Buffett, interview with Todd Finkle and students, November 9, 2009.
15. Berkeley Lovelace, Jr., "Warren Buffett: $10,000 Invested in an Index fund When I Bought My First Stock in 1942 Would Be Worth $51 Million Today," CNBC, May 7, 2018, https://www.cnbc.com/2018/05/07/warren-buffett-10000-invested-in-an-index-fund-when-i-bought-my-first-stock-in-1942-would-be-worth-51-million-today.html.
16. "GuruFocus Tracks the Stock Picks of Gurus," GuruFocus, http://www.gurufocus.com/ListGuru.php?GuruName=Warren+Buffett.
17. Julia LaRoche, "Charlie Munger Doesn't Take a Salary and Wishes Other Executives Would Do the Same," Yahoo! Finance, April 14, 2017, https://finance.yahoo.com/news/charlie-munger-doesnt-take-salary-wishes-executives-154120420.html.
18. LaRoche, "Charlie Munger Doesn't Take a Salary."
19. Equilar, "Equilar 100: CEO Pay at the Largest Companies by Revenue," 2020, https://www.equilar.com/reports/72-table-highest-paid-ceos-2020-equilar-100.html.
20. Dan Marcec, "Equilar 100: The Highest-Paid CEOs at the Largest U.S. Companies," Equilar, April 20, 2021, https://www.equilar.com/reports/80-highest-paid-ceos-2021-equilar-100.html.
21. Todd A. Finkle, "Warren E. Buffett and Berkshire Hathaway, Inc.," *Journal of the International Academy for Case Studies* 16, no. 5 (2010): 79.
22. Warren Buffett, 1994 Annual Berkshire Hathaway Shareholders' Meeting (Omaha), CNBC Warren Buffett Archive, April 25, 1994, https://buffett.cnbc.com/video/1994/04/25/morning-session---1994-berkshire-hathaway-annual-meeting.html.
23. Buffett, 1994 Annual Berkshire Hathaway Shareholders' Meeting.
24. John Prescott, "Nebraska Furniture Mart: A Pillar in Its 80th Year," *Omaha World Herald*, February 3, 2017.
25. FindLaw, "Patents, Trademarks & Copyrights," March 26, 2008, https://corporate.findlaw.com/intellectual-property/patents-trademarks-amp-copyrights.html.
26. IFI Claims Patent Services, "2021 Top 50 US Patent Assignees," January 5, 2022, https://www.ificlaims.com/rankings-top-50-2021.htm.
27. IFI Claims Patent Services, "2021 Top 50 US Patent Assignees."
28. Richard Stim, "Types of Patents Available Under U.S. Law," Nolo, 2020, https://www.nolo.com/legal-encyclopedia/types-patents.html.
29. Will Kelton, "Design Patent," Investopedia, August 20, 2019, https://www.investopedia.com/terms/d/design-patent.asp.
30. Kelton, "Design Patent."
31. Warren Buffett, 2016 Annual Berkshire Hathaway Shareholders' Meeting (Omaha), CNBC Warren Buffett Archive, April 30, 2016, https://buffett.cnbc.com/video/2016/04/30/morning-session—2016-berkshire-hathaway-annual-meeting.html.
32. Warren Buffett, 2016 Berkshire Hathaway Annual Shareholder Letter (Omaha: Berkshire Hathaway), February 25, 2017, 22, https://www.berkshirehathaway.com/letters/2016ltr.pdf.
33. Warren Buffett, 2017 Annual Berkshire Hathaway Shareholders' Meeting (Omaha), CNBC Warren Buffett Archive, May 6, 2017, https://buffett.cnbc.com/2017-berkshire-hathaway-annual-meeting/.

34. Buffett, 2017 Annual Berkshire Hathaway Shareholders' Meeting.
35. Buffett, 2016 Shareholder Letter, 22.
36. Buffett, 2016 Shareholder Letter, 23.
37. Alex Dumortier, "Warren Buffett's 13 Greatest Quotes from Berkshire Hathaway's 2016 Annual Meeting (Bonus: 11 from Charlie)," The Motley Fool, May 11, 2016, https://www.fool.com/investing/general/2016/05/11/warren-buffetts-13-greatest-quotes-from-berkshire.aspx.
38. Erik Holm and Anupreeta Das, "Recap: The 2016 Berkshire Hathaway Annual Meeting," *Wall Street Journal*, April 30, 2016, http://blogs.wsj.com/moneybeat/2016/04/30/live-analysis-of-the-2016-berkshire-hathaway-annual-meeting/.
39. Lovelace, "Warren Buffett."
40. Lovelace, "Warren Buffett."
41. "Full Transcript: Billionaire Investor Warren Buffett Speaks with CNBC's Becky Quick on 'Squawk Box' Today," interview by Becky Quick, CNBC, February 25, 2019, https://www.cnbc.com/2019/02/25/full-transcript-billionaire-investor-warren-buffett-speaks-with-cnbcs-becky-quick-on-squawk-box-today.html.
42. "Full Transcript."
43. "Full Transcript."
44. "Full Transcript."
45. Warren Buffett, Meeting with Seven Universities at Berkshire Hathaway's Corporate Headquarters, Omaha, 2009.
46. Buffett, Meeting with Seven Universities.
47. Kathleen Elkins, "Warren Buffett Simplifies Investing with a Baseball Analogy," CNBC, February 2, 2017, https://www.cnbc.com/2017/02/02/warren-buffett-simplifies-investing-with-a-baseball-analogy.html#:~:text=The%20lesson%20for%20investors%2C%20Buffett,!%2C'%20ignore%20them.%E2%80%9D.
48. John Melloy, "Buffett Slams Wall Street 'Monkeys', Says Hedge Funds, Advisors Have Cost Clients $100 Billion," *CNBC*, February 25, 2017, https://www.cnbc.com/2017/02/25/buffett-slams-wall-street-monkeys-says-hedge-funds-cost-100-billion.html.
49. Jeff Cox, " 'Peak Passive'? Money Is Gushing out of Actively Managed Funds," CNBC, January 19, 2017, http://www.cnbc.com/2017/01/19/peak-passive-money-is-gushing-out-of-actively-managed-funds.html.
50. Akhilesh Ganti, "Russell 1000 Index," Investopedia, March 8, 2021, https://www.investopedia.com/terms/r/russell_1000index.asp.
51. Warren Buffett, 2016 Annual Berkshire Hathaway Shareholders' Meeting (Omaha), CNBC Warren Buffett Archive, April 30, 2016. https://buffett.cnbc.com/2016-berkshire-hathaway-annual-meeting/.
52. 25iq, "A Dozen Things Charlie Munger Has Said about Reading," July 26, 2015, https://25iq.com/2015/07/26/a-dozen-things-charlie-munger-has-said-about-reading/.
53. 25iq, "A Dozen Things Charlie Munger Has Said about Reading."
54. Nicholas Vardy, "Why 'High Intelligence' Is a Handicap to Profitable Investing," *Seeking Alpha*, October 1, 2017, https://seekingalpha.com/article/4110909-why-high-intelligence-is-handicap-to-profitable-investing.
55. Buffett, 1994 Shareholders' Meeting.

56. Charlie Munger, *Poor Charlie's Almanack: The Wit and Wisdom of Charles T. Munger*, 3rd ed., ed. Peter Kaufman (Marceline, MO: Walsworth, 2005).
57. Johnny Hopkins, "25 Timeless Investing Lessons from Charlie Munger," *The Acquirer's Multiple*, September 11, 2017, https://acquirersmultiple.com/2017/09/25-timeless-investing-lessons-from-charles-munger/.
58. Buffett and Munger, 2008 Shareholders' Meeting.
59. Stepan Lavrouk and GuruFocus, "Warren Buffett: Why Stocks Are Like Hamburgers," Yahoo!, June 8, 2019, https://www.yahoo.com/video/warren-buffett-why-stocks-hamburgers-031629347.html.

5. BERKSHIRE'S INVESTMENT METHODOLOGY

1. Warren Buffett, 2007 Berkshire Hathaway Annual Shareholder Letter (Omaha: Berkshire Hathaway), February 29, 2008, https://www.berkshirehathaway.com/letters/2007ltr.pdf.
2. Warren Buffett and Charlie Munger, 2007 Annual Berkshire Hathaway Shareholders' Meeting (Omaha), CNBC Warren Buffett Archive, May 5, 2007, https://buffett.cnbc.com/video/2007/05/05/morning-session---2007-berkshire-hathaway-annual-meeting.html.
3. Zigfred Diaz, "The Three Most Important Words in Investing," *Business Mirror*, November 6, 2017, https://businessmirror.com.ph/2017/11/06/the-three-most-important-words-in-investing/.
4. James Chen, "Margin of Safety," Investopedia, April 21, 2021, https://www.investopedia.com/terms/m/marginofsafety.asp.
5. Chen, "Margin of Safety."
6. Investopedia, "Why Did Warren Buffett Invest Heavily in Coca-Cola in the Late 1980s?," January 16, 2021, https://www.investopedia.com/ask/answers/052615/why-did-warren-buffett-invest-heavily-cocacola-ko-late-1980s.asp.
7. Buffett, 2007 Shareholders' Meeting.
8. Buffett, 2007 Shareholders' Meeting.
9. Adam Smith, "The Modest Billionaire," *Esquire*, October 1, 1988, https://classic.esquire.com/article/1988/10/01/the-modest-billionaire.
10. Buffett, 2007 Shareholders' Meeting.
11. Warren Buffett, 2019 Berkshire Hathaway Annual Shareholder Letter (Omaha: Berkshire Hathaway), February 22, 2020, 4, https://www.berkshirehathaway.com/letters/2019ltr.pdf.
12. Buffett, 2007 Shareholder Letter, 6.
13. Buffett, 2007 Shareholder Letter, 6.
14. Buffett, 2007 Shareholder Letter, 6.
15. Buffett, 2007 Shareholder Letter, 6.
16. Warren Buffett, 1994 Annual Berkshire Hathaway Shareholders' Meeting (Omaha), CNBC Warren Buffett Archive, April 25, 1994, https://buffett.cnbc.com/video/1994/04/25/morning-session---1994-berkshire-hathaway-annual-meeting.html.
17. Warren Buffett, "Buy American. I Am," *New York Times*, October 16, 2008, https://www.nytimes.com/2008/10/17/opinion/17buffett.html.

18. J. B. Maverick, "Intrinsic Value vs. Current Market Value: What's the Difference?," Investopedia, 2019, https://www.investopedia.com/ask/answers/011215/what-difference-between-intrinsic-value-and-current-market-value.asp.
19. Buffett, 2019 Shareholder Letter, 10.
20. Buffett, 2019 Shareholder Letter.
21. Alicia Tuovila, "Net Tangible Assets," Investopedia, February 3, 2022, https://www.investopedia.com/terms/n/nettangibleassets.asp.
22. *Accounting Tools*, "Par Value Definition," February 15, 2022, https://www.accountingtools.com/articles/what-is-par-value.html.
23. Tuovila, "Net Tangible Assets."
24. Jason Fernando, "Return on Equity (ROE)," Investopedia, November 30, 2021, https://www.investopedia.com/terms/r/returnonequity.asp.
25. Adam Hayes, "Shareholder Equity (SE)," Investopedia, March 17, 2021, https://www.investopedia.com/terms/s/shareholdersequity.asp.
26. Hayes, "Shareholder Equity (SE)."
27. Ted Reed, "Buffett Decries Airline Investing Even Though at Worst He Broke Even," *Forbes*, May 13, 2013, https://www.forbes.com/sites/tedreed/2013/05/13/buffett-decries-airline-investing-even-though-at-worst-he-broke-even/?sh=4ffdb943b5e7.
28. Jason Fernando, "Debt-to-Equity (D/E) Ratio," Investopedia, February 19, 2022, https://www.investopedia.com/terms/d/debtequityratio.asp.
29. Chris Murphy, "What Is the Formula for Calculating Free Cash Flow?," Investopedia, July 4, 2021, https://www.investopedia.com/ask/answers/033015/what-formula-calculating-free-cash-flow.asp.
30. Jason Fernando, "Free Cash Flow (FCF)," Investopedia, December 4, 2021, https://www.investopedia.com/terms/f/freecashflow.asp.
31. Murphy, "What Is the Formula?"
32. Buffett, 2019 Shareholders' Meeting.
33. Theron Mohamed, "Warren Buffett's Favorite Business Is a Little Chocolate Maker with an 8000 Percent Return. Here Are 5 Reasons Why He Loves See's Candies," *Markets Insider*, December 21, 2021, https://markets.businessinsider.com/news/stocks/warren-buffett-berkshire-hathaway-dream-business-is-sees-candies-2019-7-1028348838#a-return-of-8000-1.
34. Warren Buffett, 2015 Berkshire Hathaway Annual Shareholder Letter (Omaha: Berkshire Hathaway), February 27, 2016, https://www.berkshirehathaway.com/letters/2015ltr.pdf.
35. Mohamed, "Warren Buffett's Favorite Business."
36. Warren Buffett, 2019 Annual Berkshire Hathaway Shareholders' Meeting (Omaha), CNBC Warren Buffett Archive, May 4, 2019, https://buffett.cnbc.com/2019-berkshire-hathaway-annual-meeting/.
37. Mohamed, "Warren Buffett's Favorite Business."
38. Mohamed, "Warren Buffett's Favorite Business."
39. Adam Hayes, "Dividend Payout Ratio," Investopedia, January 3, 2022, https://www.investopedia.com/terms/d/dividendpayoutratio.asp.
40. GuruFocus, "Warren Buffett Mulls $100 Billion Berkshire Share Repurchase," April 26, 2019, https://www.forbes.com/sites/gurufocus/2019/04/26/warren-buffett-mulls-100-billion-berkshire-share-repurchase/#6651546a659b.

6. CASE STUDIES: GEICO AND APPLE

1. Matthew Frankel, "5 Warren Buffett Principles to Remember in a Volatile Stock Market," The Motley Fool, June 19, 2018, https://www.fool.com/investing/2018/06/19/5-warren-buffett-principles-to-remember-in-a-volat.aspx.
2. Wedgewood Partners, "GEICO: The 'Growth' Company that Made the 'Value' Careers of Both Benjamin Graham and Warren Buffett," 2016 GuruFocus Value Conference, Omaha, April 28, 2016.
3. Wedgewood Partners, "GEICO."
4. Wedgewood Partners, "GEICO."
5. Wedgewood Partners, "GEICO."
6. Wedgewood Partners, "GEICO."
7. Wedgewood Partners, "GEICO."
8. Wedgewood Partners, "GEICO."
9. Wedgewood Partners, "GEICO."
10. Wedgewood Partners, "GEICO."
11. Wedgewood Partners, "GEICO."
12. Wedgewood Partners, "GEICO."
13. Wedgewood Partners, "GEICO."
14. Albert Crenshaw, "Buffett to Buy Rest of GEICO," *Washington Post*, August 26, 1995, https://www.washingtonpost.com/archive/politics/1995/08/26/buffett-to-buy-rest-of-geico/33f0eac8-3b53-4ab8-8cd4-ee8e8ea9947c/?noredirect=on&utm_term=.0f7f9430dcbc.
15. Carrier Management, "Berkshire's GEICO Posts 2021 Profit but Much Lower Than 2020," February 28, 2022, https://www.carriermanagement.com/news/2022/02/28/233141.htm.
16. Warren Buffett, 2021 Berkshire Hathaway Annual Shareholder Letter (Omaha: Berkshire Hathaway), February 26, 2022, 5.
17. Greg McFarlane, "How Warren Buffett Made Berkshire Hathaway a Winner," Investopedia, May 5, 2021, https://www.investopedia.com/articles/markets/041714/how-warren-buffett-made-berkshire-hathaway-worldbeater.asp.
18. Warren Buffett, 2018 Berkshire Hathaway Annual Shareholder Letter (Omaha: Berkshire Hathaway), February 23, 2019, 9, https://www.berkshirehathaway.com/letters/2018ltr.pdf.
19. Adam Hayes, "Combined Ratio Definition," Investopedia, July 31, 2020, https://www.investopedia.com/terms/c/combinedratio.asp.
20. Robert Hagstrom, *The Warren Buffett Way* (Hoboken, NJ: Wiley, 2014), 89.
21. Hagstrom, *Warren Buffett Way*, 91.
22. Jason Fernando, "Price-to-Earnings (P/E) Ratio," Investopedia, June 29, 2021, https://www.investopedia.com/terms/p/price-earningsratio.asp.
23. Warren Buffett, 2000 Annual Berkshire Hathaway Shareholders' Meeting (Omaha), CNBC Warren Buffett Archive, April 29, 2000, https://buffett.cnbc.com/2000-berkshire-hathaway-annual-meeting/.
24. Warren Buffett, 1980 Berkshire Hathaway Annual Shareholder Letter (Omaha: Berkshire Hathaway), February 27, 1981, https://www.berkshirehathaway.com/letters/1980.html.
25. Buffett, 1980 Shareholder Letter.
26. Buffett, 2021 Shareholder Letter, 7.

27. Yahoo! "Selling Apple Shares Was 'Probably a Mistake' and Munger Knew It: Buffett," May 1, 2021, https://news.yahoo.com/selling-apple-shares-last-year-was-probably-a-mistake-buffett-195811746.html.
28. "Here Is the Full Transcript of Billionaire Investor Warren Buffett's Interview with CNBC," interview by Becky Quick, CNBC, February 27, 2017, https://www.cnbc.com/2017/02/27/billionaire-investor-warren-buffett-speaks-with-cnbcs-becky-quick-on-squawk-box.html.
29. Natalie Walters, "A Look Back at Warren Buffett's Growing Love for Apple Stock," The Motley Fool, October 1, 2018, https://www.fool.com/investing/2018/10/01/a-look-back-at-warren-buffetts-growing-love-for-ap.aspx.
30. Adam Shell, "Apple Buy Sign of Change at Buffett's Berkshire," *USA Today*, May 16, 2016, https://www.usatoday.com/story/money/markets/2016/05/16/analysis-buffetts-berkshire-buys-apple/84446844/.
31. Walters, "A Look Back at Warren Buffett's Growing Love for Apple Stock."
32. Matthew Belvedere, "Warren Buffett Says Berkshire Stock Managers Weschler and Combs Have Trailed the S&P 500," CNBC, February 25, 2019, https://www.cnbc.com/2019/02/25/warren-buffett-says-berkshire-stock-managers-weschler-and-combs-have-trailed-the-sp-500.html.
33. "Full Transcript of Warren Buffett's Interview With CNBC."
34. Andrew Bary, "Big 5 Tech Stocks Now Account for 23 Percent of the S&P 500," *Barron's*, July 26, 2021, https://www.barrons.com/articles/big-tech-stocks-sp-500-51627312933?tesla=y.
35. Paul La Monica, "Apple Has $246 BILLION in Cash, Nearly All Overseas," CNN Business, February 1, 2017, https://money.cnn.com/2017/02/01/investing/apple-cash-overseas/.
36. Warren Buffett, 2017 Berkshire Hathaway Annual Shareholder Letter (Omaha: Berkshire Hathaway), February 24, 2018, 9, https://www.berkshirehathaway.com/letters/2017ltr.pdf.
37. Warren Buffett, 2018 Berkshire Hathaway Annual Shareholder Letter (Omaha: Berkshire Hathaway), February 25, 2019, https://www.berkshirehathaway.com/letters/2018ltr.pdf.
38. "Warren Buffett: I Like Apple Stock So Much 'I'd Love to Own 100 Percent' of It," CNBC, May 7, 2018, https://www.cnbc.com/2018/05/07/warren-buffett-i-dont-have-to-do-a-thing-to-own-more-of-apple.html.
39. Warren Buffett, 2019 Berkshire Hathaway Annual Shareholder Letter (Omaha: Berkshire Hathaway), February 22, 2020, 10, https://www.berkshirehathaway.com/letters/2019ltr.pdf.
40. "Warren Buffett Calls Apple 'Probably the Best Business I Know in the World," CNBC, February 24, 2020, https://www.cnbc.com/2020/02/24/warren-buffett-says-apple-is-probably-the-best-business-i-know-in-the-world.html.
41. Daniel Martins, "Buffett Sells Apple: Should Investors Worry?," TheStreet: The Apple Maven, February 18, 2021, https://www.thestreet.com/apple/news/buffett-sells-apple-should-investors-worry.
42. CNBC, "Warren Buffett Watch," August 12, 2022, https://link.cnbc.com/public/28719262.
43. Adam Seesel, "Warren Buffett Used to Avoid Tech Stocks. Now He Loves Them. Here's Why," *Money*, December 26, 2018, https://money.com/value-investing-embraces-tech/.

44. Alicia Tuovila, "Net Tangible Assets," Investopedia, February 3, 2022, https://www.investopedia.com/terms/n/nettangibleassets.asp.
45. Jason Fernando, "Debt-to-Equity (D/E) Ratio," Investopedia, February 19, 2022, https://www.investopedia.com/terms/d/debtequityratio.asp.
46. Mike Berner, "How Warren Buffett and Charlie Munger Discount Future Cash Flows," *Medium*, November 12, 2020, https://medium.com/money-clip/how-warren-buffett-and-charlie-munger-discount-future-cash-flows-3f48c376f2fb.
47. Berner, "How Warren Buffett and Charlie Munger Discount Future Cash Flows."
48. Berner, "How Warren Buffett and Charlie Munger Discount Future Cash Flows."
49. Stephanie Yang, "The Epic Story of How a 'Genius' Hedge Fund Almost Caused a Global Financial Meltdown," *Business Insider*, July 10, 2014, https://www.businessinsider.com/the-fall-of-long-term-capital-management-2014-7.
50. Warren Buffett and Charlie Munger, 2007 Annual Berkshire Hathaway Shareholders' Meeting (Omaha), CNBC Warren Buffett Archive, May 5, 2007, https://buffett.cnbc.com/video/2007/05/05/morning-session---2007-berkshire-hathaway-annual-meeting.html.
51. Warren Buffett and Charlie Munger, 2017 Annual Berkshire Hathaway Shareholders' Meeting (Omaha), CNBC Warren Buffett Archive, May 6, 2017, https://buffett.cnbc.com/2017-berkshire-hathaway-annual-meeting/.
52. Buffett and Munger, 2017 Shareholders' Meeting.
53. Akhilesh Ganti, "Terminal Value (TV)," Investopedia, December 2, 2021, https://www.investopedia.com/terms/t/terminalvalue.asp.
54. Jason Fernando, "Discounted Cash Flow (DCF)," Investopedia, September 12, 2021, https://www.investopedia.com/terms/d/dcf.asp.
55. Fernando, "Discounted Cash Flow (DCF)."
56. Fernando, "Discounted Cash Flow (DCF)."
57. Fernando, "Discounted Cash Flow (DCF)."
58. Fernando, "Discounted Cash Flow (DCF)."
59. Fernando, "Discounted Cash Flow (DCF)."
60. Akhilesh Ganti, "Terminal Value (TV)," Investopedia, March 7, 2021, https://www.investopedia.com/terms/t/terminalvalue.asp.
61. Ganti, "Terminal Value (TV)."
62. Ganti, "Terminal Value (TV)."
63. Ganti, "Terminal Value (TV)."
64. Ganti, "Terminal Value (TV)."
65. Ganti, "Terminal Value (TV)."
66. Ganti, "Terminal Value (TV)."
67. Ganti, "Terminal Value (TV)."
68. Tory Segal, "Top 3 Pitfalls of Discounted Cash Flow Analysis," Investopedia, April 15, 2020, https://www.investopedia.com/investing/pitfalls-of-discounted-cash-flow-analysis/.
69. David Ahern, "Calculating Intrinsic Value with a DCF Like Warren Buffett Would," *einvestingforbeginners*, September 7, 2021, https://einvestingforbeginners.com/intrinsic-value-warren-buffett-aher/.
70. Visit with Warren Buffett in Omaha, November 9, 2009.

71. Eric Rosenbaum, "As the Dow Tanks, Here Is Warren Buffett on the Biggest Puzzle for Investors: Intrinsic Value of a Stock," CNBC, December 5, 2018, https://www.cnbc.com/2018/12/05/warren-buffett-on-the-biggest-puzzle-for-investors-intrinsic-value.html.
72. Will Kenton, "Hurdle Rate," Investopedia, September 4, 2021, https://www.investopedia.com/terms/h/hurdlerate.asp.
73. Fernando, "Discounted Cash Flow (DCF)."
74. Ganti, "Terminal Value (TV)."

7. HOW TO MAKE BETTER INVESTMENT DECISIONS

1. Daniel Kahneman, *Thinking Fast and Slow* (New York: Farrar, Straus, and Giroux, 2013), 13.
2. Kahneman, *Thinking Fast and Slow.*
3. Joshua Teitelbaum and Kathryn Zeiler, eds., *Research Handbook on Behavioral Law and Economics* (Northampton, UK: Edward Algar, 2018).
4. Daniel Kahneman and Amos Tversky, "Prospect Theory: An Analysis of Decision Under Risk," *Econometrica* 47, no. 2 (1979): 263.
5. CFI Institute, "What Is Behavioral Finance?," January 21, 2022, https://corporatefinanceinstitute.com/resources/knowledge/trading-investing/behavioral-finance/.
6. Peter Lazaroff, "5 Biases That Hurt Investor Returns," *Forbes*, April 1, 2016, https://www.forbes.com/sites/peterlazaroff/2016/04/01/5-biases-that-hurt-investor-returns/#3bc31df1d4ac.
7. Chicago Booth, "Richard H. Thaler," https://www.chicagobooth.edu/faculty/directory/t/richard-h-thaler.
8. Richard Thaler and Cass Sunstein, *Nudge: Improving Decisions about Health, Wealth, and Happiness* (New Haven, CT: Yale University Press, 2008).
9. Richard Thaler, *Misbehaving: The Making of Behavioral Economics* (New York: Norton, 2015), 2.
10. Thaler, *Misbehaving*, 2.
11. Thaler, *Misbehaving*, 2.
12. Alex Dumortier, "9 Quotes from Nobel-Winning Economist Richard Thaler to Help You Become a Better Investor," The Motley Fool, January 5, 2018, https://nz.news.yahoo.com/9-quotes-nobel-winning-economist-193300542.html.
13. Kathleen Elkins, "Nobel Prize Winner and Hedge Fund Founder: This Is All You Need to Know to Invest Your Money," CNBC, December 13, 2017, https://www.cnbc.com/2017/12/12/richard-thaler-the-no-1-rule-to-follow-when-investing-your-money.html.
14. Vanessa Houlder, "Richard Thaler's Advice: Be a Lazy Investor—Buy and Forget," *Financial Times*, December 21, 2017, https://www.ft.com/content/90d1289e-daa9-11e7-a039-c64b1c09b482.
15. Warren Buffett, *2014 Berkshire Hathaway Annual Report* (Omaha: Berkshire Hathaway, 2015), https://www.berkshirehathaway.com/2014ar/2014ar.pdf.
16. Duke Fuqua School of Business, "Dan Ariely," https://www.fuqua.duke.edu/faculty/dan-ariely.
17. Dan Ariely, "My Irrational Life," https://danariely.com/.
18. Dan Ariely, *Predictably Irrational: The Hidden Forces That Shape Our Decisions* (New York: Harper, 2008).
19. Dan Ariely, *The Upside of Irrationality: The Unexpected Benefits of Defying Logic* (New York: Harper, 2010).

20. Lorie Konish, "The Investing Mistakes You Want to Avoid as the Market Sinks—and What to Do Instead," CNBC, August 24, 2019, https://www.cnbc.com/2019/08/24/dan-ariely-on-portfolio-mistakes-you-want-to-avoid—during-volatility.html.
21. Lorie Konish, "Two Years Ago Stocks Dropped 12 Percent in a Single Day. Here Are Lessons Investors Learned That Can Still Apply," CNBC, March 16, 2022, https://www.cnbc.com/2022/03/16/lessons-for-investors-two-years-after-the-covid-19-market-drop-of-2020.html.
22. Jeff Cox, "It's Official: The Covid Recession Lasted Just Two Months, the Shortest in U.S. History, CNBC, July 19, 2021, https://www.cnbc.com/2021/07/19/its-official-the-covid-recession-lasted-just-two-months-the-shortest-in-us-history.html.
23. Michael Boyle and Amanda Bellucco-Chatham, "The Great Recession," Investopedia, October 23, 2020, https://www.investopedia.com/terms/g/great-recession.asp.
24. Mohit Oberoi, "Warren Buffett: Growth Stocks Look Like Dot-com Bubble," *Market Realist*, September 4, 2020, https://marketrealist.com/2020/07/warren-buffett-growth-stocks-like-dot-com-bubble/.
25. Eric Rosenbaum, "What Warren Buffett's Losing Battle Against S&P 500 Says about This Market," CNBC, January 8, 2021, https://www.cnbc.com/2021/01/08/how-warren-buffetts-uphill-battle-against-the-sp-500-is-changing.html.
26. Oberoi, "Warren Buffett: Growth Stocks."
27. Rosenbaum, "Warren Buffett's Losing Battle Against S&P 500."
28. Adam Hayes, "Dotcom Bubble," Investopedia, June 25, 2019, https://www.investopedia.com/terms/d/dotcom-bubble.asp.
29. Oberoi, "Warren Buffett: Growth Stocks."
30. Rosenbaum, "Warren Buffett's Losing Battle Against S&P 500."
31. Leslie Kramer, "What Caused the Stock Market Crash of 1929?," Investopedia, December 31, 2021, https://www.investopedia.com/ask/answers/042115/what-caused-stock-market-crash-1929-preceded-great-depression.asp.
32. Gene Smiley, "Great Depression," Econlib, https://www.econlib.org/library/Enc/GreatDepression.html.
33. Will Kenton, "Moral Hazard," Investopedia, July 23, 2020, https://www.investopedia.com/terms/m/moralhazard.asp.
34. Warren Buffett, 2008 Annual Berkshire Hathaway Shareholders' Meeting (Omaha), CNBC Warren Buffett Archive, May 3, 2008, https://buffett.cnbc.com/video/2008/05/03/morning-session---2008-berkshire-hathaway-annual-meeting.html.
35. Tim Parker, "4 Behavioral Biases and How to Avoid Them," Investopedia, June 25, 2019, https://www.investopedia.com/articles/investing/050813/4-behavioral-biases-and-how-avoid-them.asp.
36. Parker, "4 Behavioral Biases."
37. CFI, "Herd Mentality," 2020, https://corporatefinanceinstitute.com/resources/knowledge/trading-investing/herd-mentality-bias/.
38. CFI, "Herd Mentality."
39. CFI, "Herd Mentality."
40. Warren Buffett, 2008 Annual Berkshire Hathaway Shareholder Letter (Omaha: Berkshire Hathaway), February 27, 2009, https://www.berkshirehathaway.com/letters/2008ltr.pdf.
41. Kahneman and Tversky, "Prospect Theory."

42. James Chen, "Prospect Theory," Investopedia, July 9, 2019, https://www.investopedia.com/terms/p/prospecttheory.asp.
43. Charlie Munger, "The Psychology of Human Misjudgment" (speech, 1995), in James Clear, Great Speeches, https://jamesclear.com/great-speeches/psychology-of-human-misjudgment-by-charlie-munger.
44. Alex Dumortier, "9 Quotes from Nobel-Winning Economist Richard Thaler to Help You Become a Better Investor," The Motley Fool, January 5, 2018, https://www.fool.com/investing/2018/01/05/9-quotes-from-nobel-winning-economist-richard-thal.aspx.
45. Houlder, "Richard Thaler's Advice."
46. CFI, "Herd Mentality."
47. CFI, "Loss Aversion."
48. Helen Edwards and Dave Edwards, "How to Invest without Regrets, According to a Nobel-Winning Economist," *Quartz*, June 28, 2018, https://qz.com/1312744/how-to-invest-without-regrets-according-to-a-nobel-winning-economist/.
49. Edwards and Edwards, "Invest without Regrets."
50. Edwards and Edwards, "Invest without Regrets."
51. Josh Hafner, "Shark Week: You're Way More Likely to Die from These Than a Shark Attack," July 24, 2017, https://www.usatoday.com/story/news/nation-now/2017/07/24/shark-week-7-things-way-more-likely-kill-you-than-sharks/506115001/.
52. 25iq, "A Dozen Lessons about Investing and Money from Dan Ariely," September 1, 2017, https://25iq.com/2017/09/01/a-dozen-lessons-about-investing-and-money-from-dan-airely/.
53. Samantha Lamas, "Is Recency Bias Swaying Your Investing Decisions?," Morningstar, April 27, 2020, https://www.morningstar.com/articles/979322/is-recency-bias-swaying-your-investing-decisions.
54. Lamas, "Recency Bias."
55. Lamas, "Recency Bias."
56. Lamas, "Recency Bias."
57. Abigail Stevenson, "Cramer: What Changed Warren Buffett's Mind about the Airlines," CNBC, November 15, 2016, https://www.cnbc.com/2016/11/15/cramer-what-changed-warren-buffetts-mind-about-the-airlines.html.
58. Theron Mohamed, "Warren Buffett's Berkshire Hathaway took a $5 Billion Hit on Its Airline Stocks Last Quarter," *Markets Insider*, April 1, 2020, https://markets.businessinsider.com/news/stocks/warren-buffett-berkshire-hathaway-lost-billions-airline-stocks-quarter-coronavirus-2020-4–1029055923.
59. Gordon Scott, "Confirmation Bias," Investopedia, June 2, 2021, https://www.investopedia.com/terms/c/confirmation-bias.asp.
60. Scott, "Confirmation Bias."
61. James Chen, "Hindsight Bias," Investopedia, April 9, 2020, https://www.investopedia.com/terms/h/hindsight-bias.asp.
62. Chen, "Hindsight Bias."
63. Theron Mohamed, " 'We Blew It': Warren Buffett Admitted He Messed up by Not Investing in Google," *Markets Insider*, January 27, 2020, https://markets.businessinsider

.com/news/stocks/warren-buffett-berkshire-hathaway-blew-it-not-investing-google-stock-2020-1-1028845920.

64. Matthew Belvedere, "Amazon's Jeff Bezos Is 'the Most Remarkable Business Person of Our Age,' Says Warren Buffett," CNBC, May 5, 2017, https://www.cnbc.com/2017/05/05/amazons-jeff-bezos-is-the-most-remarkable-business-person-of-our-age-says-warren-buffett.html.
65. Troy Segal, "Mental Accounting," Investopedia, November 27, 2020, https://www.investopedia.com/terms/m/mentalaccounting.asp.
66. Pamela Henderson and Robert Peterson, "Mental Accounting and Categorization," *Organizational Behavior and Human Decision Processes* 51, no. 1 (February 1, 1992): 92–117.
67. Amar Cheema and Dilip Soman, "Malleable Mental Accounting: The Effect of Flexibility on the Justification of Attractive Spending and Consumption Decisions," *Journal of Consumer Psychology* 16, no. 1 (January 1, 2006): 33–44.
68. Shreeta Rege, "How Can You Help Your Clients Avoid Mental Accounting Bias?," *Cafe-Mutual*, September 18, 2018, https://cafemutual.com/news/edelweiss-insights/14489-how-can-you-help-your-clients-avoid-mental-accounting-bias.
69. Rege, "Mental Accounting Bias."
70. Segal, "Mental Accounting."
71. Segal, "Mental Accounting."
72. Segal, "Mental Accounting."
73. Segal, "Mental Accounting."

8. BERKSHIRE HATHAWAY: 1967–2009

1. Warren Buffett, "Buy American. I Am," *New York Times*, October 16, 2008, https://www.nytimes.com/2008/10/17/opinion/17buffett.html.
2. Donald Kuratko, interview by Todd Finkle (February 20, 2021).
3. Robert Armstrong, Eric Platt, and Oliver Ralph, "Warren Buffett: 'I'm Having More Fun Than Any 88-Year-Old in the World,' " *Financial Times*, https://www.ft.com/content/40b9b356-661e-11e9-a79d-04f350474d62.
4. Warren Buffett, 2017 Berkshire Hathaway Shareholder Letter (Omaha: Berkshire Hathaway), February 24, 2018, https://www.berkshirehathaway.com/letters/2018.html.
5. Robert Hagstrom, *The Warren Buffett Way*, 3rd ed. (Hoboken, NJ: Wiley, 2014), 10.
6. Warren Buffett, 2004 Annual Berkshire Hathaway Shareholders' Meeting (Omaha), CNBC Warren Buffett Archive, May 1, 2004, https://buffett.cnbc.com/2004-berkshire-hathaway-annual-meeting/.
7. Matthew Frankel, "Warren Buffett and the Insurance Business: A 52-Year Love Story," The Motley Fool, February 22, 2019, https://www.fool.com/investing/2019/02/22/warren-buffett-and-the-insurance-business-a-52-yea.aspx.
8. Warren Buffett, 1983 Berkshire Hathaway Shareholder Letter (Omaha: Berkshire Hathaway), March 14, 1984, https://www.berkshirehathaway.com/letters/1983.html.
9. Warren Buffett, 2019 Berkshire Hathaway Shareholders' Meeting (Omaha), CNBC Warren Buffett Archive, May 4, 2019, https://buffett.cnbc.com/2019-berkshire-hathaway-annual-meeting/.

10. Warren Buffett, 1985 Berkshire Hathaway Shareholder Letter (Omaha: Berkshire Hathaway), March 4, 1986, https://www.berkshirehathaway.com/letters/1985.html.
11. Serena Ng and Keach Hagey, "Call It Berkshire Hathaway Ink.: Buffett's Conglomerate Adds 63 Newspapers, Right to Buy Stake in Media General," *Wall Street Journal*, May 17, 2012, https://www.wsj.com/articles/SB10001424052702303448404577409931345370866#:~:text=%22In%20towns%20and%20cities%20where,fall%20firmly%20in%20this%20mold.%22.
12. Warren Buffett, *2014 Berkshire Hathaway Annual Report* (Omaha: Berkshire Hathaway, 2015), https://www.berkshirehathaway.com/2014ar/2014ar.pdf.
13. Ng and Hagey, "Call It Berkshire Hathaway Ink."
14. Sam Ro, "Warren Buffett Says the Newspaper Business Is 'Toast,' " Yahoo! Finance, April 19, 2019, https://finance.yahoo.com/news/warren-buffett-newspapers-are-toast-exclusive-133720666.html.
15. Eugene Kim, "How Amazon CEO Jeff Bezos Reinvented the Washington Post, the 140-Year-Old Newspaper He Bought for $250 Million," *Business Insider*, May 15, 2016, https://www.businessinsider.com/how-the-washington-post-changed-after-jeff-bezos-acquisition-2016-5.
16. Warren Buffett, 1980 Berkshire Hathaway Shareholder Letter (Omaha: Berkshire Hathaway), March 4, 1981, https://www.berkshirehathaway.com/letters/1980.html.
17. Albert Crenshaw, "Buffett to Buy Rest of GEICO," *Washington Post*, August 26, 1995, https://www.washingtonpost.com/archive/politics/1995/08/26/buffett-to-buy-rest-of-geico/33f0eac8-3b53-4ab8-8cd4-ee8e8ea9947c/?noredirect=on&utm_term=.0f7f9430dcbc.
18. Max Nisen, "The Man Who Taught Warren Buffett How to Manage a Company," *QUARTZ*, October 23, 2014, https://qz.com/273797/tom-murphy-taught-warren-buffett-how-to-manage-a-company/.
19. Nisen, "The Man Who Taught Warren Buffett."
20. Minda Zetlin, "3 Times When Warren Buffett Was Absolutely Dead Wrong," *Inc.*, April 30, 2019, https://www.inc.com/minda-zetlin/warren-buffett-mistakes-berkshire-hathaway-washington-post-coca-cola-gillette.html.
21. Christine Chiglinsky, "Berkshire's Tom Murphy, 96, Resigns from Board after Getting Covid," *Bloomberg*, February 14, 2022, https://www.bloomberg.com/news/articles/2022-02-14/Berkshire-s-murphy-resigns-from-board-after-covid-revelation.
22. Wayne Duggan, "This Day in Market History: Warren Buffett Buys Nebraska Furniture Mart for 55.3M," *Benzinga*, August 30, 2021, https://www.benzinga.com/general/education/18/08/12284542/this-day-in-market-history-warren-buffett-buys-nebraska-furniture-m.
23. Theron Mohamed, "Warren Buffett Said an 89-Year-Old Carpet Seller Would 'Run Rings around' Fortune 500 CEOs. Here's the Remarkable Story of Mrs. B.," *Markets Insider*, December 14, 2019, https://markets.businessinsider.com/news/stocks/warren-buffett-berkshire-hathaway-89-mrs-b-fortune-500-ceo-2019-12-1028763487.
24. Mohamed, "The Remarkable Story of Mrs. B."
25. Carol Loomis, "Warren Buffett's Wild Ride at Salomon (Fortune, 1997)," *Fortune*, October 27, 1997, https://fortune.com/1997/10/27/warren-buffett-salomon/.
26. Loomis, "Warren Buffett's Wild Ride at Salomon."
27. Warren Buffett, Testimony before the Subcommittee on Telecommunications and Finance of the Energy and Commerce Committee of the U.S. House of Representatives, Washington, DC, 1991.

28. Buffett, "Buy American."
29. Jared Blikre, "Why Warren Buffett Invested in Coca-Cola and Its Lesson," Yahoo! News, April 29, 2021, https://news.yahoo.com/why-warren-buffett-invested-in-coca-cola-165914721.html.
30. Blikre, "Why Warren Buffett Invested in Coca-Cola."
31. Investopedia, "Why Did Warren Buffett Invest Heavily in Coca-Cola (KO) in the Late 1980s?," September 7, 2018, https://www.investopedia.com/ask/answers/052615/why-did-warren-buffett-invest-heavily-cocacola-ko-late-1980s.asp.
32. Investopedia, "Why Did Warren Buffett Invest Heavily?"
33. Anthony DeMarco, "Crazy Warren Buffett to Again Sell Jewelry at Borsheims," *Forbes*, February 29, 2012, https://www.forbes.com/sites/anthonydemarco/2012/02/29/crazy-warren-buffett-to-again-sell-jewelry-at-borsheims/?sh=6c3bc3d18d9b.
34. Janice Podsada, "Warren Buffett's Pick for Borsheims CEO Took Six-Year Break on Rise to the Top," *Omaha World Herald*, February 26, 2014, https://archive.ph/20140226215931/http://www.omaha.com/article/20131007/MONEY/131008993/1697.
35. Nicole Sinclair, "The Story behind Berkshire Hathaway's Low-Priced B Shares," Yahoo! Entertainment, April 20, 2016, https://www.yahoo.com/entertainment/berkshire-a-shares-b-shares-difference-high-low-price-buffett-120901246.html.
36. Warren Buffett, 1996 Berkshire Hathaway Shareholder Letter (Omaha: Berkshire Hathaway), February 28, 1997, https://www.berkshirehathaway.com/letters/1996.html.
37. Dairy Queen, "About Us," https://www.dairyqueen.com/en-us/about-us/.
38. "International Dairy Queen, Inc. Company History," https://www.company-histories.com/International-Dairy-Queen-Inc-Company-History.html.
39. Hermann Simon, *Hidden Champions of the Twenty-First Century: The Success Strategies of Unknown World Market Leaders* (London: Springer, 2009), 13.
40. NetJets, "NetJets History," 2009, https://web.archive.org/web/20090416085351/http://netjets.com/about_netjets/history.asp.
41. Warren Buffett, 1998 Berkshire Hathaway Shareholder Letter (Omaha: Berkshire Hathaway), March 1, 1999, https://www.berkshirehathaway.com/letters/1998htm.html.
42. Doug Gollan, "NetJets by the Numbers," March 6, 2019 (updated June 2020), https://privatejetcardcomparisons.com/2019/03/06/netjets-fleet-size-and-fast-facts/.
43. Jordan Wathen, "How Buffett Turned around a $23.5 Billion Insurance Bet," The Motley Fool, December 23, 2015, https://www.fool.com/investing/general/2015/12/23/how-buffett-turned-around-a-235-billion-insurance.aspx.
44. Gen Re, "Meet Gen Re," 2019, http://www.genre.com/aboutus/meet-genre.
45. Bloomberg News, "Berkshire Hathaway and Others Plan to Buy MidAmerican Energy," *New York Times*, October 2, 1999, https://www.nytimes.com/1999/10/26/business/berkshire-hathaway-and-others-plan-to-buy-midamerican-energy.html.
46. Bloomberg News, "Berkshire Hathaway and Others Plan to Buy MidAmerican Energy."
47. Warren Buffett, 2001 Berkshire Hathaway Shareholder Letter (Omaha: Berkshire Hathaway), February 28, 2002, https://www.berkshirehathaway.com/2001ar/2001letter.html.
48. Prem Jain, *Buffett beyond Value: Why Warren Buffett Looks to Growth and Management When Investing* (Hoboken, NJ: Wiley, 2010), 140.
49. CNNMoney, "Buffett Buys Fruit of the Loom," November 2, 2001, https://money.cnn.com/2001/11/02/deals/fruit_berkshire/.

50. CNNMoney, "Buffett Buys Fruit of the Loom."
51. Ariel Schwartz, "Clayton Homes' i-house Combines Energy Efficiency and Modular Affordability," *Fast Company*, May 4, 2009, https://www.fastcompany.com/1277559/clayton-homes-i-house-combines-energy-efficiency-and-modular-affordability.
52. Warren Buffett, *2003 Berkshire Hathaway Annual Report* (Omaha: Berkshire Hathaway, 2004), https://www.berkshirehathaway.com/2003ar/2003ar.pdf.
53. Clayton, "Statement: Reporting Mischaracterizes Clayton Homes' Treatment of Customers and Employees," December 26, 2015, https://www.claytonhomes.com/newsroom/press-releases/Statement-Reporting-Mischaracterizes-Treatment-of-Customers-and-Employees.
54. Jonathan Stempel, "Buffett Defends Clayton Homes After Critics Fault Its Lending," Reuters, February 27, 2016, https://www.reuters.com/article/berkshire-buffett-claytonhomes/buffett-defends-clayton-homes-after-critics-fault-its-lending-idUSL2N1660FS.
55. *Wall Street Journal*, "Berkshire Hathaway Agrees to Acquire Clayton Homes," April 2, 2003, https://www.wsj.com/articles/SB1049257173151638oo.
56. Logotyp.us, "Brooks Sports," https://logotyp.us/logo/brooks/.
57. Abigail Tracy, "How Brooks Reinvented Its Brand," *Inc.*, April 24, 2014, https://www.inc.com/abigail-tracy/how-brooks-running-became-an-industry-leader.html.
58. Lauren Thomas, "Brooks Running Sees Double-Digit Sales Growth Despite Unpredictability of Sports Retail," CNBC, October 30, 2017, https://www.cnbc.com/2017/10/30/brooks-running-reports-double-digit-sales-growth.html.
59. Dana Karlson, "Brooks Sprints into 2015, Holds Top Spot with Runners," *Footwear News*, January 21, 2015, https://footwearnews.com/2015/focus/athletic-outdoor/brooks-sprints-into-2015-holds-top-spot-with-runners-8738/.
60. Kate Siber, "The Frontrunner," November 2013, https://www.tuck.dartmouth.edu/uploads/content/tuck_today_fall_2013_upload.pdf.
61. Siber, "The Frontrunner."
62. Jim Weber, interview by Todd Finkle on February 28, 2022.
63. Siber, "The Frontrunner."
64. The Rational Walk, "Habit of Labor: Lessons from a Life of Struggle and Success," https://rationalwalk.com/the-remarkable-iscar-story/.
65. ISCAR, "IMC Group of Companies," https://www.iscar.com/newarticles.aspx/lang/th/newarticleid/201.
66. *Jerusalem Post*, "Warren Buffett Buys Remainder of Israel's Iscar for $2.05b," May 1, 2013, https://www.jpost.com/Breaking-News/Buffett-exercising-option-to-buy-Iscar-outright-311705.
67. Bloomberg, "Bloomberg Billionaire Index," https://www.bloomberg.com/billionaires/profiles/stef-wertheimer/?sref=c7m8pueA.
68. Vikas Bajaj, "Rapidly, Buffett Secures a Deal for $4.5 Billion," *New York Times*, December 26, 2007, https://www.nytimes.com/2007/12/26/business/26deal.html.
69. Global Restaurant Leadership, "Marmon: A Berkshire Hathaway Company," https://globalrlc.com/company/marmon-food-beverage-water-technologies-company.
70. Warren Buffett, 2013 Berkshire Hathaway Shareholder Letter (Omaha: Berkshire Hathaway), February 28, 2014, https://www.berkshirehathaway.com/letters/2013ltr.pdf.
71. *Wall Street Journal*, "NBER Makes It Official: Recession Started in December 2007," December 1, 2008, https://blogs.wsj.com/economics/2008/12/01/nber-makes-it-official-recession-started-in-december-2007/.

72. National Bureau of Economic Research (NBER), "US Business Cycle Expansions and Contractions," December 9, 2019, https://www.nber.org/cycles/.
73. Alex Crippen, "Berkshire Hathaway Down Almost 50% from All-Time High as Stock Sinks Again," CNBC, November 21, 2008, https://www.cnbc.com/2008/11/21/berkshire-hathaway-down-almost-50-from-alltime-high-as-stock-sinks-again.html.
74. Buffett, "Buy American."
75. Tami Luhby, "Buffett's Berkshire Invests $5B in Goldman," CNN Money, September 24, 2008, https://money.cnn.com/2008/09/23/news/companies/goldman_berkshire/.
76. Luhby, "Buffett's Berkshire Invests $5B in Goldman."
77. Christine Harper, "Goldman Sachs to Pay $5.65 Billion to Redeem Buffett's Stake," Bloomberg, March 18, 2011, https://www.bloomberg.com/news/articles/2011-03-18/goldman-sachs-will-buy-back-buffett-s-5-billion-preferred-stake?sref=c7m8pueA.
78. James Brumley, "Here's How Much Warren Buffett Has Made on Goldman Sachs," The Motley Fool, December 13, 2019, https://www.fool.com/investing/2019/12/13/how-much-warren-buffett-made-goldman-sachs.aspx.
79. Theron Mohamed, "Warren Buffett's Berkshire Hathaway Raked in More Than $3 Billion From Its Goldman Sachs Bailout," Markets Insider, May 18, 2020, https://markets.businessinsider.com/news/stocks/warren-buffett-berkshire-hathaway-goldman-sachs-sale-billions-return-bailout-2020-5-1029212109.
80. *New York Times*, "Buffett to Invest $3 Billion in GE," October 1, 2008, https://dealbook.nytimes.com/2008/10/01/buffett-to-invest-3-billion-in-ge/.
81. Thomas Gryta, "How Warren Buffett Made $1.5 Billion on GE," *Wall Street Journal*, August 15, 2017, https://blogs.wsj.com/moneybeat/2017/08/15/how-warren-buffett-made-1-5-billion-on-ge/?ns=prod/accounts-wsj.
82. Brad Dorfman, "Mars, Buffett Buying Wrigley for $23 Billion," Reuters, April 28, 2008, https://www.reuters.com/article/uk-wrigley/mars-buffett-buying-wrigley-for-23-billion-idUKN2847363420080428.
83. Theron Mohamed, "Warren Buffett Spent $6.5 Billion to Help Mars Acquire Wrigley during the Financial Crisis. Here's the Story of How He Made the Candy Deal Happen," *Business Insider*, July 5, 2020, https://markets.businessinsider.com/news/stocks/warren-buffett-spent-billions-help-mars-buy-wrigley-2008-crisis-2020-7-1029366581.
84. Mohamed, "Warren Buffett Spent $6.5 Billion to Help Mars Acquire Wrigley."
85. Mohamed, "Warren Buffett Spent $6.5 Billion to Help Mars Acquire Wrigley."
86. Mohamed, "Warren Buffett Spent $6.5 Billion to Help Mars Acquire Wrigley."
87. David Jolly, "Swiss Re Gets $2.6 Billion from Berkshire Hathaway," *New York Times*, February 6, 2009, https://www.nytimes.com/2009/02/06/business/worldbusiness/06swiss.html.
88. Jolly, "Swiss Re Gets $2.6 Billion from Berkshire Hathaway."
89. Jolly, "Swiss Re Gets $2.6 Billion from Berkshire Hathaway."
90. The Rational Walk, "Buffett Seizes Opportunities during Financial Crisis," https://rationalwalk.com/buffett-seizes-opportunities-during-financial-crisis/.
91. The Rational Walk, "Buffett Seizes Opportunities during Financial Crisis."
92. Ravi Nagarajan, "Berkshire Hathaway: In Search of the 'Buffett Premium,'" The Rational Walk, LLC, March 1, 2011, https://rationalwalk.com/wp-content/uploads/2010/02/InSearchOfBuffettPremiumSample.pdf.

93. Swetha Gopinath, "Dow Chemical to Convert $4 Billion of Preferred Shares into Equity," Reuters, 2016, December 15, https://www.reuters.com/article/us-dowchemical-preferred-shares-berkshir-idUSKBN1442UX.
94. Gopinath, "Dow Chemical to Convert $4 Billion of Preferred Shares into Equity."
95. The Rational Walk, "Revisiting Berkshire Hathaway's Acquisition of BNSF," 2019, http://www.rationalwalk.com/?p=13350.
96. The Rational Walk, "Revisiting Berkshire Hathaway's Acquisition of BNSF."
97. The Rational Walk, "Revisiting Berkshire Hathaway's Acquisition of BNSF."

9. BERKSHIRE HATHAWAY: 2010–2020

1. Marcel Schwantes, "Warren Buffett Says Doing Your Job This Way Is What Separates Successful People from Everyone Else," *Inc.*, August 20, 2020, https://www.inc.com/marcel-schwantes/warren-buffett-career-advice-success.html.
2. Ben Winck, "Warren Buffett's Berkshire Hathaway Made $800 Million on Snowflake's First Day of Trading as the Stock Spiked," *Business Insider* , September 17, 2020, https://markets.businessinsider.com/news/stocks/warren-buffett-berkshire-hathaway-800-million-snowflake-stock-price-ipo-2020-9–1029599049.
3. Winck, "Berkshire Hathaway Made $800 Million on Snowflake's First Day."
4. Serena Ng, Susan Pulliam, and Gregory Zuckerman, "Buffett: Combs Is a 100 Percent Fit," *Wall Street Journal*, October 26, 2010, https://www.wsj.com/articles/SB100014240527023033419045755763730088607754?ns=prod/accounts-wsj.
5. *Stamford Advocate*, "Local Hedgie to Become Berkshire Investment Head," October 26, 2010, https://www.stamfordadvocate.com/business/article/Local-hedgie-to-become-Berkshire-investment-head-724947.php.
6. Ng, Pulliam, and Zuckerman, "Buffett."
7. Alex Crippin, "$5.3 Million Dinners with Warren Buffett Lead to Dream Job for Money Manager," CNBC, September 12, 2011, https://www.cnbc.com/2011/09/12/53m-dinners-with-warren-buffett-lead-to-dream-job-for-money-manager.html.
8. Carol Loomis, "Meet Ted Weschler: Buffett Auction Winner, Berkshire's New Hire," *Fortune*, June 4, 2017, http://fortune.com/2011/09/12/meet-ted-weschler-buffett-auction-winner-berkshires-new-hire/.
9. Julia LaRoche, "Meet Ted Weschler, the Guy Who Just Got an Investing Dream from Warren Buffett," *Business Insider*, September 12, 2011, https://www.businessinsider.com/ted-weschler-2011-9.
10. *Institutional Investor*, "Warren Buffett Deputy Ted Weschler Makes His Mark," July 21, 2016, https://www.institutionalinvestor.com/article/b14z9npww3drst/warren-buffett-deputy-ted-weschler-makes-his-mark# %2F.WTQnhlKZN-U.
11. Steve Jordan, "Buffett Entrusts a Growing Role to Lieutenants Combs and Weschler," *Omaha World Herald*, April 30, 2016, https://www.omaha.com/money/buffett-entrusts-a-growing-role-to-lieutenants-combs-and-weschler/article_732e9e31-c56b-539e-983d-12ee88c375d7.html.
12. Andy Serwer, "EXCLUSIVE: Warren Buffett's Money Managers, Todd Combs and Ted Weschler, Speak," Yahoo! Finance, April 28, 2017, https://finance.yahoo.com

/news/warren-buffetts-money-managers-todd-combs-ted-weschler-speak-142643892.html.

13. Helen Thomas, "Berkshire Hathaway in $9bn Lubrizol Deal," *Financial Times*, March 11, 2011, https://www.ft.com/content/c6290078-4e30-11e0-a9fa-00144feab49a.
14. Brett Arends, "Why Warren Buffett Just Spent $10 Billion," *Wall Street Journal*, March 18, 2011, https://www.wsj.com/articles/SB10001424052748703328404576207040639038696.
15. Louise Story and Gretchen Morgenson, "A.I.G. Sues Bank of America Over Mortgage Bonds," *New York Times*, August 8, 2011, https://www.nytimes.com/2011/08/08/business/aig-to-sue-bank-of-america-over-mortgage-bonds.html.
16. Ben Protess and Susanne Craig, "Buffett Invests $5 Billion in Bank of America," *New York Times*, August 25, 2011, https://dealbook.nytimes.com/2011/08/25/buffett-to-invest-5-billion-in-bank-of-america/.
17. Adam Shell, "Warren Buffett is Now Bank of America's Top Shareholder," *USA Today*, August 30, 2017, https://www.usatoday.com/story/money/business/2017/08/29/warren-buffett-now-bank-americas-top-shareholder/614150001/.
18. Matthew Belvedere, "This Decade Saw Warren Buffett Finally Turn His Back on IBM and Jump Big Time into Apple," CNBC.com, December 31, 2019, https://www.cnbc.com/2019/12/31/this-decade-saw-warren-buffett-finally-exit-ibm-jump-big-into-apple.html.
19. Belvedere, "This Decade Saw Warren Buffett Finally Turn His Back on IBM."
20. Belvedere, "This Decade Saw Warren Buffett Finally Turn His Back on IBM."
21. Oriental Trading Company, "Mission" (2016), http://corp.orientaltrading.com.
22. Dawn McCarty, "Oriental Trading Co. Files for Bankruptcy in Delaware," Bloomberg, August 25, 2010, https://www.bloomberg.com/news/articles/2010-08-25/oriental-trading-co-files-for-bankruptcy-with-as-much-as-1-billion-debt.
23. Michael De La Merced, "Berkshire to Buy Oriental Trading Company," *New York Times*, November 2, 2012, https://dealbook.nytimes.com/2012/11/02/berkshire-to-buy-oriental-trading-company/.
24. Heesun Wee, "10 Top Brands Warren Buffett's Berkshire Hathaway Owns," CNBC, May 5, 2014, https://www.cnbc.com/2014/05/05/10-top-brands-warren-buffetts-berkshire-hathaway-owns.html.
25. Michael De La Merced and Andrew Ross Sorkin, "Berkshire and 3G Capital in a $23 Billion Deal for Heinz," *New York Times*, February 14, 2013, https://dealbook.nytimes.com/2013/02/14/berkshire-and-3g-capital-to-buy-heinz-for-23-billion/.
26. Kevin Dowd, How 3G Capital and a $50B Buyout Turned Kraft Heinz Upside Down," *PitchBook*, May 23, 2019, https://pitchbook.com/news/articles/how-3g-capital-and-a-50b-buyout-turned-kraft-heinz-upside-down.
27. De La Merced and Sorkin, "Berkshire and 3G Capital in a $23 Billion Deal for Heinz."
28. Mathew Belvedere, "Warren Buffett Gets into Auto Dealers in Big Way," CNBC, October 2, 2014, https://www.cnbc.com/2014/10/02/warren-buffett-gets-into-auto-business buying-big-car-dealership-group.html.
29. Belvedere, "Warren Buffett Gets into Auto Dealers in Big Way."
30. Patrick Morris and The Motley Fool, "Why Warren Buffett Just Bought Duracell," November 14, 2014, *Money*, https://money.com/warren-buffett-duracell/.

31. Morris and The Motley Fool, "Why Warren Buffett Just Bought Duracell."
32. Morris and The Motley Fool, "Why Warren Buffett Just Bought Duracell."
33. Craig Giammona and Matthew Boyle, "Kraft Will Merge with Heinz in Deal Backed by 3G and Buffett," Bloomberg, March 25, 2015, https://www.bloomberg.com/news/articles/2015-03-25/3g-capital-berkshire-to-buy-kraft-foods-merge-it-with-heinz.
34. Tom DiChristopher, "Buffett's HJ Heinz to Merge with Kraft Foods," CNBC, March 25, 2015, https://www.cnbc.com/2015/03/25/kraft-foods-group-and-hj-heinz-merge-to-create-the-kraft-heinz-co.html.
35. DiChristopher, "Buffett's HJ Heinz."
36. DiChristopher, "Buffett's HJ Heinz."
37. Josh Barro, "What's Wrong at Kraft? There Are Two Theories, Both Bad for Warren Buffett," *Intelligencer*, February 28, 2019, http://nymag.com/intelligencer/2019/02/whats-wrong-at-kraft-the-answer-is-bad-for-warren-buffett.html.
38. Barro, "What's Wrong at Kraft?"
39. Fred Imbert, "Buffett, After Last Week's Stock Plunge, Says Berkshire Hathaway 'Overpaid' for Kraft," CNBC, February 25, 2019, https://www.cnbc.com/2019/02/25/buffett-says-berkshire-hathaway-overpaid-for-kraft-following-last-weeks-stock-plunge.html.
40. Jonathan Stempel, "Warren Buffett's $10 Billion Mistake: Precision Castparts," Reuters.com, February 27, 2021, https://www.reuters.com/article/us-berkshire-buffett-precision castparts/warren-buffetts-10-billion-mistake-precision-castparts-idUSKCN2AR0MZ.
41. Stempel, "Warren Buffett's $10 Billion Mistake: Precision Castparts."
42. Todd Finkle, "Warren Buffett: Entrepreneur, Investor, and Philanthropist," *Journal of Business Cases and Applications*, 19 (2018), 1–19.
43. Chelsey Dulaney, "Buffett's Berkshire to Buy Precision Castparts for $32 Billion," *Wall Street Journal*, August 10, 2015, https://www.wsj.com/articles/berkshire-hathaway-to-buy-precision-castparts-1439205293.
44. Nidhi Singh, "Guess the Top #5 Investors of the World's Biggest Company," *Entrepreneur*, February 28, 2017, https://www.entrepreneur.com/article/289859.
45. Philip van Doorn, "Apple Is Berkshire's Largest Stock Holding, but Buffett and Co. Own a Bigger Share of These Companies," MarketWatch, February 19, 2022, https://www.marketwatch.com/story/apple-is-berkshires-largest-stock-holding-but-buffett-and-co-own-a-bigger-share-of-these-companies-11644962524.
46. Warren Buffett, 2007 Annual Berkshire Hathaway Shareholder Letter (Omaha: Berkshire Hathaway, February 2008), https://www.berkshirehathaway.com/letters/2007ltr.pdf.
47. Ted Reed, "Buffett Decries Airline Investing Even Though at Worst He Broke Even," *Forbes*, May 13, 2013, https://www.forbes.com/sites/tedreed/2013/05/13/buffett-decries-airline-investing-even-though-at-worst-he-broke-even/?sh=4ffdb943b5e7.
48. GuruFocus.com, "Why Did Warren Buffett Sell Some of Berkshire's Airline Holdings?," April 6, 2020, https://finance.yahoo.com/news/why-did-warren-buffett-sell-181224820.html.
49. NPR, "The 'Nasty, Rotten' Airline Business," *Planet Money*, December 9, 2011, https://www.npr.org/sections/money/2011/12/09/143466204/the-Friday-podcast-the-nasty-rotten-airline-business.

50. Warren Buffett and Charlie Munger, 2018 Annual Berkshire Hathaway Shareholders' Meeting (Omaha), CNBC Warren Buffett Archive, May 5, 2018, https://buffett.cnbc.com/video/2018/05/05/morning-session—2018-berkshire-hathaway-annual-meeting.html.
51. Buffett and Munger, 2018 Shareholders' Meeting.
52. Buffett and Munger, 2018 Shareholders' Meeting.
53. Jen Wieczner, "Berkshire Hathaway, Amazon and JP Morgan Are Close to Hiring a CEO for Their Healthcare Venture," *Fortune*, May 5, 2018, https://fortune.com/2018/05/05/warren-buffett-berkshire-hathaway-amazon-jmorgan-healthcare/.
54. Reuters, "CEO to Be Named Soon for Berkshire, Amazon, JP Morgan Healthcare Venture," June 7, 2018, https://www.reuters.com/article/us-berkshire-buffett-healthcare/ceo-to-be-named-soon-for-berkshire-amazon-jpmorgan-healthcare-venture-idUSKCN1J31MV.
55. Buffett and Munger, 2018 Shareholders' Meeting.
56. Becky Quick, "Berkshire Hathaway Has Been Buying Shares of Amazon: Warren Buffett," CNBC, May 2, 2019, https://www.cnbc.com/2019/05/03/berkshire-hathaway-has-been-buying-shares-of-amazon-warren-buffett.html.
57. Clifford Krauss, "Warren Buffett Backs Occidental's Bid for Anadarko with $10 Billion Investment," *New York Times*, April 30, 2019, https://www.nytimes.com/2019/04/30/business/energy-environment/warren-buffett-occidental-anadarko.html.
58. Mark Kolakowski, "Why Buffett Is Betting $10 Billion on Occidental in the Anadarko Bidding War," Investopedia, June 25, 2019, https://www.investopedia.com/why-buffett-is-betting-usd10-billion-on-occidental-in-anadarko-bidding-war-4685821.
59. Anadarko, "Anadarko Agrees to Be Acquired by Occidental," May 9, 2019, https://www.prnewswire.com/news-releases/anadarko-agrees-to-be-acquired-by-occidental-300847771.html.
60. Berkshire Hathaway, "Committed to Clean Energy," https://www.brkenergy.com/environment/renewables.aspx.
61. Rich Duprey, "Warren Buffett Acquires $549 Million Stake in Kroger," The Motley Fool, February 18, 2020, https://www.fool.com/investing/2020/02/18/warren-buffett-acquires-549-million-stake-in-kroge.aspx.
62. Duprey, "Warren Buffett Acquires $549 Million Stake in Kroger."
63. Jim Sloan, "Reverse-Engineering Buffett's Thinking about Those Japanese Trading Companies," *Seeking Alpha*, September 8, 2020, https://seekingalpha.com/article/4373016-reverse-engineering-buffetts-thinking-those-japanese-trading-companies.
64. Yun Li and Maggie Fitzgerald, "Warren Buffett's Berkshire Hathaway Just Made a Fast $800 Million on Snowflake's Surging IPO," CNBC, September 16, 2020, https://www.cnbc.com/2020/09/16/warren-buffetts-berkshire-hathaway-just-made-a-fast-1-billion-on-snowflakes-surging-ipo.html.
65. *Irish Times*, "Warren Buffett Pulls Back on Banks and Bets on Drug Makers," November 17, 2020, https://www.irishtimes.com/business/markets/warren-buffett-pulls-back-on-banks-and-bets-on-drug-makers-1.4411581.
66. David Kass, "Major Changes to Berkshire Hathaway's Stock Portfolio during Fourth Quarter of 2020," February 17, 2021, https://blog.umd.edu/davidkass/2021/02/17/major-changes-to-berkshire-hathaways-stock-portfolio-during-fourth-quarter-of-2020/.

10. BUFFETT'S INVESTING MISTAKES

1. Aksapada, *Open Secrets of Warren Buffett: Lessons for Business and Personal Success* (self-published, 2018), 42.
2. Catherine Clifford, "Warren Buffett Bought $114.75 in Stock at Age 11—Here's How Much It Would Be Worth Now If He'd Bought a Low-Cost Index Fund," CNBC, February 25, 2019, https://www.cnbc.com/2019/02/25/warren-buffett-bought-114point75-in-stock-at-11--what-itd-be-worth-now.html.
3. Joshua Kennon, "How Warren Buffett Became One of the Wealthiest People in America," *The Balance*, January 3, 2022, https://www.thebalance.com/warren-buffett-timeline-356439.
4. Kennon, "How Warren Buffett Became One of the Wealthiest People in America."
5. Gurufocus.com, "Warren Buffett's Biggest-Ever Loss: 20 Percent of His Net Wealth," January 16, 2020, https://finance.yahoo.com/news/warren-buffetts-biggest-ever-loss-192041138.html.
6. Noreen Malone, "Salad Oil Swindle!," *New York*, May 30, 2012, https://nymag.com/news/features/scandals/salad-oil-2012-4/.
7. Alex Crippen, "Warren Buffett: Buying Berkshire Hathaway Was $200 Billion Blunder," CNBC, October 18, 2010, http://www.cnbc.com/id/39710609.
8. Warren Buffett, "1966 Buffett Partnership. Ltd. (1966)," http://csinvesting.org/wp-content/uploads/2012/05/complete_buffett_partnership_letters-1957-70_in-sections.pdf.
9. Buffett, "1966 Partnership," 97–98.
10. Buffett, "1966 Partnership," 97–98.
11. David Shahrestani, "Investment Theory #11: Buffett's 1966 Letter," *Wiser Daily*, September 16, 2016, https://wiserdaily.wordpress.com/2016/09/02/investment-theory-11-buffetts-1966-letter/.
12. Shahrestani, "Investment Theory #11," 3.
13. Sean Williams, "3 of Warren Buffett's Biggest Billion-Dollar Blunders," The Motley Fool, April 14, 2021, https://www.fool.com/investing/2021/04/14/3-warren-buffetts-biggest-billion-dollar-blunders/.
14. Williams, "3 of Warren Buffett's Biggest Billion-Dollar Blunders."
15. Warren Buffett, 1998 Annual Berkshire Hathaway Shareholders' Meeting, CNBC Warren Buffett Archive, May 4, 2018, https://buffett.cnbc.com/1998-berkshire-hathaway-annual-meeting/.
16. Williams, "3 of Warren Buffett's Biggest Billion-Dollar Blunders."
17. Silicon Valley Historical Association, "Intel," March 24, 2022, https://www.siliconvalleyhistorical.org/intel-history.
18. Warren Buffett, 2014 Annual Berkshire Hathaway Shareholder Letter, Warren Buffett Archive, https://www.berkshirehathaway.com/letters/2014ltr.pdf.
19. Laura Woods, "Warren Buffett's Failures: 15 Investing Mistakes He Regrets," CNBC, December 15, 2017, https://www.cnbc.com/amp/2017/12/15/warren-buffetts-failures-15-investing-mistakes-he-regrets.html.
20. Ted Reed, "Buffett Decries Airline Investing Even Though at Worst He Broke Even," *Forbes*, May 13, 2013, https://www.forbes.com/sites/tedreed/2013/05/13/buffett-decries-airline-investing-even-though-at-worst-he-broke-even/?sh=4ffdb943b5e7.

21. Reed, "Buffett Decries Airline Investing Even Though at Worst He Broke Even."
22. Reed, "Buffett Decries Airline Investing Even Though at Worst He Broke Even."
23. Reed, "Buffett Decries Airline Investing Even Though at Worst He Broke Even."
24. Reed, "Buffett Decries Airline Investing Even Though at Worst He Broke Even."
25. Carol Loomis, "Warren Buffett's Wild Ride at Salomon a Harrowing, Bizarre Tale of Misdeeds and Mistakes That Pushed Salomon to the Brink and Produced the 'Most Important Day' in Warren Buffett's Life," CNN Money, October 27, 1997, https://money.cnn.com/magazines/fortune/fortune_archive/1997/10/27/233308/index.htm.
26. Exchange Act Release No. 34-31554, "In the Matter of John H. Gutfreund, Thomas W. Strauss, and John W. Meriwether, Respondents Administrative Proceeding," File No. 3-7930, December 3, 1992, https://www.lw.com/admin/Upload/Documents/in-re-john-gutfreund-51-sec-93-release-no-34-31554.pdf.
27. Rob Wells, "Mozer Sentenced to Four Months in Salomon Treasury Scandal," Associated Press, December 14, 1993, https://apnews.com/article/0d8432126425 71ffe244c82b0b906bd2.
28. U.S. Department of Justice, "Department of Justice and SEC Enter $290 Million Settlement with Salomon Brothers in Treasury Securities Case," May 20, 1992, https://www.justice.gov/archive/atr/public/press_releases/1992/211182.htm.
29. Wells, "Mozer Sentenced to Four Months in Salomon Treasury Scandal."
30. *Wall Street Journal*, "Buffett's 1991 Salomon Testimony," May 1, 2010, https://blogs.wsj.com/marketbeat/2010/05/01/buffetts-1991-salomon-testimony/.
31. Carol Loomis, "Warren Buffett's Wild Ride at Salomon (Fortune, 1997)," *Fortune*, October 27, 1997, https://fortune.com/1997/10/27/warren-buffett-salomon/.
32. Theron Mohamed, "Warren Buffett's 'Most Gruesome Mistake' Was Buying Dexter Shoe. Here's the Story of His $9 Billion Error," *Markets Insider*, January 18, 2020, https://markets.businessinsider.com/news/stocks/warren-buffett-most-gruesome-mistake-dexter-shoe-9-billion-error-2020-1-1028827359.
33. Warren Buffett, 2015 Annual Berkshire Hathaway Shareholder Letter, Warren Buffett Archive, https://www.berkshirehathaway.com/letters/2015ltr.pdf.
34. Mohamed, "Warren Buffett's 'Most Gruesome Mistake.' "
35. Woods, "Warren Buffett's Failures."
36. Warren Buffett, 2009 Annual Berkshire Hathaway Shareholders' Meeting, Warren Buffett Archive, May 2, 2009, https://buffett.cnbc.com/2009-berkshire-hathaway-annual-meeting/.
37. Rupert Hargreaves, "Reviewing the Mistakes Buffett Made Acquiring Gen Re," Gurufocus, October 9, 2020, https://www.gurufocus.com/news/1253307/a-look-back-at-warren-buffetts-gen-re-mistake.
38. Woods, "Warren Buffett's Failures."
39. Woods, "Warren Buffett's Failures."
40. Rupert Hargreaves, "Looking Back at Some of Buffett's Biggest Errors," Gurufocus, December 19, 2019, https://www.gurufocus.com/news/1003439/what-we-can-learn-from-warren-buffetts-2-10-billion-mistakes.
41. Woods, "Warren Buffett's Failures."
42. Motley Fool Staff, Leo Sun, Jordan Wathen, and Patrick Morris, "Warren Buffett's 3 Biggest Mistakes," November 24, 2014, The Motley Fool, https://www.fool.com/investing/general/2014/11/24/warren-buffetts-3-biggest-mistakes.aspx.

43. Warren Buffett, 2004 Annual Berkshire Hathaway Shareholders' Meeting, Warren Buffett Archive, May 1, 2004, https://buffett.cnbc.com/2004-berkshire-hathaway-annual-meeting/.
44. Hargreaves, "Some of Buffett's Biggest Errors."
45. Hargreaves, "Some of Buffett's Biggest Errors."
46. Woods, "Warren Buffett's Failures."
47. Buffett, 2014 Annual Berkshire Hathaway Shareholder Letter.
48. Laura Woods, "What You Can Learn from Warren Buffett's 15 Biggest Money Mistakes," *Las Vegas Review-Journal*, April 13, 2021, https://www.reviewjournal.com/life/what-you-can-learn-from-warren-buffetts-15-biggest-money-mistakes-2327972/.
49. Ben Eisen, "Warren Buffett's Big Mistake Ends up in Bankruptcy Court," MarketWatch, April 29, 2014, https://www.marketwatch.com/story/warren-buffetts-big-mistake-ends-up-in-bankruptcy-court-1398778775.
50. Alex Crippen, "What Has Warren Buffett Been Buying? 'Harold,' " CNBC, September 13, 2013, https://www.cnbc.com/2011/11/14/what-has-warren-buffett-been-buying-harold.html.
51. Becky Quick, "Warren Buffett Has Sold IBM Shares, and 'Revalued' Tech Icon Downward, Cites 'Big Strong Competitors,' " CNBC, May 4, 2017, https://www.cnbc.com/2017/05/04/warren-buffett-has-revalued-ibm-downward-cites-big-strong-competitors.html.
52. Buffett, 2008 Annual Berkshire Hathaway Shareholder Letter.
53. Eisen, "Warren Buffett's Big Mistake."
54. Warren Buffett, 2013 Annual Berkshire Hathaway Shareholder Letter, Warren Buffett Archive, https://www.berkshirehathaway.com/letters/2013ltr.pdf.
55. Craig Giammona and Matthew Boyle, "Kraft Will Merge with Heinz in Deal Backed by 3G and Buffett," Bloomberg, March 25, 2015, https://www.bloomberg.com/news/articles/2015-03-25/3g-capital-berkshire-to-buy-kraft-foods-merge-it-with-heinz.
56. Steve Watkins, "Kroger Private Brand Hits Major Milestone," *Cincinnati Business Courier*, March 10, 2021, https://www.bizjournals.com/cincinnati/news/2021/03/10/kroger-private-brand-hits-major-milestone.html.
57. Praveen Chawla, "Investor Disgust May Have Created an Opportunity in the Kraft Heinz Company," GuruFocus.com, February 25, 2019, https://www.yahoo.com/now/investor-disgust-may-created-opportunity-172150890.html.
58. Nathaniel Meyersohn and Alicia Wallace, "Costco's Kirkland and Other Store Brands Are Having a Moment," CNN.com, May 12, 2020, https://www.cnn.com/2020/05/12/business/private-label-costco-walgreens-coronavirus/index.html.
59. Fred Imbert, "Buffett, After Last Week's Stock Plunge, Says Berkshire Hathaway 'Overpaid' for Kraft," CNBC, February 25, 2019, https://www.cnbc.com/2019/02/25/buffett-says-berkshire-hathaway-overpaid-for-kraft-following-last-weeks-stock-plunge.html.
60. Jonathan Stempel, "Warren Buffett's $10 Billion Mistake: Precision Castparts," Reuters, February 27, 2021, https://www.reuters.com/article/us-berkshire-buffett-precisioncastparts/warren-buffetts-10-billion-mistake-precision-castparts-idUSKCN2AR0MZ.
61. Stempel, "Warren Buffett's $10 Billion Mistake: Precision Castparts."
62. Becky Quick, "Berkshire Hathaway Has Been Buying Shares of Amazon, Warren Buffett Says," CNBC, May 2, 2019, https://www.cnbc.com/2019/05/03/berkshire-hathaway-has-been-buying-shares-of-amazon-warren-buffett.html.
63. Benjamin Graham, *The Intelligent Investor*, revised ed. (New York: HarperCollins, 2006), viii.

11. SHAREHOLDER MEETINGS, LIFE ADVICE, AND PHILANTHROPY

1. James Altucher, "8 Unusual Things I Learned from Warren Buffett," Altucher Confidential (blog), 2016, http://www.jamesaltucher.com/2011/03/8-unusual-things-i-learned-from-warren-buffett/.
2. Robert Armstrong, Eric Platt, and Oliver Ralph, "Warren Buffett: 'I'm Having More Fun Than Any 88-Year-Old in the World,'" *Financial Times*, April 24, 2019, https://www.ft.com/content/40b9b356-661e-11e9-a79d-04f350474d62.
3. Claudia Assis, "Warren Buffett Makes Less Than Twice the Typical Berkshire Employee," MarketWatch, March 16, 2018, https://www.marketwatch.com/story/warren-buffett-makes-less-than-twice-the-typical-berkshire-employee-2018-03-16-1810346.
4. Todd A. Finkle, "Warren E. Buffett and Berkshire Hathaway, Inc." *Journal of the International Academy for Case Studies* 16, no. 5 (January 2010): 81.
5. Peter Buffett, *Life Is What You Make It: Find Your Own Path to Fulfillment* (New York: Crown, 2011), 11.
6. P-I Staff, "Bidding Begins on Warren Buffett's Car," SeattlePI.com, September 13, 2006, https://www.seattlepi.com/business/article/Bidding-begins-on-Warren-Buffett-s-car-1214487.php.
7. Andy Kilpatrick, *Of Permanent Value: The Story of Warren Buffett* (Mountain Brook, AL: Andy Kilpatrick Publishing Empire, 2008), 16.
8. Kathleen Elkins, "Warren Buffett's Best Advice for Young People Has Nothing to Do with Business," CNBC, January 30, 2017, https://www.cnbc.com/2017/01/30/warren-buffetts-best-advice-for-young-people.html.
9. Richard Kirkland, "Should You Leave It All to Your Children?," *Fortune*, September 29, 1986, http://archive.fortune.com/magazines/fortune/fortune_archive/1986/09/29/68098/index.htm.
10. Minda Zetlin, "How Warren Buffett's Son Spent the $90,000 of Berkshire Stock He Got at 19—Worth $200 Million Now: 'I Don't Regret It,'" CNBC, January 15, 2021, https://www.cnbc.com/2020/05/07/warren-buffett-son-doesn't-regret-spending-berkshire-stock-he-got-at-19-worth-200-million-now.html.
11. Zetlin, "How Warren Buffett's Son Spent."
12. Buffett, *Life Is What You Make It*, 113.
13. Buffett, *Life Is What You Make It*, 124.
14. NPR.org, "Buffett's Lasting Legacy: Immaterial Wealth," May 6, 2010, https://www.npr.org/templates/story/story.php?storyId=126538348.
15. Buffett, *Life Is What You Make It*, 125.
16. NPR.org, "Buffett's Lasting Legacy."
17. Oliver Staley, "Warren Buffett Gives His Employees 'Principles of Behavior' and Trusts Them to Do the Right Thing," *Quartz*, May 8, 2017, https://qz.com/978339/warren-buffett-gives-berkshire-hathaway-brka-employees-principles-of-behavior-rather-than-rules-and-trusts-them-to-do-the-right-thing/.
18. Todd Finkle and Paul Buller, "Wisdom from Warren Buffett," *Research in Higher Education Journal* 16 (2012): 1–10.
19. Finkle and Buller, "Wisdom from Warren Buffett."

20. "Full Transcript: Billionaire Investor Warren Buffett Speaks with Becky Quick on 'Squawk Box' Today," CNBC, February 25, 2019, https://www.cnbc.com/2019/02/25/full-transcript-billionaire-investor-warren-buffett-speaks-with-cnbcs-becky-quick-on-squawk-box-today.html.
21. "Warren Buffett, the Pragmatist," *Esquire*, June 1, 1988, 159.
22. Warren Buffett, "Speech to Seven Universities at Berkshire Hathaway Corporate Headquarters," Omaha, November 6, 2009.
23. Natasha Bach, "Warren Buffett Just Made His Largest Donation to Date," *Fortune*, July 17, 2018, http://fortune.com/2018/07/17/warren-buffett-giving-pledge-donation-2018/.
24. *Forbes*, "America's Top Givers 2022: The 25 Most Philanthropic Billionaires," January 19, 2022, https://www.forbes.com/sites/forbeswealthteam/2022/01/19/americas-top-givers-2022-the-25-most-philanthropic-billionaires/?sh=788b26fa3a6c.
25. Investopedia, "How Does Warren Buffett Plan to Bequeath His Estate?," January 31, 2020, https://www.investopedia.com/ask/answers/021615/who-does-warren-buffett-plan-bequeath-his-estate.asp.
26. "Warren Buffett's Final Charity Lunch Draws Record $19M Bid," Associated Press, June 18, 2022, https://apnews.com/article/warren-buffett-new-york-city-omaha-5805bbcd0bacb5c7930d6d71dfaa2247.
27. Steve Jordon, "Warren Buffett's 2006 Cadillac Goes for $122,500 in Charity Auction That Benefits Girls Inc.," *Omaha World Herald*, February 20, 2015, https://www.omaha.com/money/buffett/warren-buffett-s-cadillac-goes-for-in-charity-auction-that/article_3aa310de-b89e-11e4-9948-3f28a3daea73.html.
28. Girls, Inc., "Programs," 2020, https://girlsincomaha.org/about/programs/.
29. Kilpatrick, *Of Permanent Value*, 26.
30. Kathleen Elkins, "Warren Buffett's Partner Charlie Munger Says There Are '3 Rules for a Career,'" CNBC, August 17, 2017, https://www.cnbc.com/2017/08/16/warren-buffetts-partner-charlie-munger-has-3-rules-for-a-career.html.
31. Finkle and Buller, "Wisdom from Warren Buffett."
32. wikiHow, "How to Be Lovable," June 3, 2019, https://www.wikihow.com/Be-Lovable.
33. Todd A. Finkle, "Lessons Learned from 'The Oracle of Omaha' Warren Buffett," *Journal of Instructional Pedagogies* 2 (March 2010), https://www.aabri.com/manuscripts/09397.pdf.

12. A DAY WITH WARREN BUFFETT

1. *Inc.*, "Warren Buffett Says What Separates Successful People from Everyone Else Really Comes Down to a Two-Letter Word," November 12, 2021, https://www.inc.com/marcel-schwantes/warren-buffett-says-what-separates-successful-people-from-everyone-else-really-comes-down-to-a-2-letter-word.html.
2. Jade Scipioni, "Warren Buffett's Diet Still Includes 5 Cans of Coke, McDonald's, and Dairy Queen," Fox Business, April 6, 2020, https://www.foxbusiness.com/features/inside-warren-buffett-junk-food-diet-which-includes-5-cans-of-coke-mcdonalds-and-dairy-queen.

13. BERKSHIRE HATHAWAY LOOKING FORWARD

1. Warren Buffett, 1996 Berkshire Hathaway Annual Shareholder Letter, February 22, 1997, https://www.berkshirehathaway.com/letters/1996.html.
2. Sean Williams, "Apple Now Makes up 45 Percent of Buffett's Invested Assets," The Motley Fool, August 4, 2020, https://www.fool.com/investing/2020/08/04/apple-now-makes-up-45-of-buffetts-invested-assets.aspx.
3. Julia Kagan, "Financial Technology–Fintech," Investopedia, August 27, 2020, https://www.investopedia.com/terms/f/fintech.asp.
4. Kagan, "Financial Technology–Fintech."
5. Alex Wilhelm, "The Berserk Pace of Fintech Investing Outshines the Global VC Boom," *TechCrunch*, January 19, 2022, https://techcrunch.com/2022/01/19/the-berserk-pace-of-fintech-investing-outshines-the-global-vc-boom/.
6. Jake Frankenfield, "Cryptocurrency," Investopedia, January 11, 2022, https://www.investopedia.com/terms/c/cryptocurrency.asp.
7. Frankenfield, "Cryptocurrency."
8. Frankenfield, "Cryptocurrency."
9. Frankenfield, "Cryptocurrency."
10. Frankenfield, "Cryptocurrency."
11. Frankenfield, "Cryptocurrency."
12. PwC, "Making Sense of Bitcoin, Cryptocurrency and Blockchain," https://www.pwc.com/us/en/industries/financial-services/fintech/bitcoin-blockchain-cryptocurrency.html.
13. Adam Hayes, "Blockchain Explained," Investopedia, March 5, 2022, https://www.investopedia.com/terms/b/blockchain.asp.
14. PwC, "Making Sense of Bitcoin, Cryptocurrency and Blockchain."
15. Hayes, "Blockchain Explained."
16. IBM, "Smart Contracts Defined," March 21, 2022, https://www.ibm.com/topics/smart-contracts.
17. "Mark Cuban Explains Blockchain Game Changer," North American Bitcoin Conference, YouTube, January 17, 2022, https://www.youtube.com/watch?v=vjwBfVRQPt4, at 1:15.
18. Evan Conrad, interview by Todd Finkle, March 19, 2022.
19. Frankenfield, "Cryptocurrency."
20. Tae Kim, "Warren Buffett Says Bitcoin Is 'Probably Rat Poison Squared,'" CNBC, May 5, 2018, https://www.cnbc.com/2018/05/05/warren-buffett-says-bitcoin-is-probably-rat-poison-squared.html.
21. Eamon Barrett, "Even After Berkshire Hathaway Sank $1 Billion into Crypto-Friendly Bank, Vice Chairman Charlie Munger Calls Coins Like Bitcoin a 'Venereal Disease,'" *Fortune*, February 16, 2022, https://fortune.com/2022/02/17/charlie-munger-calls-crypto-venereal-disease-bitcoin-warren-buffett-nubank/.
22. Barrett, "Berkshire Hathaway Sank $1 Billion into Crypto-Friendly Bank."
23. Luc Olinga, "Russia Wants to Ban Crypto. Here Are Countries Where Crypto Is Illegal," *TheStreet*, January 21, 2022, https://www.thestreet.com/investing/russia-wants-to-ban-crypto-these-countries-outlaw-crypto.

24. Dan B., "Crypto Hater Warren Buffett Invested $1 Billion in a Crypto-Friendly Bank," *Bitcoinist*, February 17, 2022, https://bitcoinist.com/warren-buffett-invested-1-billion-in-a-digital-bank/.
25. Barrett, "Berkshire Hathaway Sank $1 Billion into Crypto-Friendly Bank."
26. Holly LaFon and GuruFocus, "Warren Buffett Takes 11 Percent Stake in Stoneco," Yahoo!, November 9, 2018, https://www.yahoo.com/now/warren-buffett-takes-11-stake-232347717.html.
27. David Kass, "Did Berkshire Hathaway Sell Its Shares in StoneCo Ltd. during the Third Quarter?," University of Maryland, November 11, 2021, http://blog.umd.edu/davidkass/2021/11/11/did-berkshire-hathaway-sell-its-shares-in-stoneco-ltd-during-the-third-quarter/.
28. Neha Chamaria, "Warren Buffett's Berkshire Hathaway Might Have Found an Amazon-like Opportunity in India's Paytm," The Motley Fool, August 29, 2018, https://www.fool.com/investing/2018/08/29/warren-buffets-berkshire-hathaway-might-have-found.aspx.
29. Jessica Bursztynsky, "Snowflake More Than Doubles in Market Debut, Largest Ever Software IPO," CNBC, September 16, 2020, https://www.cnbc.com/2020/09/16/snowflake-snow-opening-trading-on-the-nyse.html.
30. Snowflake, "Snowflake Launches the Financial Services Data Cloud to Accelerate Customer-Centric and Data-Driven Innovation in the Financial Services Industry," September 14, 2021, https://www.snowflake.com/news/snowflake-launches-the-financial-services-data-cloud-to-accelerate-customer-centric-and-data-driven-innovation-in-the-financial-services-industry/.
31. Bursztynsky, "Snowflake More Than Doubles in Market Debut."
32. Andres Engler, "Berkshire Hathaway Invests $1B in Brazilian Digital Bank Nubank, Reduces Mastercard, Visa Positions," CoinDesk, February 15, 2022, https://www.coindesk.com/business/2022/02/16/berkshire-hathaway-invests-1b-in-brazilian-digital-bank-nubank-reduces-mastercard-visa-positions/.
33. Dan B., "Crypto Hater Warren Buffett Invested $1 Billion."
34. Ian Smith, "Central Bank Digital Currencies: Which Countries Are Using, Launching or Piloting CBDCs?," Euronews.next, March 9, 2022, https://www.euronews.com/next/2022/03/09/cbdcs-these-are-the-countries-are-using-launching-or-piloting-their-own-digital-currencies.
35. Bank of England. "Central Bank Digital Currency: Opportunities, Challenges and Design," March 12, 2020, https://www.bankofengland.co.uk/paper/2020/central-bank-digital-currency-opportunities-challenges-and-design-discussion-paper.
36. Bank of England, "Central Bank Digital Currency: Opportunities."
37. Smith, "Central Bank Digital Currencies."
38. Smith, "Central Bank Digital Currencies."
39. Smith, "Central Bank Digital Currencies."
40. James Areddy, "China Creates Its Own Digital Currency, a First for Major Economy," *Wall Street Journal*, April 5, 2021, https://www.wsj.com/articles/china-creates-its-own-digital-currency-a-first-for-major-economy-11617634118.
41. Christina Majaski, "Yuan vs Renminbi: What's the Difference?," Investopedia, April 29, 2021, https://www.investopedia.com/articles/forex/061115/yuan-vs-rmb-understanding-difference.asp.

42. Jonathan Cheng, "China Rolls out Pilot Test of Digital Currency," *Wall Street Journal*, January 2, 2020, https://www.wsj.com/articles/china-rolls-out-pilot-test-of-digital-currency-11587385339.
43. Eustance Huang, "China's Digital Yuan Could Challenge the Dollar in International Trade This Decade, Fintech Expert Predicts," CNBC, March 15, 2022, https://www.cnbc.com/2022/03/15/can-chinas-digital-yuan-reduce-the-dollars-use-in-international-trade.html.
44. Evan Freidin, "China's Digital Currency Takes Shape," The Interpreter, September 8, 2021, https://www.lowyinstitute.org/the-interpreter/china-s-digital-currency-takes-shape.
45. Freidin, "China's Digital Currency Takes Shape."
46. Freidin, "China's Digital Currency Takes Shape."
47. Huang, "China's Digital Yuan Could Challenge the Dollar."
48. Huang, "China's Digital Yuan Could Challenge the Dollar."
49. CNA, "Biden Orders Government to Study Digital Dollar, Other Cryptocurrency Risks," March 9, 2022, https://www.channelnewsasia.com/business/joe-biden-orders-us-government-study-digital-dollar-cryptocurrency-risks-2553071.
50. CNA, "Biden Orders Government to Study Digital Dollar."
51. Derek Anderson, "MIT, Boston Fed Give Digital Dollar CBDC a Modest Test Run," Cointelegraph, February 11, 2022, https://cointelegraph.com/news/mit-boston-fed-give-digital-dollar-cbdc-a-modest-test-run.
52. Anderson, "MIT, Boston Fed Give Digital Dollar CBDC."
53. Anderson, "MIT, Boston Fed Give Digital Dollar CBDC."
54. Anshu Siripurapu, "Cryptocurrencies, Digital Dollars, and the Future of Money," Council on Foreign Relations, September 24, 2021, https://www.cfr.org/backgrounder/cryptocurrencies-digital-dollars-and-future-money.
55. Jonathan Stempel, "Buffett's Berkshire Posts Record Annual Profit, Extends But Slows Buybacks," *Reuters*, March 21, 2022, https://www.reuters.com/business/buffetts-berkshire-posts-record-annual-profit-extends-slows-buybacks-2022-02-26/.
56. Stempel, "Buffett's Berkshire Posts Record Annual Profit."
57. Alex Crippen, "Warren Buffett Scoops up Another $1 Billion in Occidental Shares, Bringing Total Stake to $7 Billion," CNBC, March 17, 2022, https://www.cnbc.com/2022/03/17/warren-buffett-scoops-up-another-1-billion-in-occidental-shares-bringing-total-stake-to-7-billion.html.
58. Shubham Kalia, "Berkshire Hathaway Buys 9.6 Mln More Occidental Shares, Raises Stake to Over 16%," Reuters, June 22, 2022, https://www.reuters.com/markets/deals/berkshire-hathaway-buys-96-mln-more-occidental-shares-raises-stake-over-16-2022-06-23/.
59. Noor Zainab Hussain and Jonathan Stempel, "Buffett Ends Drought with $11.6 Billion Alleghany Purchase," Yahoo! Finance, March 21, 2022, https://finance.yahoo.com/news/berkshire-hathaway-acquire-alleghany-11-094234451.html.
60. Jonathan Stempel, "Berkshire Bought $51 Billion in Stock as Buffett Combats Supply Chain," Reuters, April 30, 2022, https://www.reuters.com/business/buffetts-berkshire-bought-51-bln-stock-first-quarter-operating-results-flat-2022-04-30/.
61. Anderson, "MIT, Boston Fed Give Digital Dollar CBDC."
62. James Leggate, "Warren Buffett Acknowledges He Won't Live Forever," FOX Business, February 22, 2020, https://www.foxbusiness.com/money/warren-buffett-annual-letter-prepares-shareholders-death.

63. "Forty U.S. Billionaires Pledge to Give Half Their Money to Charity," Xinhua News Agency, August 5, 2010, https://web.archive.org/web/20100811032238/http://news.xinhuanet.com/english2010/world/2010-08/05/c_13430367.htm.
64. Scott Hensley, "What We Can Learn from Warren Buffett's Prostate Cancer," NPR, April 18, 2012, https://www.npr.org/sections/health-shots/2012/04/18/150892066/what-we-can-learn-from-warren-buffets-prostate-cancer.
65. Lawrence Cunningham, "Berkshire Hathaway's Fate after Buffett Will Be up to Its Board Members. Are They up to the Task?," MarketWatch, November 6, 2021, https://www.marketwatch.com/amp/story/berkshire-hathaways-fate-after-buffett-will-be-up-to-its-board-members-are-they-up-to-the-task-11636013151.
66. Jonathan Stempel, "Berkshire Hathaway Nominates Wally Weitz to Fill Open Board Seat," Reuters, March 11, 2022, https://www.reuters.com/business/berkshire-hathaway-nominates-wally-weitz-fill-open-board-seat-2022-03-11/.
67. Allen Lee, "20 Things You Didn't Know About Ajit Jain," *Money Inc.*, 2019, https://moneyinc.com/20-things-you-didnt-know-about-ajit-jain/.
68. Warren Buffett, 2016 Berkshire Hathaway Annual Shareholder Letter, February 24, 2018, https://www.berkshirehathaway.com/letters/2016ltr.pdf.
69. Becky Quick, "When Warren Buffett Eventually Is No Longer Berkshire Hathaway CEO, Greg Abel Will Succeed Him," CNBC, May 3, 2021, https://www.cnbc.com/2021/05/03/when-warren-buffett-eventually-steps-down-as-berkshire-hathaway-ceo-greg-abel-will-succeed-him.html.
70. Adam Mead, "Berkshire Hathaway after Buffett: Who Will Be CEO, What Else Will Change—and What Won't," MarketWatch, May 2, 2021, https://www.marketwatch.com/story/Berkshire-hathaway-after-buffett-who-will-be-ceo-what-else-will-change-and-what-wont-11619179467.
71. Horatio Alger Association, member profile, 2018, https://horatioalger.org/members/member-detail/gregory-e-abel.
72. Horatio Alger Association, "2018 Horatio Alger Award Winner Gregory E. Abel," https://horatioalger.org/members/member-detail/gregory-e-abel/.
73. Horatio Alger Association, "2018 Horatio Alger Award Winner Gregory E. Abel."
74. Tae Kim, "Warren Buffett Takes a Step Closer to Naming a Successor as Berkshire Appoints Abel and Jain to Board as Vice Chairs," CNBC, January 10, 2018, https://www.cnbc.com/2018/01/10/berkshire-hathaways-warren-buffett-appoints-greg-abel-and-ajit-jain-as-vice-chairmen.html.
75. Marcel Schwantes, "Warren Buffett Says Your Greatest Measure of Success at the End of Your Life Comes Down to 1 Word," *Inc.*, September 13, 2018, https://www.inc.com/marcel-schwantes/warren-buffett-says-it-doesnt-matter-how-rich-you-are-without-this-1-thing-your-life-is-a-disaster.html.
76. "Annual Meetings," CNBC Warren Buffett Archive, https://buffett.cnbc.com/annual-meetings/.
77. Benjamin Graham, *The Intelligent Investor*, revised ed. (New York: Harper Business, 2006), 524.
78. Robert Arffa, *Expert Financial Planning: Investment Strategies from Industry Leaders* (New York: Wiley, 2021), 110.
79. Eva Mathews and Jonathan Stempel, "Warren Buffett Resigns from Gates Foundation, Has Donated Half His Fortune," June 24, 2021, Reuters, https://www.reuters.com/business/buffett-resigns-trustee-gates-foundation-2021-06-23/.
80. Bloomberg Billionaire's Index, Bloomberg, March 28, 2022, https://www.bloomberg.com/billionaires/.

INDEX